Working Communally

Working
Communally
Patterns and Possibilities

David French
and
Elena French

Russell Sage Foundation   New York

PUBLICATIONS OF RUSSELL SAGE FOUNDATION

Russell Sage Foundation was established in 1907 by Mrs. Russell Sage for the improvement of social and living conditions in the United States. In carrying out its purpose the Foundation conducts research under the direction of members of the staff or in close collaboration with other institutions, and supports programs designed to develop and demonstrate productive working relations between social scientists and other professional groups. As an integral part of its operation, the Foundation from time to time publishes books or pamphlets resulting from these activities. Publication under the imprint of the Foundation does not necessarily imply agreement by the Foundation, its Trustees, or its staff with the interpretations or conclusions of the authors.

Russell Sage Foundation
230 Park Avenue, New York, N.Y. 10017

Acknowledgments

We and this book owe much to:

Lanier Graham, who planted the seed;

Russell Sage Foundation, which financed much of our research;

Joel Dorkam, Lee Goldstein, Howie Romero and Professor Henri Desroche, all of whom provided invaluable counsel on specific issues;

Rodney, Marilyn, John, Steve, and Roger Smith, who gave us the joy and friendship that allowed us to keep our work on the book in (more or less) proper perspective;

Glenda Haskell, John and Connie McFarlane, and Sharon Metcalf, who did necessary things ranging from typing to searching through back issues of underground magazines for obscure pieces of information;

Dr. Patterson H. French and Professor Albert O. Hirschman, whose extensive comments on our manuscript saved us from at least some of our worst blunders; and

the hundreds of "alternative-seekers" whose contacts with us over the last four years have been reduced, if only for the purposes of this book, to the line of argument set forth in the pages that follow.

Contents

Part I: Context

Chapter 1: The Work System as Oppression—Roots of Discontent

During 1973, a series of conferences was held across the United States to ponder the "changing work ethic" in this country (Shabecoff, 1973:22). The conferees, who included national political figures as well as business and labor leaders, were plainly worried. And with good reason, for the diagnosis of a "changing work ethic" was simply a polite way of noting that large numbers of people were becoming increasingly fed up with the way they earned their living. Earlier in the year, a task force of the Department of Health, Education, and Welfare had released a report showing that only 43 percent of white-collar workers, and only 24 percent of blue-collar workers, would choose the same line of work if given a chance to start their careers anew (1973:15). Workers' discontent, long a theme of American radicals, had become a matter of national concern.

As usual, the convening of task forces and high-level conferences indicated only that a pervasive problem of long standing had finally become a serious nuisance to the power structure. At the work place, this particular problem was showing itself in unacceptable levels of absenteeism, in-plant crime, vandalism, drug abuse, declining productivity, and active rebellion against traditional management prerogatives. More dramatically, the previous decade had seen the emergence of an entire "counterculture," one of whose tenets was that available work was alienating, unnecessary, and therefore to be avoided altogether—preferably by moving to some rural commune. Although the counterculture was not large, it included a disproportionate number of the most "promising" members of its generation, and its attitudes spread broadly through the society as a whole. With rebellion against conventional work situations arising on every side, something clearly had to be done, though nobody seemed to know quite what.

It is the thesis of this book that an appropriate "something" was in fact available, if all but universally ignored. If communards do not work, and workers do not commune, the answer may lie simply in bringing the two together—in communal work. In brief, the productive aspects of the work place would be combined with the modest size and highly personal content of the commune. In such an environment, work becomes tangibly related to the entire process of living, on a scale that is within human ability to comprehend and master. The structural bases for the sorts of alienation which have led to our "changing work ethic"—alienation of workers from each other, their work, their superiors, themselves; and alienation of work itself from other aspects of life—are largely eliminated. In all these respects, the communal work place is a social unit superior to those in which we now try to function.

Of course, this remedy has not yet reached far into the national consciousness, partly because of the ways in which the problem itself has generally been set forth. For those who define it in terms of glaring disparities in economic status between rich and poor, the solution is simply to redistribute national income more equitably. For those who see the numbing routines of the work place as the root of the problem, it can be avoided by creating autonomous work teams or by implementing other "work-enrichment" programs. More radical critics see a latent class struggle at work, one whose resolution should have the proletariat (variously defined) seize the instruments of power. The limitation of all such approaches is that they are either too abstract or too narrowly based to embrace the range of immediate issues which has led people to be unhappy with their lives. To begin the case for the communal work place as a logical response to these issues, let us first establish what they are.

THE ROOTS OF DISCONTENT

Production and Consumption. To find full meaning in their work, people must feel that some relationship exists between their labor and the satisfactions that accrue to those consuming the products of that labor. Only in a profoundly alienated system would people find themselves producing everincreasing quantities of dubious goods and then delivering these goods into a distribution network whose end points—the buyers—are always out of sight. Such a system would give rise to two problems. Makers would be severed from users and would thus be unable to draw pleasure from the joy that use of their products might provoke. And joy itself would wither away, crippled by the spiritually corrosive qualities of the goods involved. It is a somber image—and a precise description of the economic system within which we live.

To arrive at this point, our society has had to purge its definition of a "rational" economic order of any taint of personal contact. We work, and the things we make are placed into boxes by strange hands and sent out into the void. We shop, and from the void miraculously appear other boxes. Oh, brave new world: "More or less automatically and impersonally . . . the market mechanism . . . directs and coordinates the decisions and activities of millions of independent, dispersed economic units and agents. With all of its problems and imperfections, it is surely one of the most remarkable of social institutions" (Grossman, 1967:15). It is remarkable indeed, allowing us all to live without ever making contact around the acts through which we keep each other alive. The chilling touch of the "invisible hand" (Adam Smith's felicitous phrase to describe the workings of the capitalist market) transmutes us all into profits and losses, the only things to which attention must be paid. Little wonder that we begin to feel uneasy with the work we do.

And that is only the beginning, for much of what we produce would be intrinsically without meaning no matter how it was delivered to its final user. According to Murray Bookchin:

> Roughly seventy percent of the American labor force does absolutely no productive work that could be translated into terms of real output or the maintenance of a rational system of distribution. Their work is largely limited to servicing the commodity economy—filing, billing, bookkeeping for a profit and loss statement, sales promotion, advertising, retailing, finance, the stock market, government work, military work, etc., *ad nauseam*. Roughly the same percentage of goods produced is such pure garbage that people would voluntarily stop consuming it in a rational society. (1971:236)

We can quibble with Bookchin's figures, but his point is nonetheless a strong and valid one. The number of people actually working to make those goods and services that we buy, and that enhance our lives, is a minor fraction of the labor force. For the rest, perhaps the modal worker of our time is the book-keeper tallying data on some advertising agency's new campaign for its low-calorie laxative account. Most of us are involved in work that is the functional equivalent of this. And although we tend to avoid thinking about it very much, it is the sort of reality which, if allowed to surface, can help drive us to seek alternatives to what we are doing.

Curiously enough, the only respite from production of meaningless goods seems to have become massive consumption of those same goods—or, in the jargon, consumerism. According to Thomas Weisskopf, "Consumerism derives from a fundamental tenet of capitalist ideology: the assertion that the primary requirement for individual self-fulfillment and happiness is the possession and consumption of material goods" (1972:369). Again, under irrational circumstances, such thinking becomes rational. Were our work to have meaning, and were it carried out in a supportive social context, we would not be driven wholly to identify our fulfillment with consumption. As Herb Gintis has argued, however, where "work, community, and environment become sources of pain and displeasure rather than inviting contexts for social relations, [the] reasonable individual response . . . is . . . to emphasize consumption *per se*" (1972:128). Our powers of discernment are directed to distinguishing between brands of cars, beers, and television sets, rather than to surrounding ourselves with sources of beauty and enlightenment. Our energies carry us to movies, book stores, and stadiums rather than to dance, participant sports, or the making of music. Here again, it takes relatively little self-awareness for us to wonder if our priorities are sound.

If our work severs us from those who use our products and our consumption severs us from ourselves, the final folly—rational only in our Alice-in-Wonderland world—is the search to quench our thirsts through more and more of the same thing. But that the object of this search is a torrent of salt water is an idea whose time may now have come. As far back as 1970, for example, even *Time* magazine discovered that "the glitter of growth has begun to tarnish." And *Time* went on to quote a puzzled President Nixon, worrying over the fact that "never has a nation seemed to have had more and enjoyed it less" (1970:72–73). Little wonder. Consumption for many people has already surpassed—or become divorced from—their ability to enjoy their worldly goods.

In *Report From Engine Co. 82,* Dennis Smith talks of a Puerto Rican bodega owner in the South Bronx who worked for eleven years to buy his wife a new Cadillac:

He attached a garage [to his bodega] to protect the Cadillac from the neighborhood kids, and he double padlocked it, and built a mesh wire fence around it, and padlocked that. He never gets to drive the Cadillac though, because he works the bodega fourteen hours a day, seven days a week. His wife doesn't get to drive it much either, because it takes two to run the store. The garage proved to be a good investment for them. (1972: 198–199)

In kind, if not degree, it is a familiar situation, one whose inevitability is increasingly being questioned.*

The Nature of Work. When people begin to question the value of consumption, they quickly move on to question the need for much of the work that finances that consumption. Thus, companies as diverse as General Motors and the Wales Manufacturing Company of Gastonia, North Carolina, have been troubled by workers who have anticipated the four-day work week by simply refusing to show up on the fifth day. The Wales management went so far as to offer a twenty-cent hourly bonus for workers who put in a full week; they found it made no difference (*Newsweek,* 1972:87). Relative affluence seems increasingly to be innoculating large numbers of people against the lure of money, the traditional enforcer of work behavior in the capitalist way of life. And so liberated, people will announce by their absence their innermost feelings about the work places themselves: boredom, irritation, and a general sense that in work lies no fulfillment at all.

While never much of a secret, such discontent with work has taken on the proportions of a major social issue over the last few years. In 1972, worried businessmen began to speak of a "Lordstown Syndrome" after the General Motors workers in Lordstown, Ohio, took one look at what GM executives were calling their new "plant of the future," said the hell with it, and went out on strike. Were the problem to stop there, we might be able to bemoan the effects of the assembly line and go on about our business— assuming our business to be other than on the line. But the disease is far more pervasive. Seashore and Barnowe have found that *"vulnerability to blue-collar blues is endemic in the whole work force and rests only slightly on the stereotyped attributes of the middle-mass worker"* (1972:80; italics in original). In other words, none of us is immune. For every report of striking workers, there are hints of widespread executive absenteeism.** For

---

* For a more thorough analysis of the costs of growth, see E. J. Mishan, 1969. Mishan's arguments are summarized in Greene and Golden, 1971.
** For an anecdotal account of absenteeism in advertising, see Della Femina, 1970: 109.

every story of a worker shooting up during coffee break, there are tales of the heavy, sweet smell in the halls of some corporate headquarters. Where our work does not turn us on, we will turn on to other things or not show up at all.

The sources of this discontent have become truisms, and not only in the United States. Looking at the industrial scene in France, for example, Yvon Bourdet says: "Everything happens as though the worker had been decerebrated; his hands, sometimes tied to the machine, seem to receive orders from another brain; his own brain is no more than an organ for recording and relaying" (1970:143–144). In the usual cliché, we appear to have become interchangeable cogs in a great industrial machine.* In fact, the problem is often more complex than that. We are given just enough scope for initiative to keep us from losing our minds, but not enough to be fully satisfied. We are neither one place nor the other, lost in a set of contradictions inherent in the situation:

> It has been shown that the hands of millions of workers cannot be correctly directed by the brain of one engineer, that the worker in this system can be neither passive nor active. He cannot be *passive* because without his constant ingenuity the system breaks down; it is enough for the worker to follow the rules and regulations scrupulously to effect a sort of strike by zeal. Nor can he be *active* since he is expected not to think but to obey orders.... (Bourdet, 1970:12)

Stated this way, it is clear that the problem is not limited to "workers" alone. For practically everyone, the balance between work activity and work passivity is a constantly shifting reality of our jobs. We are passive much more of the time than we admit to ourselves, but we admit enough to be troubled by what we see.

Passivity might be bearable if the organizing principles toward which we are expected to be passive made due allowance for varieties of people and situations. But this is exactly what bureaucratic organization cannot do. It is absurd to expect a worker on the verge of the flu to tighten bolts as rapidly as a worker at the peak of condition, but this is what the system demands. It is absurd to expect every piece of learning to come in fifty-minute segments, but this is what the schedules of our schools assume. It is absurd to expect any standard reporting procedure to allow for all possible contin-

---

* We run the risk of forgetting how precisely this image can reflect reality. See Langer, 1972:16 for a personal account of the machine and its cogs in the New York Telephone Company.

gencies, but this is the assumption behind most of the tables, forms, or grade sheets we fill out. In such conditions, much of our "activeness" takes the form of trying to reconcile our jagged edges with a work process that expects us to be smooth. That we tend to become accustomed to this over time is but a measure of our degradation.

An example: At the same time every year, every United States economic aid mission in the world compiles data, according to standard forms, on the economic conditions of the country in which it operates. Among these forms is one that summarizes the gross national product in the preceding year. We went through this little exercise in Ethiopia one summer; it was a paradigm of the bureaucratic way. For eight hours a day during the appropriate (that is, bureaucratically specified) weeks, members of the program office were to think GNP. Drunk, sober, or enfeebled by chronic diarrhea, entranced by the exercise or preoccupied with problems at home, the program officers worried over investment figures and disposable income Monday through Friday, from 8:00 to 12:00 each morning, and from 12:30 to 4:30 each afternoon. As it happens, nobody has even a clue to the *population* of Ethiopia, much less to what it is that those however many people are producing. Nonetheless, numbers were dreamed up, forms filled out and duplicated, and copies sent to everyone from the Department of Commerce to the CIA (which subsequently sent them back to us as part of a secret report on the Ethiopian state of things). Oddly enough, everyone went through the process in total seriousness; they seemed to feel there was nothing particularly strange in what they were doing.*

Control. If the conditions and nature of our work are more than enough to bring us to a point of quiet desperation, the final indignity rests in the fact that we as workers have little to say about any of these things. In most of the institutions in which we most directly participate—and not only our places of business—we feel ourselves to be more or less impotent. Considering a range of institutions including the political party, the economic enterprise, the trade union, and the university, Robert Dahl observes that even "where the ostensible claim to legitimacy by those who wield authority is that leaders are democratically chosen, as in the political party and the trade union, everyone knows that internal democracy is mainly a fake" (1970:7). And nobody would even pretend to a democratic basis for selection of those holding power in the corporate enterprise.

---

* For a general statement of this process, see Goodman, 1972:31–32.

It is not that we are wholly without voice. Once again, the system listens with just enough of an ear to provide us the barest illusion of participation in its business, enough of an ear to ward off active revolt. Workers may band together to influence a change in the overhead lighting system that is giving them headaches. They will have nothing to say about the product they make or the basic conditions—the assembly line, for example—under which it is produced. Civil servants may act to change procedures under which eligibility for welfare programs is determined. They will have little or no influence on the *criteria* for eligibility or on the conditions that drive people to welfare offices in the first place. Faculty senates may tinker with grading systems, instituting pass-fail for their classes instead of letter grades. They are unlikely to be given the option of dispensing with grades or classes altogether. That we have grown accustomed to living within such narrow boundaries does not negate their narrowness. In virtually every one of the moments of choice which set the context for our lives, we find the choice is not ours.

Most critics, radical and liberal alike, have been prone to analyze such questions in terms of the class-based, unequal distribution of power which they see around them. For example, the ultimate power of decision in a company like General Motors appears to rest in a few private hands, thereby disenfranchising the millions of workers and consumers who are equally bound up with what GM does. Private interest is substituted for the public will, an incurably bourgeois and unfair way of handling such an extensive operation:

> General Motors is as much a public enterprise as the U.S. Post Office. With gross receipts approximately equal to Sweden's Gross National Product; with employees and their families about as large as the total population of New Zealand; with outlays larger than those of the central government of France or West Germany . . . General Motors is de facto the public business. . . . In the circumstances, to think of General Motors as *private* instead of *public* is an absurdity. (Dahl, 1970:120)

To unburden ourselves of this particular absurdity, we might conclude, we have only to transfer ownership and control of General Motors to some worthy agent of the public interest, whether government ministry or workers' council or consumer-based board of directors.

The problem, however, lies not in the *ownership* of General Motors but in the *scale* of General Motors—and of virtually every institution (outside the family) within which we function. With few exceptions, *all* these institu-

tions are simply too large for us ever, under any conceivable system of ownership and direction, to have more than a marginal part in their affairs. When
the scope of the institutions which support us grows beyond that which we
can personally know, we are forced to accept means of coordinating these
institutions—the market, committees, legislatures, the law, tyrants, or whatever—that are impersonal to us, beyond our immediate control.

The greater the size of the unit involved, the greater will be the power
of the coordinating mechanism—and the less will be the power of those
being coordinated, singly or together. Even in the most democratic systems,
the ballot primarily serves the function of delegating sovereignty over our
lives to our "representatives," who will then make our decisions for us
during their two- or four-year terms of office. Instead of governing ourselves,
we become the governed, with consequences that Pierre-Joseph Proudhon
roundly denounced more than a century ago:

> To be governed is to be watched over, inspected, spied on, directed, legis-
> lated, regimented, closed in, indoctrinated, preached at, controlled, assessed,
> evaluated, censored, commanded. . . . To be governed means that at every
> move, operation, or transaction one is noted, registered, entered in a census,
> taxed, stamped, priced, assessed, patented, licensed, authorized, recom-
> mended, admonished, prevented, reformed, set right, corrected. Govern-
> ment means to be subjected to tribute, trained, ransomed, exploited, mono-
> polized, extorted, pressured, mystified, robbed; all in the name of public
> utility and the general good. Then, at the first sign of resistance or word of
> complaint, one is repressed, fined, despised, vexed, pursued, hustled, beaten
> up, garroted, imprisoned, shot, machine-gunned, judged, sentenced, de-
> ported, sacrificed, sold, betrayed, and to cap it all, ridiculed, mocked,
> outraged, and dishonored. (Quoted in Guérin, 1970:15–16)

Proudhon assumed all this to be done by "creatures that have neither the
right, nor wisdom, nor virtue"; but this is hardly central to his argument.
We may find virtue or wisdom in the particular bosses, chairmen, congress-
men, or presidents who govern us, without feeling any better about the fact
that we are out of control of our own lives.

Ecology: Physical and Human. Finally, the separation of our work in time
and space from other aspects of our being is a symptom of the general
fragmentation of our lives. In simpler societies, work, play, worship, and
learning take place in the same limited geographical space, and are often
indistinguishable from each other. Even in the Vermont village where we
recently lived, many families continued to lead largely integrated lives.

Book learning had been moved from the local one-room schoolhouse to an academy over the hills, and "recreation" had emerged in the form of the bowling alley ten miles in one direction and the club twenty miles in another. But the core of all work, learning, and play took place in the house, dooryard, barn, and fields, where members of the family-community were seldom out of one another's sight. In their ignorance, the trendier minds of our society condescend to such a life style, finding it limiting, inward-looking, and dull. They did not know our neighbors.

Whatever its merits, the simple life in America—as everybody knows—is doomed. Instead, we have cities, suburbs, office buildings, factories, churches, stadiums, movie theaters, and all the other appurtenances of modern industrial life. Where a single place—say, the farm—once served many social functions, these functions have now become specialized, with a separate place and separate groups of people for each. Community is destroyed, and we have instead many communities in which we participate. As Martin Buber observed, "work forges other personal links than does leisure, sport again others than politics, the day is cleanly divided and the soul too" (1958:136).

We live in a Disneyland of social spaces: The Wonderful World of Work over here; Fantasyland on the tube or at the cinema down the street; Adventureland in a summer visit to Yellowstone Park, or perhaps in a suburban fling at spouse-swapping; The House of Magical Moments, ten days at Esalen or an evening around the water pipe in our living room. In none of this is there continuity, since people and events are constantly changing. And in very little is there even much sense of emotional reality. How could we allow ourselves to become involved when this show is about to close, the one at the next booth about to begin—and we with a pocketful of tickets?

Naturally, the system spins off its own apologetics, and many would take exception to our gloomy view of current realities. In May, 1972, for example, Kenneth Gergen published an article in *Psychology Today* entitled "Multiple Identity: The Healthy, Happy Human Being Wears Many Masks." *Psychology Today* was sufficiently delighted with the piece to make a television special out of it. Obviously, Gergen had touched a sensitive nerve, a need felt by many for theoretical justification of the fragmented life styles about which they felt somehow uneasy. And Gergen supplied soothing balms: "I believe we must abandon the assumption that normal development equips the individual with a coherent sense of identity." Instead, "we should learn to play more roles, to adopt any role that seems enjoyable—a baron, a princess, a secret agent, an Italian merchant" (Ibid.:64, 66). All this, presumably, in addition to our more familiar roles as parent, husband, wife, worker, boss, underling, sports enthusiast, movie-goer, tourist, consumer, politico, investor, correspondent, intellectual, gardener, craftsperson, and so on. It would be a busy and diverting life.

But to what end? Gergen speaks of the "storehouse of novel self-images" we may accumulate, but why should we want to? His experiments show nothing of the psychological, much less spiritual, impact of having many masks; they show only that in a highly diverting society we are easily diverted. Finally, all he can really conclude is that such malleability is functional. The worst thing that could happen would be for us to have a strong sense of our selves: "Identity may become coherent in this fashion, but it may also become rigid *and maladaptive*" (our italics). And adapt we must; it is the traditional, final refuge of thought in the social sciences. But if that is the stick, Gergen's carrot is no more enticing. We are to become little bundles of television productions on feet and in living color, changing channels in response to our shifting audiences. If we work hard at it, we may end up with all the varied glitter of a joint ABC/CBS/NBC/PBS marathon spectacular. It is a glamorous extension of the way we now live, but it does little to make that way appealing.

If our masks are many, they are also being shifted at an ever dizzier pace. Alvin Toffler, who has called this "future shock," is "driven to a relentless conclusion: man's ties with the invisible geography of organization turn over more and more rapidly, exactly as do his relationships with things, places, and the human beings who people these ever-changing organizational structures" (1970:123). In such a world, enduring relationship with any of the forces which make up our kaleidoscopic vision is increasingly a luxury that we cannot afford. It is all we can do to keep inventory of the "storehouse of novel self-images" which results. For Toffler, the prescription is training in faster absorption of images, lest they overwhelm us. Left always unexamined are the consequences of being driven ever further back into ourselves, into a giddy, self-preoccupied world of transitory events and disposable people. If this has become the path of least resistance, almost a necessity for adaptation to our social environment, there are those who find it nonetheless obscene.

The obscenity becomes palpable when we smell our air, taste our waters, or walk our land. After all, our environmental degradation follows from our social degradation, from our unwillingness to become *connected* with the things around us. If we find it limiting to be involved on a continuing and intimate basis in the lives of other people, it is hardly surprising that we should find little basis for involvement in the lives of our rivers. If we feel it hopeless to try to comprehend the social organizations through which we pass, there is no more reason to expect we should understand the complex ecology of the land over which we drive. It was not always this way. As Murray Bookchin has argued, "it was not until organic community relations, be they tribal, feudal or peasant in form, dissolved into market relationships that the planet itself was reduced to a resource for exploitation" (1972:391). As we view other people, so do we view the world. The fact that the earth has become an object for our consumption mirrors the degree to which we have become objects of consumption for each other, sources of diversion removed from any long-term organic context or—which is to say the same thing—from any sense of continuing responsibility for those around us.

Severed from our fellow human beings and our ties to the earth, we apply Band-aids to mutilations: we chlorinate our water and strengthen the police, bury our wastes somewhere and split when things get heavy, build highways through forests and hire encounter leaders to introduce us to strangers. It is all very haphazard in a driven sort of way, all motion and no center. In such conditions, everything we make is evanescent, from love to paper towels to social policy. Little wonder that people search for some other way to live.

THE "POSTSCARCITY" ERA—AND BEYOND

Through the early part of this decade, there was a strong current of belief that our problems were all but over. The drive and efficiencies of our economy, so the argument went, had brought us to a point of affluence where anything was possible. More specifically, this age in which we had finally moved beyond material scarcity promised us three things.

First, we were to have possessions in great measure. The cornucopia was spilling over, and there was no practical limit to the booty with which we could surround ourselves.

Second, little or no effort was necessary on our parts to produce all this. Robert Theobald, for example, announced that "the cybernated era will allow everybody a reasonable standard of living without toil" (1970:106). And Murray Bookchin promised us "a wide range of luxuries" at the same low price (1971:10).*

---

* See also Platt, 1972:26–27. These views were becoming sufficiently widespread to appear in popular fiction; see Herlihy, 1971:250.

Third, the millennium was to follow, more or less automatically. For Charles Reich, "it is just this simple: when there is enough food and shelter for all, man no longer needs to base his society on the assumption that all men are antagonistic to one another" (1970:415). For such adherents of the "new culture," Philip Slater reported, "there is no reason outside of human perversity for peace not to reign and for life not to be spent in the cultivation of joy and beauty" (1970:104). It was a pretty picture. Somewhere beyond our vision, the Great Cybernomachine would churn out goods, while we gamboled together in the grass.

To what extent was such a euphoric vision really warranted? True, we were a nation of staggering wealth. Personal disposable income was approaching $4000 per person annually, or $16,000 on the average for a family of four, and our output increased year by year. But such figures grow less impressive when examined. For one thing, they are grossly inflated by the huge incomes of the wealthy few. The vast majority of us make appreciably less; and postscarcity reasoning is likely to ring a little hollow for the twenty million or so Americans whom the government acknowledges to be living in poverty, as well as for the dozens of millions more who are barely surviving from one installment payment to the next. Moreover, significant advances in this picture are likely to be slow in coming. Over the period 1950–1970, disposable income per person (corrected for inflation to show actual purchasing power) grew by an average of only 2.9 percent a year (U.S. Bureau of the Census, 1972:315). And the steady deterioration of our economy in the years since 1970 gives notice that we may consider ourselves fortunate to achieve as much over the next twenty years. Wishful thinking aside, economic scarcity would seem to be alive and well in the United States.

A more sophisticated version of postscarcity thinking argues that all this misses the point. According to this view, *affluence is already ours,* were we only to recognize the fact. Instead of chasing after more goods to feed our material appetites, we should reassess our appetites to bring them more in line with the goods we have. Who really needs two color television sets, the argument goes, or two cars or snowmobiles, or Florida vacations or sirloin steaks or expensive new clothes or elaborate hi-fi systems? We can make our own music and grow our own food, hitchhike where we want to go and buy our clothes at the Goodwill store, and we will be the happier for it. Given this perspective, the problem with all those installment-ridden Middle Americans is not that their incomes are too low to pay cash for their major purchases, but rather that they were duped into making those purchases in the first place.

There is truth to this, of course; many of the things we buy *do* cripple rather than enhance our lives. But reducing our needs to fit our incomes is hardly a general solution as long as those incomes continue to vary greatly from person to person, a problem that the postscarcity theorists tend to leave untouched. More important for the purposes of this book, however, during the period of transition to the Great Cybernomachine (twenty years? fifty years? never?), those incomes will continue largely to be the result of work, whose nature cannot simply be ignored. Even if we were no longer to "want" and produce great quantities of junk, our lives would be only marginally improved if our work places continued to be demeaning and undemocratic, and if their separation from the rest of our lives helped perpetuate our current lack of organic ties with others and with our environment. In other words, virtually none of the problems we have talked of above as afflicting us in our daily lives would necessarily be solved by our becoming, or believing that we have become, affluent.

But this is perhaps to deal with postscarcity thought at too abstract a level. What our national wealth has tended to mean in practice is that increasing numbers of people have been offered the choice of doing well or dropping out and existing on the considerable leavings of society. The life styles that have resulted—the counterculture was the most prominent—have given some specific content to the idea of what a truly affluent society might actually involve. Most notably, these practitioners of "postscarcity" life patterns have asserted that no relationship need exist between work (which is to be avoided) and income (which might just as well come, and often does come, from welfare, savings, checks from home, inheritances, or gifts). We obviously cannot all live this way yet; but in the meanwhile, as Judson Jerome has argued, "those who are satisfied by acquisition should be enabled to acquire at the same time that we make possible survival for those who have less interest in acquisition or success through a career."* Liberated from hang-ups about success or any felt need to produce as much as we consume, we are to live for the time being off the work of others. And with the arrival of the Great Cybernomachine, none of us would have to work at all.

None of this postscarcity thinking is particularly new. Writing in 1793, William Godwin proposed that his contemporaries reassess their attitudes toward the accumulation of goods. Given more modest material desires, "the necessity for the greater part of the manual industry of mankind would

---

* Quoted from a 1972 draft of Jerome's *Families of Eden: Communes and the New Anarchism* (New York: The Seabury Press, 1974).

be superseded; and the rest, being amicably shared among all the active and vigorous members of the community, would be burthensome to none" (quoted in Woodcock, 1962:87). Ultimately, with advances in technology, the "burthens" would be even further reduced. And in the meantime, the enlightened could at least adopt a postscarcity life style of their own: Godwin himself was "one of the most notorious and unashamed spongers of his time, constantly borrowing money which he rarely repaid" (Joll, 1964:38). Godwin's argument parallels much recent postscarcity argument, notably with respect to the conclusions he drew as to the appropriate sources of his own income.

At least until the millennium arrives, such attitudes are treading perilous political ground. Many people would agree on the need for some sort of dole for those whom society has left behind. Fewer are likely to find appeal in permanent subsidies for those who have left society behind. It is one thing to believe our values to be superior ones; it is quite another to feel that our superior consciousness entitles us to be supported by others.

This is especially true where the working poor and middle classes are expected to support the dropout children of the wealthy (or the dropout wealthy themselves). The political realities can be obscured by dismissing, as "those who are satisfied by acquisition," the people who will keep the economic machine clicking along. But the argument remains a class-based one. Walter Weisskopf, for example, eagerly anticipates the coming era "in which most people will have to live on an 'independent' fixed income like the precapitalist aristocracy. . . . This income they will receive even if they do nothing but enjoy themselves" (1971:175). Even if the aristocrats became numerically preponderant, as Weisskopf assumes, the All-New Postscarcity America would remain rooted in the serfdom of those who continued to work.

There is a more fundamental point still. Suppose that we could *all* lay down our tools and retire from the "productive" scene—would eternal glory be ours? We think not. Although we can agree that work for its own sake is an outmoded notion, we continue to believe that the spirit profits from a felt connection between the expenditure of our energies and the maintenance of our lives. Whether the "work" that supplies our food, clothing, and shelter takes us twelve hours a day or two (we prefer the latter), a direct link between our acts and our survival seems preferable to a life dependent on manna from the Great Cybernomachine. This latter path subsumes us totally within a highly-rationalized technological structure whose integrity is obviously then more fundamental than our own. This is but an extension of our present social realities. And as such, it is a further move in the wrong direction.

Assuming that our current economic problems fade away and "affluence" is once more ours, we should perhaps view this less as a solution in itself than as an opportunity to choose specific modes of living that will ennoble our days, and potentially the days of all of our fellows. Some years ago, Percival and Paul Goodman noted that "for the first time in history we have, spectacularly in the United States, a surplus of technology, a technology of free choice, that allows for the most widely various community-arrangements and ways of life" (1960:11). If our choices have in practice tended toward a free rein for technology and/or a permanent vacation for ourselves, these are not the only possibilities. Our vision could also be one of small, organic groups, united in play and meaningful work, so constituted that most of the decisions which affect us are within the range of our comprehension and our touch.

If on first look this vision seems a good one, there remains the question of whether we are moving to achieve it. And this question in turn becomes one of what we cherish. Are the elements of such a life style congenial to the system of values we hold? Equally important, if we aspire to such goals, are our values such as to allow us to get there? The answers are not easy, nor are they reassuring. There is at least the strong likelihood that we are now torn between incompatible values, the most tenacious of which are imposed by our culture in such a way as to condemn us indefinitely to play out the sordid drama we claim to be trying to flee.

Chapter 2: The "New Values"

During the late 1960s, the United States went through what many people took to be a profound assault on its most cherished beliefs. In keeping with the expansiveness of the times, reports of what was happening tended toward the hyperbolic. The carriers of the new values were mutations, a more advanced form of life. In them was reposited Consciousness Three. Some observers, Murray Bookchin among them, saw the roots of the new order in technological developments extending back at least thirty years. But the point, for Bookchin as for others, was that our vastly altered technological condition "negates all the values, political schemes and social perspectives held by mankind throughout all previous history" (1971:93). The negation was coming alive before our eyes, and our destiny was to be part of it, whatever the cost:

> We must apply the blade to ourselves and cut back the outer skin to expose the pulsing flesh. And then we must harrow and pulverize the outer skin and use our egos for compost. Then, in the new flesh, we must plant the seeds of the people we wish to become. (Gardner, 1970:15)

The Aquarian Age was upon us, in all its torment and glory.

And now it is gone, or so one would think from a tour through the media. Instead of running stories about dope-fed communards dancing in flowering meadows, your weekly news magazine is likely to be telling you of the communards' return to law school. The media early on had become pre-occupied with the most extreme expressions of the "new values," particularly as acted out by the younger Aquarians. When the extremes either faded (as did the rush to rural communes) or became routine (as did the dope-smoking), the media simply lost interest. "Youth is not making the scene the way it used to," noted *Time* in an article entitled "The Graying of America" (1973:76). By implication, it would seem, we were getting back to normal.

But "normal" is a bit different these days. The earthquake of the youth revolt had a more lasting counterpart in lesser tremors that shook people throughout the social structure. Whatever the media's treatment of this era may suggest, the results endure. And necessarily so, since the seismic roots of all these phenomena were precisely the sorts of continuing problems we raised at the outset of this book. The problems once confronted, as the paroxysms of the 1960s forced many people to do for the first time, they are not easily forgotten. And the "new values" adopted in response tend to stick. The thrust of our argument is that the "new values" are not in fact new enough to allow the sorts of action which would solve the underlying problems themselves. But in terms of the glacial pace of social change we have come to expect in this country, they represent a fresh way for many people to view their lives.

There is no clearly-defined group, we should note, within which such people exist. The "new values" have been embraced by commune dwellers, college professors, shop keepers, business executives, blue-collar workers, and government officials. Not everyone in these categories is a carrier of the "new values," of course, and not every carrier is equally devoted to each of the values we discuss. Some people have embraced the whole package of attitudes. But these emerge more commonly in less sweeping forms of self-assertion, from an executive's refusal to carry work home to an antique dealer's move from the city to a shop in a rural village. The fevers of the 1960s broken, the "new values" remain with us, if now in more diffuse and muted form.

THE "NEW VALUES"

The most important among the constellation of values to remain from the turbulence of the 1960s seem to be a search for pleasure and joyfulness, concentration on the moment here and now, release from work, the pursuit of aesthetic, natural, and spiritual goals, and individualism. Noble objectives all—or are they? In our discussion, we present these values in their strongest form, as if they had captured the public imagination in somewhat more pervasive and coherent fashion than has been the case. To do this is to understand more clearly their limitations. If the existing system has led people to be discontented with their lives, general adoption of the "new values" which have resulted from this discontent would do little to move us forward.

Pleasure and Joy. Perhaps the basic insight of the new consciousness is that few people in America seem to be having a good time, and that something should be done about it. Trapped in an extended hangover from our Puritan past, we are guilty of the "repression of drives, passions, emotions, feelings, sentiments, sensuality, sensuousness; of fantasy, spontaneity, creativity, joy, play, nonpurposive, expressive behavior" (W. Weisskopf, 1971: 36). Quite rightly, this degree of repression is seen to have given our lives a dreary cast, and there seems to be no good reason not to have fun instead. But what is fun to consist of? Some of its elements, such as sensuality and creativity, are relatively straightforward, but others must be inferred from what people choose to leave behind. Here, as with many of the new values, the process originally began with a sweeping rejection of the old order (our lives will no longer be dreary) and took form in the negation of specific aspects of that order (we will no longer do the following dreary things . . .). It is with some of these negations that we begin to follow the search for joy.

First, what is no longer satisfying is the restless attempt to buy pleasure in the marketplace. In most cases, the carriers of the new values are affluent enough to have become saturated with cars and television sets and all the rest, and it is logical that by now they would simply have lost interest in such things. But then there is a further trap to be avoided. Standing ready in the wings are a thousand commercial brokers of nonmaterial paths to joy: peddlers of sex manuals and yoga courses, lavishly-paid leaders of sensitivity sessions, light-show entrepreneurs, and so on. As Toffler has noted, "From a system designed to provide material satisfaction, we are rapidly creating an economy geared to the provision of psychic gratification" (1970: 195). It is all too easy to fall back into this economic mainstream. At least for the purists, this is no solution. Instead, they have retreated to the hills, or at least to a state of mind, where pleasure is to be made, not bought.

Whatever pleasurable things we are to make, however, do not include the products of our minds, for a second negation is that of reason, or, broadly defined, "the scientific world view." For all too long, we have been bottled up inside our heads, rationalizing our experiences and therefore remaining detached from them, instead of responding freely and joyfully to the world around us. The remedies are extreme. For Theodore Roszak, "nothing less is required than the subversion of the scientific world view . . . In its place, there must be a new culture in which the non-intellective capacities of the personality . . . become the arbiters of the good, the true, and the beautiful" (1969:50). And Roszak is something of a moderate on such matters, allowing science at least a role as one "school of consciousness" among others, albeit one of greatly reduced importance (1972:222). There are those who would deny it even that degree of legitimacy.

Third, pleasure is not to come from involvement in large social issues. To be sure, political radicals are still among us, waging the good fight against the structural bases of bureaucracy, alienation, racism, sexism, inequality, imperialism, and the other symptoms of a technologically advanced capitalist system. And even among our most resolutely back-to-the-earth communards, there has occasionally surfaced the sort of cry that would be immediately understood by social activists. Thus, Ray Mungo, speaking of his life on Total Loss Farm, asserts that "We till the soil to atone for our fathers' destruction of it" (1970:17).

But by and large, activism is assumed to provide little pleasure and less joy, and therefore coexists uneasily with the new consciousness. In part, this springs from the political disillusionments of the 1960s. The war in Vietnam long outlasted massive actions to end it, and policies of "benign neglect" triumphed effortlessly over attempts to pursue domestic justice. But equally important, politics proved largely to be an exercise in either rage or reason—the delineation of objectives, selection of tactics, concern over logistics—and in neither case was there much joy to be found. To some degree, at least, the playful new consciousness is an escape from the earnestness of social concern.

Release from Work. For our purposes here, the new values involve a further negation that is worth looking at separately. It has come to be almost universally believed that pleasure, and virtually all other values worthy of allegiance, require our release from work. This is implicit in the drive in straight society for a four- (or three-) day week, which would free more of our time for the things we enjoy. Those with more visionary programs for reconstituting society would go the straight world one better, and do away with work altogether. But the tendencies are the same; and in the most diverse sources the theme is repeated:

MURRAY BOOKCHIN: "My suspicion is that the workers, when they get into revolutionary motion, will demand even more than the control of the factories. I think they will demand the elimination of toil, or what amounts to the same thing, freedom from work." (1971:16)

SUSAN SHAFFNER: "If what someone wants to do most in life is to work full time to attain material wealth, fine; let him work in happiness. But many people would rather go with a little less so that they can spend their life doing what they want to do most (not their jobs)." (1972:4)

HENRI GOUGAUD (on communes in France): "People work together in many collectives.... But it is important to understand that common work is not then the essential part of the group's life. Work ensures material survival, that's all. The important things are elsewhere." (1971:24)

R. BUCKMINSTER FULLER: "We must do away with the absolutely specious notion that everybody has to earn a living . . . that everybody has to be employed at some kind of drudgery because, according to Malthusian-Darwinian theory, he must justify his right to exist.... The true business of people should be to . . . think about whatever it was they were thinking about before somebody came along and told them they had to earn a living." (Quoted by Davidson, 1970:96)

There are four closely related assumptions here. First, work is drudgery, enslavement, toil; it has no redeeming social value. Second, it logically follows that work is something one does only to earn a living. Third, as noted in Chapter 1, technological advances have made work obsolescent. Many of us already need not work, and it is only a matter of time until we all are so blessed. Finally, given the unpleasantness of work and the lack of necessity for doing it, why not just stop? We may have to overcome our "Malthusian-Darwinian" or other hang-ups about its value, but the message is plain for us to see: drop out, have a good time.

Here and Now. One way to know that we are having a good time—and we are dealing here in negatives again—is that we are not in pursuit of some distant goal. Philip Slater has noted that in our society "The answer to 'what are you doing?' can be 'nothing' only if one is a child. An adult's answer must always imply some ulterior purpose—something that will be fed back into the mindless and unremitting productivity of the larger system" (1970:91). And if this is undesirable in itself, it has other negative implications as well. We must reason our way through the system in a way that holds our attention always to the future rather than the present, which is obviously the only place where pleasure and joy are to be experienced. Better to become "purposeless" and focus on the moment at hand. As one countercultural cliché had it, "Getting there isn't half the fun, it's *all* the fun." It matters less where we are going, in other words, than how we act on the way. In the current jargon, we have become "process-oriented," rather than goal-directed. We are to live fully in the here and now.

There is something else implied in the idea of "process," however. We may head in no particular direction, but neither will we stay where we are. Tomorrow's "here and now" will be different from today's, which in turn is something other than yesterday's. This tendency is rooted in assumptions that are basic to our sense of self and society. As Erich Fromm said, "What holds true for the individual holds true for society. It is never static; if it does not grow, it decays; if it does not transcend the *status quo* for the better, it changes for the worse" (1968:16). Fromm's statement suggests something of an idea of the "better" toward which we aspire. But his sense that one way or another we must be engaged in restless, perennial change is one that the new consciousness accepts as well.

Given the importance we attach to a shifting here and now, it is inevitable that many of the "new values" should be coextensive with, or at least derived from, those of the "youth culture." Our national preoccupation with youth has been widely noted, of course. Keith Melville puts it this way:

> Rather than respecting the subtle values of maturity, we celebrate the physical strength, spontaneity, and vitality of youth. Why is it, after all, that everyone over thirty is encouraged to commit cosmetic camouflage to disguise the fact? And why are the media constantly attacking us with the world view of the Now Generation? Is it because our best consumers are fairly young, or because we have no other conception of what values we might revere than those of youth? (1972:94–95)

Naturally, both answers are correct. We cannot conceive of values other than those of the young precisely *because* the young are our best consumers, and this is an age where the "consumption" of an endlessly changing stock of pleasurable experiences, people, and things has become a value for most of us. Viewed in this fashion, the "generation gap" takes on somewhat different meaning. It is not so much that the values of the young differ from those of their parents, but that the young are better able to act out those values. After all, somebody has to mind the store. The young can postpone this, while their parents—regretting it all the while—cannot, at least not yet.

Still unanswered, however, is the basic question, what *are* the values that the young are better able to realize than the old, but to which the old aspire as well? So far, we have only discussed what they are *not*. They do not lie in the future; they are not things rational, material, or political; they are not to be found in work. Our negative approach to the question is intentional, for the new values themselves were born of reaction to an existing society felt to be in many ways unpleasant. The very negation of values, however, implies at least some sense of direction. In this case, we may assume from the above that what people value must lie in the immediate experience of pleasures of an intuitive or ecstatic sort. But this is simply to push the question one step further. Of what sort are the ecstasies or intuitions we prize, and what conditions are required to achieve them?

Aesthetics, Nature, and Religion. The first source of pleasure for the new consciousness lies in aesthetics, loosely defined to include art, handicrafts, and the design of living space. Although hardly a spokesman for the new values, John Kenneth Galbraith anticipated this tendency several years ago in looking to the future of our industrial system: "Aesthetic goals will have pride of place; those who serve them will not be subject to the goals of the industrial system; the industrial system itself will be subordinate to the claims of these dimensions of life" (1967:405). Whether or not the industrial system has been brought into line as yet, the years since Galbraith wrote have seen the emergence of thousands of painters, leather workers, silversmiths, designers of inexpensive but imaginative housing (especially on rural communes), workers in macramé and leaded glass, potters, cabinet-makers, and others. To be sure, we have always had our craftspeople, but never before has it been so central to us to surround ourselves with beautiful objects that we or our friends have created.

A second thrust of the new values lies in everything "natural," as in "natural foods" or the "return to nature." Away with plastics, chemical additives in our food, and the ubiquitous concrete of parking lots and free-ways. Instead, we want to walk barefoot through the grass under the stars, and harvest our own food from soil untainted by pesticides. There is a *real* world out there, so the message goes, one not of human making, in whose vistas and imperatives we need again to become involved. And this is serious business. According to Ray Mungo:

> We are never higher or nobler than when we are weeding the eggplants, and all concern for literature and society disappears there in our greater concern for life. . . . [We] are going to die on Total Loss Farm, we will die very soon with the rest of the race, and yet live here forever. That is how

we survive, in our souls, and in the beauty in earthly nature which seizes our bodies for organic waste. (1970:164, 169)

Not everyone would wax that lyrical, and it is in any case hard to find eggplants to weed in most of urban America. But even there, people can and do make their own yogurt and buy stone-ground flour to bake their bread.

The vision of nature which Mungo and others have embraced is at root a spiritual one; and it is in the realm of the spirit that a further value of the new consciousness is to be found. Our materially-oriented culture is directing itself more and more toward a search for cosmic values. The transformation has many causes, but it got perhaps its biggest push from the Swiss chemist Albert Hoffman, who in 1943 discovered, quite by accident, the hallucinogenic properties of lysergic acid diethylamide: LSD. Through the 1960s, thousands of people "dropped acid" and experienced what they could only describe as transcendence. Keith Melville, for example, quotes an Oregon communard whose acid trip had taken him "cell for cell, vibration for vibration, back to the common denominator, that one seed which we all came from" (1972:162). Turning on became almost a moral imperative. For Jerry Garcia,

> To get really high is to forget yourself. And to forget yourself is to see everything else. And to see everything else is to become an understanding molecule in evolution, a conscious tool of the universe. And I think every human being should be a conscious tool of the universe. That's why I think it's important to get high. (1972:36)

If the use of psychedelic drugs seemed to many a violation of all that America stood for, the lessons of the drug experience filtered quickly into consciousnesses that were primed to receive them. By the early 1970s, the pursuit of transcendence found testimony in the popularity of an astonishing range of books whose common denominator was the drive for greater spiritual understanding: the Richard Wilhelm translation of the *I Ching,* Paramahansa Yogananda's *Autobiography of a Yogi,* Theodore Roszak's *Where the Wasteland Ends,* John C. Lilly's *The Center of the Cyclone,* Carlos Castaneda's books about the *brujo* Don Juan, the Lama Foundation's *Be Here Now,* even Richard Bach's *Jonathan Livingston Seagull.* It began to seem that the "pleasure" the new consciousness was ultimately seeking was that provided by an enlarged spirit.

Individualism. If we have been peeling back the layers of the new consciousness one by one, we have not yet reached its core. For the emphasis on cosmic understanding conceals an even more basic assumption about how that understanding is to come about. Thus, Dick Fairfield comments that "Each of us, as we are one with all, is totally alone. Solitary. Separate" (1971: 177). In a word, each of us is an *individual* even as we are One; and never forget it, for in that lies our glory. William Kaysing states, "The age of individuality has dawned" (1972:10). Theodore Roszak, writing on the "politics of the visionary commonwealth," maintains that "Its field of play is the individual soul" (1972:435). Roszak, the scholar, finds points of reference in the visionary works of the Romantic poets. But we need never have read a Romantic line to be conscious of the pervasive message of today: Spiritual insight comes to us one by one, solitary, separate. Look to yourself, for only there can vision be found.

This is often difficult to achieve since there is not enough privacy in our lives, a fact that sharply limits our individual growth. According to Charles Reich, "The self needs, above all, privacy, liberty, and a degree of sovereignty to develop" (1970:150). And Erich Fromm concurs that "privacy still seems to be an important condition for a person's productive development. First of all, because privacy is necessary to collect oneself and to free oneself from the constant 'noise' of people's chatter and intrusion . . ." (1968:45). Most people would take this for granted. The new consciousness reaffirms it, providing a more explicitly spiritual rationale for tendencies toward separateness.

Our use of language underscores this fundamental sense of separation from each other (except at the mystical—abstract?—level at which we are One). The English language is not rich in collective forms of expression. We seem to feel that such forms imply immersion in the faceless mass at the expense of our individuality, and thus are loath to use them.

A good example of this is the Great Pronoun Debate fueled by the women's liberation movement. With justice, feminists complain about the discrimination inherent in the habitual use of the masculine pronoun in sentences such as: "Anyone can join the choir if *he* can carry a tune"; "If anybody you know has a bad drug trip, have *him* call the Crisis Center"; "If someone looks hard enough, *he* will find God." Since English has no pronouns that mean "he or she," "him or her," we should therefore invent them—or so the argument goes. "Tey" and "tem" have been proposed for this purpose, as has "co": "Anyone can join the choir if *co* can carry a tune."

All this would be largely academic, however, were it not for our dogged individualism, since virtually every instance where this problem arises could be dealt with by use of plural forms: * *"All those* who can carry a tune may join the choir"; "If you know people on bad drug trips, have *them* call the Crisis Center"; "If we look hard enough, *we* will find God." But the fact that the problem persists is no accident. The assumption that human possibilities are fundamentally individual ones is too deeply rooted for us to be comfortable with collectivizations of our language. As representatives of the new consciousness would be the first to affirm, it is as individuals that we carry tunes, trip out, or find God.

"NEW VALUES" AT AN IMPASSE

In the next chapter, we stress the degree to which the new values are destructively parochial in their view of human nature and the paths to truth. And we suggest an orientation to values and social structure, rooted in communal work, that could more readily lead to radically transformed, humane styles of living. For the moment, however, let us accept the new values as legitimate ones and ask only this question: Are they likely to lead people where they want to go?

Value Systems. For individualism to hold sway, we obviously must avoid accepting any socially-given, overriding value system that might interfere with our personal search for truth. That is, our values are our own and must be fully respected as such. There is no higher code through which judgment might be brought against us, save only in the case where we do direct harm to others. Charles Reich calls this the "second commandment" of Consciousness Three: "No one judges anyone else" (1970:243). And Fritz Perls has provided the definitive statement of this "commandment": "I do my thing and you do your thing. I am not in this world to live up to your expectations, and you are not in this world to live up to mine. You are you and I am I; and if by chance we find each other, it's beautiful" (quoted in Greenburg, 1972:250). But don't hold your breath waiting. The idea is that individual points of moral reference are different, so that there is no common ground from which mutual expectations might arise. Under the circumstances, what we can best do is avoid breathing down one another's necks as we follow our separate paths to self-actualization.

---

* Except for the examples just used, and in quotations from other sources, neither the awkward "he or she" nor "he" as a substitute for this appears in these pages. There may be occasions where one of these usages is called for, but we have written an entire book without finding one.

In a way, this is a case of morality trailing along behind economic theory. Describing how economists approach the measurement of the general welfare, Walter Weisskopf notes:

> Welfare economics eliminates the social and moral context of the concept of economic welfare and finds welfare only in an increase of the welfare of the individuals; but the welfare of individuals is also denuded of any objective content and defined in purely value-empty terms . . . which, at least in theory, can include anything that the individual desires. No idea of the individual good, the "common good," the "public interest" or the good as such, no concept of right and wrong, is left in the modern concepts of common welfare. (1971:93–94)

In other words, whether we choose to consume pushpin or poetry, as Jeremy Bentham once put it, is of no interest to the economist, as long as we enjoy what we are doing. Welfare economics caught up with this version of nineteenth-century utilitarianism some time ago. More recently, our approach to interpersonal relationships has followed suit. Everyone is to be happy, but our personal sense of what comprises happiness cannot be generalized to anyone else.

There are two problems here. First, to say that each individual is to have an independent value system is, in fact, to impose one basic value on everyone, the necessity for psychological apartness. In this sense, the new values are an exercise in hypocrisy, saying in effect: "You are free to believe anything you want, as long as you cherish the One True Way—individualism—along with everybody else." Someone who brings to personal contacts a desire for *inter*dependence, commitment over time, and the search for common understandings is therefore in trouble. Such a person would constantly encounter the refrain, "But that way you lose your freedom, which requires being separate like me. Go ahead and be interdependent, but on your own time. Don't try to involve anyone else." So much for freedom of choice.

A second problem arises in the extent to which a refusal to accept explicit common values means that such values simply slip in through the back door. Obviously, no society can exist where no assumptions are shared by its members. A host of shared perceptions and beliefs are required for us to carry out the simplest social functions: planting the garden together, talking, looking for work, dancing, making love. To pretend that we are morally self-contained cannot do away with this fact. It can only allow our common understandings to drift in, unexamined, from our social environment. This is what has happened with the new consciousness. In reality, few of its attitudes are truly new, a point we pursue in our chapter on counterculture communes. Instead, such values as individualism, aesthetic experience, and the avoidance of work were already implicit in the ethos of industrial America out of which the "new values" grew. The new consciousness made these values explicit, codified them, and insisted on living them more fully. It did not invent them.

This is not to say that the new culture is synonymous with the old. It is doubtless better that individual self-actualization, for example, is now measured more in spiritual than in material terms. And we can prefer that people in the process of avoiding toil make music rather than watching televised football games while drinking at the corner bar. But the fact remains that at key points the new values are just more fully articulated versions of the old. To the extent that this is true, considerable doubt is cast on our ability to create environments that point in the directions we want to go, rather than back toward the place from which we, and our values, came.

Attitudes Toward Community. The danger is perhaps most clearly evident in our attitudes toward group experience. Obviously, if we are to create living situations that are radically different from those of the "straight" world, we must do this together. The more isolated we are from one another, the more pieces of our daily lives will take place within the contexts we would like to shed. If we live alone, for example, our personal contacts are far more likely to take place at Functions, By Appointment, than if we are living together. If we rely solely on ourselves for material sustenance, our working lives will be bound up at more points with the System than if we work together. And a greater portion of our time will be devoted to "earning a living," since solitary life styles—or their nuclear-family variant— are an extraordinarily costly way to live. To escape all this, we need each other.

But it is precisely this about which the new consciousness is most dubious. To recognize that "each of us, as we are one with all, is also totally alone" is to make our real "community" the Community of Everyone, while preserving our individualism in our direct personal dealings. Gar Alperovitz, for example, asserts that: "Within the best communities one major point deserves emphasis: Individual responsibility—to act, to take initiative, to build cooperation voluntarily—is a necessary precondition of a community of mutual, reciprocal obligation" (1972:528). It is an image of community as a series of contractual relationships, stated or unstated, designed to meet each individual's sense of private need. We still resist the idea of organic community as having *in itself* transcendent meaning from which (and from which alone) we can find meaning in our individual lives. For us, it is always the other way around: the individual precedes the group.

This particular assumption of our culture is so powerful that it seems an ineradicable part of our consciousness. The extent of its power over us can be felt in the way we view cultures of different persuasion. Thus, Erich Fromm speaks of "primitive" societies whose members feel integrally bound into the being of the things around themselves—people, animals, land:

> By remaining bound to nature, to mother or father [or group], man indeed succeeds in feeling at home in the world, but he pays a tremendous price for this security, that of submission, dependence, and a blockage to the full development of his reason and of his capacity to love. He remains a child when he should become an adult.

Happily, we are adults now:

> The new bond which permits man to feel at one with all men is fundamentally different . . .; it is the harmonious bond of brotherhood in which solidarity and human ties are not vitiated by restrictions of freedom, either emotionally or intellectually. (1968:66–67)

Exactly, and there lies the hook. For if only our relationships with ourselves are holistic, while those with the people around us remain primarily functional, then our group life is attenuated to a point of extreme fragility. And such is the case where we tolerate the group only as long as it does not impinge on our emotional or intellectual "freedom." There will be two results. First, we will expose to the group only those parts of ourselves which we feel the group can feed. Basically, we will remain intact and distinct. This implies that we may "belong" to a number of groups, each of which offers us separate things and to each of which our allegiance remains partial, at best. Second, such groups are likely to be either transitory (folding as members grow bored with them) or stable only in an institutional sense (members come, members go). In neither case will the group come to have any real organic meaning for those involved in it.

Objections will quickly be raised to this gloomy view of the new values and their implications for group experience. Roszak, for one, looks at the new spirituality and comes to very different conclusions: "The relationship is ancient and indisputable—the politics of eternity has always automatically become communitarian politics." But there is an immediate, and telling, qualification: "The stronger the mystical sensibility, the stronger the longing for *anarchist* brotherhood and sisterhood" (1972:425; our emphasis). These days, "anarchist" has come to imply the condition where we are all to do our own things, unfettered by binding ties to other people or to particular groups. What Roszak is doing, then, is robbing us with one hand of the promise of communitarianism he has given us with the other. We are back to fulfilling our separate destinies again, though we may feel brotherly and sisterly in so doing. "Communitarian politics," in other words, may have little to do with community.

The point is an important one, since many "new-values" people are equally guilty of muddying the distinction between mystical insight and its social expression. True mystical experience may well be the same at all times and in all places, and a sense of cosmic unities may be its essence. But after we come down from our mystical high, the implications we draw for our social relationships, and even the language in which we try to tell others of where we have been, will be conditioned by our cultural environment. That is, African mystics are likely to find new meaning in their organic units, while American mystics may simply find new meaning in their individualism. In the latter case, a sense of fellowship with humankind may follow; but there is no reason to believe that strong group experiences will do the same.

A stronger objection to our pessimism about the American cultural "revolution" comes from those who feel that significant group activities have in fact been arising everywhere in the past several years. We deal with this more fully in other chapters, but it deserves a few words here. First, this is hardly a new phenomenon, especially among the young. More than a decade ago, in college, we were ourselves striving for "self-actualization" through living in "communes," belonging to political "collectives," and achieving "higher states of consciousness" with groups of friends. We did not know we were doing these things, of course, because the jargon had not yet been invented. But we did them just the same, along with hundreds of thousands of our peers. At the same time, our parents were choosing between civic centers, bridge clubs, and a whole range of political groups as social foci of their own lives. Group activities—even "new" ones—have been around for a long time. The new consciousness did not create the idea.

What *has* changed, to some degree at least, is the tone of group life. The youth have expanded on their traditional role of bringing to groups a sense of the playful, the open, the adventurous, and their parents are increasingly doing the same. But this is more a mellowing of group dynamics than an increase in group solidarity. People have rejected—and happily so—the quality of brittle intensity that had come to be identified with the social life of the old culture. And they have replaced it with a simplicity, directness, and easy good fellowship that is reminiscent, say, of evenings spent with the Vermont dairy farmers who until recently comprised our immediate community. It is all to the good, but it is less the forging of a new group consciousness than a drift into something akin to the spirit of preindustrial New England townships. No more than ever are our communities the central fact of our lives. Instead, they continue to be subordinate to our individual senses of need, readily discarded or ignored if our attention should happen to move elsewhere.

Where we seek out groups only for what they may provide for a part of ourselves, however, members of these groups will have to be alike, at least in those areas of common concern on which the groups are based. And as we accentuate our similarities to allow such intercourse to occur, the groups themselves will become increasingly alike in a lowest-common-denominator form of social osmosis. Conformity, in other words, is inherent in the social life of an individualistic culture. As we show in the next chapter, *individualism,* the most basic of the "new" values, is therefore one of the worst ways to allow for maximum growth and integrity of the *individual,* in whose interests the new culturists claim to be acting.

Americans may be reluctant to accept this, but there is a further problem whose implications are more obvious. As we assert throughout this book, and as most bearers of the new consciousness would agree, the society we are striving for must have certain features: greater interpersonal directness, increased control over our own lives, less dehumanizing patterns of production and consumption, a touch of the divine in daily life. All of these features suggest a reduction in the variety and scale of the social units of which we are a part. But here the new values are caught in a hopeless contradiction. Attachment to a limited number of small groups appears to bear the threat of oppression, of a diminished individuality. And where individualism is the ultimate value, it seems easier to participate in a number of larger systems—job, cooperative, political collective, living "community"—each of whose claims are sufficiently limited to leave us apparently intact. Just as the "new" values at many points resemble the old, so does the "new" social structure mimic the forms of the past. As "revolutionaries," we prove to be deeply conservative, embracing the lineaments of a society we pretend to reject. So bound, we are unlikely to achieve what we want.

Design of the Future. Contributing to our complicity with the old ways is the fact that we are reluctant to design new ones. To be sure, we have our Buckminster Fullers and our Paolo Soleris, but they are unrepresentative of the new values. As we are uncomfortable with reason, so do we resist its social expression: planning and design of our environment. To some degree, this might seem an appropriate response to the society in which we live. We have only to look around us to realize what a rationalized economy can do to our environment, our heads, our lives. But finding attempts to "design" our lives wanting, the new consciousness has tried to make a cosmic principle of doing nothing of the sort. As Judson Jerome puts it, "Finally what the counterculture has come to realize is that design itself is the evil."* Better to focus on the here and now, we may conclude, and let the future take care of itself.

In both diagnosis and prescription, however, this approach is almost pathologically culture-bound. "Planning" and "design" are inherent in the human situation itself, as close to universals as we can expect to find. But the roots of design vary enormously in different cultures. In the United States, we plan according to the requirements of technological development and economic growth. In simpler societies, design follows the contours of the land and the social realities of the tribe. One approach requires immersion in the machine; the other, immersion in life. To suggest that "design itself is the evil" only reveals that our consciousness is unable to transcend our cultural boundaries.

But the issue here is not degree of sociological insight. Rather, what is important are the social consequences of rejecting "designing" in favor of an eternal here and now. To be fully involved in a moment is a noble state of being. But there are different sorts of moments. To be fully involved in a moment on an assembly line is not the same thing as being involved in a kiss. Metaphorically speaking, to surround ourselves with kisses instead of auto chassis may require a period of planning, perhaps even deferred involvements, to provide the environment we want. To resist this, as the new values would have us do, is to condemn ourselves in fair measure to the moments society chooses to give us, the very moments that led us to proclaim the need for a new consciousness in the first place. If we keep coming back to the place where we began, we should begin to suspect our map.

Implications for Change. In the latter part of the 1960s, it was widely

---

* Quoted from a 1972 draft of Jerome, 1974.

assumed that we needed basic changes in the ways in which American society functioned and in which we lived. Revolutionary movements were everywhere. There were the ethnic power movements (black, brown, yellow, and red), the new marriage forms, the revolution in ecological awareness, the new populism, the youth revolution, the new consciousness, the sexual revolution, the women's liberation movement, the commune movement, the psychedelic revolution, the student power movement, the natural foods craze, the counterculture, the peace movement, and the new spiritualism, to name only the most obvious. The mass media, always alert to trumpet the Biggest, the Newest, the Best, nearly went crazy trying to keep up. But their job is easier these days. We seem to be running short of revolutions.

This is not, however, because we are busy consolidating the successes of the 1960s. Our political terrain, for example, is of an almost unimaginable bleakness, with the best that can be said of it all being that we have become too numb to mind. And it would take a delicate instrument indeed to measure any widespread changes in the ways we work or live from day to day. For most of us, our lives continue to be fragmented; our work is of no greater value than before, nor is its context more personal; we consume many of the same things, deficient in both conception and workmanship, at many of the same places; and our relationships with each other and our surroundings remain relatively distant.

Nor do the "new values" groups themselves really stir the blood. At the farthest edge of the movement, there are surely a few scattered people who have created whole alternatives to America. But what prevails of the new culture tends to be severely compromised. Women become conscious of their full humanity and assert their rights, within the System. Craftspeople make beautiful objects, which decorate the homes of those whom the System has made wealthy enough to afford them. People buy rural property together, forming "communities" or land trusts, and then scatter their private homes about the land in an ecologically-conscious version of the suburbs. People seek spiritual and psychological revelation, purchased from such growth industries as encounter and sex therapy foundations or the Cosmic Consciousness divisions of the major publishers. People struggle over the formulation of new ideas and insights, backed by foundation money and with a promise of publication through normal System channels (witness this book). As bearers of the new consciousness and social order, we have not come very far.

Or perhaps we never started. It has been chilling to see the ease with which new consciousness phenomena have been co-opted by the surrounding culture. Your local supermarket carries crunchy granola, Tamari sauce, and whole wheat flour. Your local junior executive smokes dope and wears the current countercultural fashions to work. Your local bank offers loans to back your change of life style from urban job to refurbisher of old chairs for sale from your rural garage. And insistence on spiritual uplift has taken hold everywhere: in 1972, the acting director of the FBI made *Jonathan Livingston Seagull* more or less required reading for his top associates "because I want their minds to soar" (quoted in *Newsweek*, October 16, 1972:34). Rather than being a radical break with the past, perhaps the new consciousness has been only a designer of fashions, all of which were but a step ahead of where the culture was anyway.

In sum, what we needed in the late 1960s and early 1970s were groups of people willing to make the commitments to each other and to transcendent values that would have forced change: change in the body politic and, perhaps even more important, change in the form of organic working-living-playing-praying units which could have been the cells of a new social order and of a transformed consciousness. What we got instead were individuals seeking separate paths to "self-actualization" or pursuing their own momentary "trips." All the rest followed: the avoidance of common points of moral reference, the related inability to form organic groups, the unwillingness to plan where such groups might have gone in any case, and the inevitable reaffirmation of most of the social patterns of the straight society. If the "new consciousness" has provided people with what they take to be fresh perspective on their lives, it has not basically changed them.

People seem content just to survive these days. The deeper social problems have not gone away, however, and people have not completely forgotten them. It might take another Vietnam War—not all that unlikely—or maybe just the right conjunction of the stars, and then they will be ready for another try. But there is much to be learned. If people are to make the break they need the next time around, they will have to avoid the mistakes of the last time. Might there not be new models to reflect on, different ideas of meaning and wholeness, that could suggest ways out of this cultural impasse? We think there are.

Chapter 3: The Communal Work Place—
Vision and Values

To illustrate the structure and values of a social order responsive to the problems outlined in Chapter 1, we begin below with a description of one communal work place. Should you follow the clues we provide to its location, however, you may be disappointed. If you inquire at the local general store or post office as to where the commune can be found, they may look at you strangely and suggest you have lost your way. At some point, you may begin to wonder whether the group exists at all, whether we have invented the tales we tell of it. In the face of such doubts, we would quote Black Elk: "This they tell, and whether it happened so or not I do not know; but if you think about it, you can see that it is true" (in Neihardt, 1961:5). Approach it that way. Think of the traditional societies we describe, of communal life in Israel, China, and the United States. Consider what men and women have aspired to and, at their best, have been, and you will see that it is true.

THE TANA COMMUNE

Three miles up the Branch Road from Toby's General Store, in the Craftsbury Township of northern Vermont, live the fifty members of the Tana Commune. Tana began in the summer of 1968, when three families moved to Vermont from Cambridge, Massachusetts. It had been an awful spring. Martin Luther King and Robert Kennedy had been murdered, local campuses were in turmoil, the forces of "order" were growing ever more brutally repressive. Cambridge had become an armed camp, with everyone expecting some sort of Armageddon in which The System—or The People— would finally have to fall. For those who were to become the Commune, there seemed no hope in any of this. And so they moved, naming their new home after the Ethiopian lake, Tana, the source of the Blue Nile. The name expressed their hopes: a new beginning, fertility of body and spirit, peacefulness. In the years since Tana's founding, much of this promise has been fulfilled, in ways that are extraordinarily suggestive for those seeking alternatives to the contemporary social patterns of America.

People, Land, and Buildings. What is now the Tana Commune was once the Manning Place, a moderate-sized dairy farm that succumbed in the mid-1960s to the pressures that are forcing small farmers out of business across the country. In the Mannings's time, the farm consisted of a barn big enough for forty cows and a winter's supply of hay, a garage for the tractors, a couple of outbuildings, and the main house. Surrounding this were 200 acres of woods and meadows, sloping down from a maple grove at the top of the hill to the Wild Branch River, a half-mile walk below. The woods and the river and the buildings remain, but all the rest has changed. The barn has been transformed into living space for twenty-six people. Eight more live in the farmhouse, the bottom floor of which has been rebuilt to serve as communal dining room and living space. Four others live in what was once the garage, and twelve people occupy a new "dormitory" building that commune members built in the summer of 1972. One large outbuilding has become a well-equipped wood shop. Working farm has become working commune.

This is not a commune in the stereotyped media mold of the 1960s, however. For one thing, work is a central part of life for Tana people. And Tana is conspicuously multigenerational. Thirty of its members are between twenty-two and forty-five years old. Ten others, eight of them parents of younger commune members, are what outsiders might call "senior citizens." And there are ten children below the age of twelve. Those within the commune would not think of themselves in such categories; they prefer to deal with each other in terms of what each person can add to the group, a consideration that is often only marginally related to age. Where age and experience do imply knowledge or wisdom, however, Tana members are wholly open to this, in a further departure from prevalent communal attitudes of the period. One older man is a "retired" businessman. Another couple are veterans of several earlier communitarian experiments including the Macedonia colony, which had a brief life in Georgia during the 1940s and 1950s. Tana's receptiveness to what these people, among others, have to teach is an important factor in its survival and success.

Meaning. Tana is a "religious" group, though not according to any categories that a visitor can readily comprehend. Members speak of "The Knowledge." In browsing through the commune's library, one soon sees that the most-thumbed books are those dealing with various forms of higher understanding: the Bible, Black Elk, Jung, the Tao, Castaneda, a volume of African myths. But if this is a meager guide to the commune's spirituality, the members are hardly of greater help in explaining it. Work with us, they say, be part of our life. Only then will you understand.

One thing members will say something about is the twofold role of Tana itself in their "religion." First, the group is an expression of this religion. As one member puts it:

> What The Knowledge involves is a sense of the unity and continuity of all things (most religious traditions would agree). We *live* that sense in our relations with each other, in the fact that every day we are close to death (Art had another heart attack last week) and rebirth (Sara/Paul is due next month), in the way we deal with the passing of the seasons and the harvesting of our crops and the making of our tables, in how we play together . . . We are not so much "seeking" The Knowledge as doing it, however imperfectly; and we have to do it fully because we are fully with each other, fully *here*.

Second, the group is a means to greater understanding:

> What any of us comes to know is contagious, given how closely we live together. If Jesse or Sylvie or Jim or Barbara see something new, I am likely to see it as well—not because they *tell* me (that never works) but because they are seeing something in what is common to our lives (so much is!), and I can *feel* it happen. It is as if we were all continuously making love to each other's souls.

For both reasons, its members have come to feel that Tana is a fundamental part of their spiritual search.

This group sense shows itself also in the commune's insistence on consensus in the making of major decisions. Such decisions are normally made in the course of the group's regular Sunday meeting, which may extend through the day if especially difficult questions are on the agenda. But consensus here is far more than simply a political technique. Rather, it is a manifestation of the commune members' deepest feelings about their group life. The Sunday meetings themselves are a combination business session, meditation period, tribal ritual, and encounter meeting, sensitively conducted to bring those participating into closer tune with one another's needs and feelings, as well as the "needs" of their work and environment. The expectation is clear: over time, the common ground within Tana of shared understandings and perceptions will be enlarged, to the point where these are congruent with The Knowledge.

At Tana today, such an endeavor seems a sufficient communal goal. The group itself has no ambitions for expansion, either in numbers or in wealth. Individual members have little interest in the mobility and relentless experiential change that have been dominant values in other contemporary communes. Rather than wishing to make "progress" in the linear terms that prevail in the world outside, the people within Tana appear to look for meaning in the repetitive. They want to understand, for example, the cycle by which vegetable becomes, in turn, meal, garbage, compost, and once again vegetable; or the rhythm within which raw lumber is transformed into pieces of wood, which then become a finished product; or the recurrent patterns of excitement and fatigue which characterize interpersonal relations within the group. Change in such a situation becomes less an accretion of shifting external influences than a series of inner illuminations of the familiar. All this may seem relatively opaque—to the visitor, Tana members sometimes seem to be speaking a foreign language in describing how they live—but the qualities of joy and creative intensity which Tana embodies are inescapable to the most casual observer of the commune.

Work and Income. Tana supports itself by making simple, but sturdy, wood products: desks, tables, book cases, cabinets. The group prefers to barter such goods for the produce of other communards or local farmers. But although most of its milk and eggs, and some of its meat and clothing, are currently being acquired in this way, the larger part of Tana's business involves sales for cash. Some of these are to buyers who come to the commune itself, but most are through urban retail outlets. Recently, Tana contracted with a small-scale housing development in a nearby village to "customize" kitchen cabinets, around its standard line, according to the tastes of the buyers.

Some twenty commune members work regularly in Tana's wood shop.

The other adults take responsibility for maintenance of buildings and vehicles, cooking, laundering, bookkeeping, gardening, and the more formal aspects of educating the children. Although there is some interchange of people between these positions, job rotation is considerably more limited than that which many other communes have assumed to be necessary for personal fulfillment. When reminded of this, the Tana people respond that members having strong feelings about changes in job assignments are generally accommodated, but that change for its own sake is discouraged. For one thing, some of the commune's tasks require considerable skills. Tana, operating at close to subsistence, simply could not afford the time and resources that would be needed to give each member proficiency in every job. And equally important, the group does not feel, as one member put it, that growth comes from "an endless series of personal diversions." Rather, being at one with a task whose value and connection to the group as a whole is always felt is self-fulfillment of the highest order.

Those in the wood shop calculate the return on their labor as being less than two dollars an hour, a major factor in making Tana's products competitive with comparable mass-produced items. The resulting income, close to $75,000 in 1972, allows the commune a per capita expenditure of approximately $1500 a year. Given the substantial economies of communal living, this represents a surprisingly comfortable level of consumption. (Instead of twenty families' worth of sewage and water systems, furniture, electrical and phone hookups, vehicles, kitchen and laundry equipment, toys, typewriters, book and record collections, tools, and so on, Tana is able to live for the most part on what three or four families might ordinarily require. Food and some other items are bought at quantity discounts.) The group has experimented with various ways of distributing its income, finally arriving at a strikingly simple system. Collective expenditures such as food and maintenance of the buildings, which claim the bulk of total revenues, are given first priority on communal funds. Money remaining is provided by a "Budget Master" to individual members on their request. Any conflicts that arise from this system are resolved at Sunday meetings.

Education. Five of the Tana adults have primary responsibility for child care and education of the commune's children. (One of the five spent three semesters earning a teaching credential at a nearby college in order to satisfy state requirements for creation of "The Tana School.") The school itself is a fluid series of activities around a basic schedule that varies according to season. During the six-month Vermont winter, mornings are spent in "class" learning the basics of reading, writing, and arithmetic. All these skills are closely related to the commune's life. Children may learn to count by helping with an inventory of the wood shop's products. Reading and writing often involve stories about communal activities and events. Afternoons are more flexible; the children participate in whatever is happening in the commune that day, be it cross-country skiing, cleaning the house, stacking lumber, skating on the pond, or shoveling the walk. During the other six months, the time devoted to "classes" is cut back (to an hour or so in summer), and more time is spent in gardening and other outdoor pursuits.

What unifies all of these activities is the commune itself. Education anywhere consists of transmitting the values and skills of adults to their children, and this is no less true of The Tana School than it is of either public education or the "free school" movement in the United States. Just as Tana is culturally distinct from both the "straight" world and the counterculture out of which the free schools arose, so does the content of its education differ from other contemporary patterns. Tana is more playful than the larger society, more inclined to work than the counterculture, and more concerned with interpersonal responsibility than either. These qualities are passed on to the children both in and out of "class." In sharp contrast to most American communes, perhaps the most notable element here is Tana's commitment to resolving interpersonal or financial difficulties that might threaten its success. As one member put it: "This is a place where certain things have to be done, or we wouldn't survive as a group. Of course, the children feel this, and they do what they can. How else could it be?"

Outside Relationships. Tana communards have not retreated from the world outside. Adults and children travel regularly to Burlington, Boston, and New York to transport goods to retail outlets. Members often work for neighbors in exchange for farm produce, and they contributed much of the labor for a barn raising following a fire on a nearby farm in the spring of 1973. In addition, several once served on a town planning committee that joined statewide efforts to bring order to Vermont land development.

The commune also attracts a steady flow of visitors from outside: friends of members, students commune-hopping over summer vacations, media people looking for a story, other communards looking for ideas, researchers, and a small flood of the curious, anxious to see a self-supporting commune at work. Far from being too isolated, Tana has often found itself so involved in external events that its work and intracommunal relationships have suffered. In partial response, the commune has been forced to limit overnight visitors to no more than five at a time.

In the future, Tana hopes to concentrate its outside energies on neighbors and on other productive communes, and to devote less attention to casual passersby. Members see particular potential in links between communes, which could barter goods and services among themselves, as well as cooperating for food purchases, transport of produce, financial support, and provision of legal and health services. Ultimately, Tana would like to see the creation of a regional federation of working communes, formed roughly along the lines of the federations of Israeli kibbutzim, to give greater strength to what members hope will be a movement toward widespread establishment of serious communal enterprises. Although Tana doesn't talk about this much—so far, there are few comparable communal groups with which to ally—expansion of their movement is clearly a dream the members would like to see realized. "People all over the country are looking for a better way to live," says one. "But they have few models to help them know what they can do. We think we've found the way, but we can't show it to everyone ourselves. Just suppose there were fifty groups like ours, or a hundred. . . ." He was silent for a while, and then he changed the subject.

VALUES OF A RADICAL COMMUNALISM

A communal work place such as Tana would be responsive to the full range of problems to which this book is addressed. Work would take on new meaning, people would feel in control of their lives, and a sense of deep involvements—among people, with the land—would grow over time. But to get to this point requires a radical break with conventional assumptions about social organization and purpose. As we indicated in Chapter 2, the "new values" that emerged in the late 1960s and early 1970s did not represent such a break. At critical points, however, the Tana example does express the changes required. Among the issues posed here, perhaps the most important lie in four areas: the relationship between individual and group, the concept of "progress," attitudes toward work, and approaches to education.

Person and Group. For Tana communards, the group itself became a "we" of great potency. In general, Americans have grave doubts about social involvements that imply a "we," suspecting these of inherent tendencies toward erosion of personal integrity. To overcome this suspicion is the first necessary step toward creating the Tanas which can make our lives whole again.

All societies claim to function in the interests of the people who comprise them, but such assertions conceal great differences between cultures in controlling assumptions as to the relationship between person and group. In the United States, the appropriate balance is expressed in the idea of "individualism," which holds that meaning and satisfactions cannot make sense except as received or interpreted by sovereign individuals. Society therefore exists primarily to gratify individual desires or to mediate between individuals in conflict. Life is most real in the first-person singular. For Erich Fromm, "identity is the experience which permits a person to say legitimately 'I'—'I' as an organizing active center of the structure of all my actual or potential activities" (1968:82–83). The weak among us may abandon the "I" in search of the support of "we." But this is a perversion that right thinking can cure. In one countercultural view, for example, "as your self-confidence develops, you'll come to realize . . . that security rests in the self" (Thomas, 1972:13).

If individuals are most complete when independent, then the opportunity for isolation from others in the most vital parts of living must be jealously guarded. Thus, the "right to privacy": private homes, private bedrooms, private incomes, private reflection, private offices. The search can become almost obsessive. Serge Chermayeff and Christopher Alexander—who speak of privacy as "that marvelous compound of withdrawal, self-reliance, solitude, quiet, contemplation, and concentration"—pose the following questions as criteria for the "ideal" home:

1. Is there an entry "lock" to give the house as a whole an adequate buffer zone against intrusion? . . .
2. Is the children's domain directly accessible from outside so as not to interfere with the adult's private and family domains? . . .
3. Is there a buffer zone between the children's private domain and the parents' private domain? . . .
4. Is there a "lock" to the parents' private domain? . . .
5. Can a "living room" be isolated . . . from the rest of the house? . . .
6. Are the outdoor spaces private and differentiated? (1963:37, 219–220)

This detailed vision of the private life illustrates a deeply American "need." Not even within the family is there to be a fully operative "we." Even there, our primary concern is to protect our individual selves from one another.

We take this so much for granted that it is generally assumed in this country that privacy is a universal human need. And yet the very concept exists in virtually no language other than English. You simply cannot say "privacy," for example, in French, Italian, Amharic, Korean, Russian, Spanish, or Arabic. These languages have words to express the state of being apart from others: *solitude* in French, say, or the Spanish *aislamiento* and its Italian equivalent, *isolamento*. But such words invariably carry a strong emotional connotation of aloneness or painful separation from one's natural group. They are in no way equivalent to the neutral "privacy," which simply expresses a condition (like "bachelorhood") with no such connotations. As far as we know, such matter-of-fact linguistic provision for routine separation from others in the course of daily life is an affectation of the English-speaking world alone.

For most Americans, the social arbitrariness of the "need" for privacy does not make this "need" any less potent. In *Freedom and Culture,* Dorothy Lee analyzes the extensive social conditioning that guarantees we will grow up as seekers of privacy. From the earliest moments of a child's life,

> we see suckling merely as a matter of nutrition, so that we can then feel free to substitute a bottle for the breast and a mechanical bottle-holder for the mother's arms; thus we ensure privacy for the mother and teach the child self-dependence. We create needs in the infant by withholding affection and then presenting it as a series of approvals for an inventory of achievements or attributes. On the assumption that there is no emotional continuum, we withdraw ourselves, thus forcing the child to strive for emotional response and security. And thus, through habituation and teaching, the mother reproduces in the child her own needs, in this case the need for privacy . . . (1959:75; see also pp. 30–31)

And the process continues. Where possible, the child is given a bedroom of its own, sent off to a school where it gets its own locker for private possessions and is installed in a separate chair which isolates it from physical contact with other children—and so on, endlessly. Little wonder that by adulthood Americans have come to think of privacy as a basic requirement of their lives. But it does not follow that privacy is a natural human "need." Rather, the search for privacy is only a symptom of the extreme individualism which our environment imposes on us.

Such individualism has deep social roots. America was settled by individual misfits in flight from their home cultures, and the tradition of flight from others across various "new frontiers" remains with us to this day.

This tendency in turn has recently been aggravated by at least three other phenomena. First, there is the sensory overload that urban civilization carries with it. In their architectural design for privacy, for example, Chermayeff and Alexander argue that "only physical insulation against the dangers and pain of invasion—interruption by people, traffic, and noise—can inhibit chaos and confusion" (1963:75). Second, there are the effects of the depersonalized forms of control through which all this confusion is organized. As Charles Reich laments, "Beginning with school, if not before, an individual is systematically stripped of his . . . personal uniqueness, in order to style him into a productive unit for a mass, technological society" (1970: 7–8). Finally, there are the obvious perils of political centralism. The specter of Stalinism hangs over every page of David Riesman's *Individualism Reconsidered* (1954, recently reissued), for example. And virtually every part of the American political spectrum suspects its enemies of secret tendencies toward totalitarianism. On all these counts, individuals in America feel their integrity to be in a continual state of siege.

If Americans have legitimate fears of submersion in a faceless mass, however, it does not necessarily follow that the only appropriate response is one of dogged individualism. Such a response presupposes a false dichotomy—individualism versus mass conformism—which merely reflects our stunted perceptions of cultural alternatives. It may make sense to retreat to our locked, private bedrooms when we are walling out the din of strangers; it would make little or no sense were we to be hiding from the gentleness of friends and lovers. Similarly, it may be healthy to wave the lonely banner of individualism in the face of The Great Industrial Machine; to cling to the same obsession in a worker-controlled communal enterprise would be pathetic, if not mad. Intensely close groups such as the Tana Commune have found that there is little real conflict between individual self-realization and strong group life. Indeed, the two are felt to be inseparable. But this is a lesson that Americans for the most part cannot accept.

The result of our social paranoias has been a seeping away of our capacity for intimate group life. This process has been so gradual that we can hardly recall just what it is that is missing. As René Dubos points out, "when changes occur progressively in social life, the quality of human contacts can degenerate without the persons involved being conscious of the loss this entails" (1968:173). To some extent, allowing such degeneration has been a logical response to a world whose groups seem invariably to be oppressive. But this has been just to make the best of an intolerable situation:

An analogy:
If you tear the wings from a butterfly
He will not
Flutter his stubs
Forever:
He will begin to walk
To get where he wants to go.
Is it rational
That a butterfly
Walk?
No.
Is it rational
That
The
Butterfly walk?
Yes.

                                                    (Gintis, 1970:17–18)

If we could overcome the belief that all groups necessarily diminish those persons within them—a belief that results from the traumas of visible models such as corporation or government agency—perhaps we could return to the butterfly its wings.

To look more closely at the impact on the individual of intense group life, let us start with the most intense of all groups, the traditional tribe.* Philip Slater has suggested that we might benefit from a more "tribal" life style, arguing that American culture frustrates a natural human desire "to live in trust and fraternal cooperation with one's fellows in a total and visible collective entity" (1970:5). But for most of us, the idea of tribal unity suggests only tyrannies happily long past. Jean-François Revel, for example, reminds us that "in the past, the diversity of cultures was balanced by the uniformity of individuals within those cultures" (1970:74). And Alvin Toffler looks back with horror on "the imprisonment of the past— a past when individuals may have been more tightly bound to one another, but when they were also more tightly regimented by social conventions, sexual mores, political and religious restrictions" (1970:89).

Revel and Toffler, and those who agree with them, are accurate in finding distinctly un-American qualities in the traditional group: the ego-centered

_____

* To talk of "the traditional tribe" is a little like referring to "the contemporary family"; any single model does violence to complex realities. Nonetheless, this discussion is accurate within the limits of its scope.

individualist simply had no place there. Instead of seeking out a private identity, the person in such groups found meaning primarily through communal interactions, to the extent that the line between self and society became extremely indistinct. Speaking of the Wintu Indians, Dorothy Lee notes that "the Wintu conceive of the self not as strictly delimited or defined, but as a concentration, at most, which gradually fades and gives place to the other" (1959:134).* The result was an extremely strong group consciousness. Reflecting on his childhood in an Indian village, Wilfred Pelletier notes that such a group "can exist and function and solve all its problems without any kinds of signals, like a school of fish. All of a sudden you see them move; they shift together" (1971:29). People raised in this way would be mystified by Descartes's "I think, therefore I am." Their equivalent statement of self would be very different. As the African philosopher John Mbiti puts it: "The individual [in a tribal setting] can only say: 'I am, because we are; and since we are, therefore I am'" (1969:108–109).

This intrusion of the group into every aspect of living was most noteworthy in two areas that Westerners have come to assume to be the natural province of the individual: religious experience and artistic creation. Among tribal groups, "religion" and the ethical precepts derived from it were inextricably linked with daily life,** and they therefore necessarily took on the communal character of that life. Commenting on the Zuni Indians, for example, Irving Goldman notes that in religion,

> only group ritual is effective. The masked katcina dances are group dances, and it is the collective rhythmic movement of a mass of men that will bring the rain. When the priests go into retreat into the ceremonial houses . . . they go in groups. . . . In addition to the collective performance, all the blessings asked for are collective; it is rain for the group, fecundity for the group, long life for the group. (1961:336–337)

Even where visionary experience was assumed to be more personal, as with the Plains Indians, individual vision was prepared for and interpreted with the help of older, wiser tribesmen and was thus routinely incorporated into the collective group wisdom.

And similarly with art. As one character in Ali Mazrui's *The Trial of*

---

* As in other tribal groups, the Wintu self "faded" into natural surroundings as well as other people. Facing south, the Wintu has a "west arm" and an "east arm," not right and left arms, and these are reversed when the person turns around (Ibid.: 139). See also Margaret Mead on the Arapesh, who "are conceived as *belonging to* the land and the trees," rather than the other way around (1961:21).

** See, for example, Radin, 1957:72.

Christopher Okigbo points out, "Great art in Europe may have been at best a mode of communication; great art in Africa had always been a flow of interaction" (1971:77). In his autobiography, the African writer Camara Laye provides an evocative description of this flow, as his father makes a gold ornament for a woman of the village (1954:31–41). Rather than being a private act of creation, the working of the gold becomes a ritual in which workman, apprentices, friends, and customers take part. When the ornament is completed, the "praise-singer" who has been participating throughout delivers a chant of homage, and the entire group is transformed into a festive knot of people exchanging praise, gifts, and the kola nuts which throughout West Africa are distributed at ceremonial occasions. It is a joyous scene, but one whose implications of pervasive groupness would make the solitary Western artist distinctly uncomfortable.

As a displaced tribesman laments in a novel by Ayi Kwei Armah, "Outside community, what justification in life? The spirit dies . . ." (1972: 114). Almost by reflex, we might conclude that people living in such environments must have been interchangeable ciphers, compressed by the totality of group demands into a standardized mold. In reality, however, members of traditional tribal societies were conspicuously strong, distinct individuals. We have seen this in our own extensive contacts with African tribal life, and support for this view comes from a number of authoritative sources. For example:

PAUL RADIN: "I think every one competent to judge will admit that in primitive societies free scope is allowed for every conceivable outlet. . . . Every man and woman seeks individuation—outer and inner individuation—and this is the psychological basis for their otherwise bewildering and unintelligible tolerance of the fullest expression of personality." (1957: 32–33)

DOROTHY LEE (on the Navaho): ". . . we find a tightly knit group, depending on mutual responsibility among all its members, a precisely structured universe, *and a great respect for individual autonomy and integrity.*" (1959:10; our emphasis)

MARGARET MEAD (on the Arapesh): "Conspicuous also is the diffuseness of the goals set up by the society, the number of ways in which a satisfactory functioning may be attained, the freedom left to the individual to choose or reject a skill, the lack of any single scale by which success can be measured." (1961:50)

JOHN MBITI (on African religions): "Individuals hold differences of opinion on various subjects; and the myths, rituals and ceremonies may differ in detail from area to area. But such ideas or views are not considered as either contrary or conforming to any orthodox opinion. . . . In traditional religions there are no creeds to be recited; instead, the creeds are written in the heart of the individual, and each one is himself a living creed of his own religion." (1969:3)

For most of us, it seems an almost insupportable contradiction: thorough individuation within an intensely strong group. But it is true.

We need not have returned to "primitivism" to make this point. Contemporary examples abound of communal groups comprised of strong, self-confident individuals: the Israeli kibbutzim (see Chapter 7), or the Chinese work brigades (Chapter 8), or the Society of Brothers (Chapter 9), as well as the Tana Commune. How explain this recurrent paradox, which the tribal model embodies in its purest form? Perhaps a leap of understanding is called for. *There is in truth no paradox here at all; individuation and strong group life are inseparable, not contradictory.* Tribal groups could hardly have flourished over the centuries, remaining culturally and spiritually progressive, if they had crushed the spirit of their members. As Dorothy Lee points out, "Group effort and community of ends does not mean totalitarianism and the loss of individual uniqueness. In fact, the group can prosper only to the extent that this uniqueness is fully actualized" (1959:24). For people in traditional tribes, the option was always open of abandoning their groups and homesteading in the manner of the settlers of the American West. But the tribes endured.*

If individuation is a requirement for durable communal life, it may be equally true that communal life is a requirement for full individuation. Martin Buber speaks of "the need of a man to feel his own house as a room in some greater, all-embracing structure in which he is at home, to feel that the other inhabitants of it with whom he lives and works are all acknowledging and confirming his individual existence" (1958:140). Buber concludes that these requirements can only be fully met within a structure of communal living. But this need to be in intimate enough contact with

---

* There is a current tendency to explain away tribal communalism as a necessary function of poverty. Howard Sherman, for example, asserts that "the 'communist' features observed in some primitive societies are imposed by dire necessity for bare survival" (1972:17). Margaret Mead, in a massive study of cooperation and competition among "primitive" peoples, concludes however that the degree of cooperation in such groups is a function of their cultural values and has little to do with economic factors (1961:16). If tribes are communal, in other words, it is because they choose to be.

others that they can know, and respect, our full being is only part of the story. Equally important is the fact that communal units, by the very comprehensiveness of their structures, can find "respectable" an extremely wide range of human types, all of which have their place in the general enrichment of the group. It is in the tribal framework, after all—not in the groups with which we have become familiar in the United States—that people of almost any inclination find a niche: artisans, poets, farmers, drunkards, prophets, idiots, craftspeople, cripples. It is precisely the strong communal bond that allows all of these to be themselves without fear of rejection by the group.

The same point can be made by considering what happens to individuation when communal life is absent, as in the United States. Here, we cannot allow ourselves full allegiance to any single group; our sense of definition must be pursued independently. Since we continue to be social beings, however, we must find some way of realizing the various aspects of our personalities in group life. If we feel ourselves to be scholars, aesthetes, and politically concerned citizens, for example, we will teach at universities, buy tickets to the local chamber ensemble, and attend meetings on issues of national concern. If our self-image involves being countercultural liberation-seekers working to shed the poisons of technological civilization, we will join an urban commune, participate in sex-role discussion groups, and work two days a month at the local organic food co-op. If our inner beings thrill to financial success, civic leadership, and the task of preserving the Republic, we will take seriously our corporate duties and join the Chamber of Commerce and the Republican Party. Whichever of these paths we follow, we will see ourselves as acting in the interest of our special, individual beings.

But will we have become individualized? Social life along this model is almost invariably a matter of like meeting with like. All these groups are dependent on a sameness of concerns and a uniformity of behavior on the part of those within them. Those at your ad hoc meeting on The Current Social Crisis will hardly be interested in your views on reality therapy, even if that is what is really on your mind. And they are likely to become hostile if, captured by momentary ecstasy, you take off your clothes and dance down the aisle. Similarly, your yoga class will be less than entranced by a summary of the dollar's position on world markets. And considerable uneasiness will result if you abandon the lotus position on impulse to do calisthenics instead. Since our groups are organized around narrowly-based interests, in other words, they have little tolerance for deviation from the norm. And as a result, we grow accustomed to being "normal" throughout our group relationships in order to have any social life at all.

We may, of course, express our felt eccentricities by joining groups to which our neighbor does not belong. But in addition to the fact that these of necessity will be as conformist as any others, there is the question of how distinctive they are likely to be. In a climate where people grow unfamiliar and uncomfortable with the experience of heterogeneous groups, the tendency of society as a whole will be toward greater uniformity. It has become a truism, for example, to note that our political system offers us choices between virtually identical quantities. When oppressed groups such as women and blacks seek "liberation," it is revealing that this generally takes the form of demanding the opportunity to be more like the dominant white men. And even where the system spins off a "counterculture," the movement's most striking feature is the extent to which it resembles the society at large (see Chapter 5). There are conspicuous exceptions to all this, of course—any land of 200 million people and sufficient affluence to allow many of them free rein for fancy must expect some oddballs. But we tend to exaggerate our differences beyond their due. Any culture that can tell the difference between a Ford and a Chevrolet has developed a fine eye for subtlety, but it takes only a return from decompression within a foreign culture to be struck by the overwhelming sameness of it all.

These tendencies are hardly new to the United States. David Riesman noted twenty years ago that "the fear of being intellectually out of step . . . seems to be considerably greater here than in Europe [not to mention in cultures with even stronger group bonds]; this was true even in the nineteenth century" (1954:73), and it remains true today. Barring some sudden flash of national insight, it could remain true indefinitely, since the dynamics of this process are strongly self-perpetuating. Since we sense that none of our existing groups can acknowledge our total selves, we strike a pose of individualism which allows us to keep our distance from them. As we have indicated above, this means that the groups we deal with must be narrowly based and conformist. Since they thus cannot acknowledge our total selves, we must keep our distance from them. And so on, a nation of conformist individualists forever.

As groups like Tana have shown, however, it is possible to break free from this cycle, replacing it with a more healthy one. If people can give allegiance to a strong "tribal" commune, the commune will develop familial ties that far transcend the coincidence of limited interest which binds groups in the outside culture. Given such "family" ties, the commune can then acknowledge the distinctness of the personalities it includes. Their full humanness thus acknowledged, members will feel all the more comfortable in their allegiance to the group. And so on, into an individualized communalism.

This pattern does not function with total predictability. There may be oppressive communal situations, just as there may be fully-realized individuals even in the most individualistic cultures. But as a social tendency, the association between communalism and a high degree of individuation is supported by both common sense and a mass of examples. We have noted some of the evidence in talking of tribal situations. We will add more through our discussion in later chapters of successful communes of the present.

The Concept of "Progress." The Tana example involves yet another sharp departure from prevalent cultural assumptions in the United States. As the members found, there can be considerable meaning and growth in the repetitive, the cyclical, the mundane events of daily life. Above, we spoke of the attention given such acts as gardening, cooking, woodworking, childbirth—events whose leitmotif is the fact of recurrence—and of the commune's sense that personal progress involves an ever-deeper understanding of the meaning of these things. Missing here is the surrounding culture's belief that nothing is worthwhile unless it has never happened before.* In the straight world, it is the ALL NEW miracle detergent, the ALL NEW 8-cylinder Detroit Economy Special, the ALL NEW scholarly formulation of social truth. And the "new culture" has its own, less material, equivalents: "It keeps changing, this thing called Earth People's Park. . . . It changes every time someone else hears, thinks, or talks about it. It keeps changing—but that's what it's all about anyway—changing" (Reim, 1970: 7). For most of us, God forbid that anything should ever be the same two days in a row, or that it should happen a second time.

If change in the straight world is a matter of economic obsolescence designed to keep the industrial machine spinning insanely along, change in the counterculture is a matter of experiential obsolescence designed to keep its members from getting bored: "If a system is stable, it is intolerable

---

* This belief explains our fascination with things like the *Guinness Book of World Records,* a massive compendium of the biggest, strongest, smallest, fattest, fastest, etc. (McWhirter, 1973), as well as the appearance of articles such as that in the *New York Times* (February 8, 1973) announcing that one Susan Starr had become the first concert pianist to play Prokofiev in Korea. A fixation on "firsts" and "onlies" has become one of our most prominent national characteristics.

to human spirit, a kind of death-in-life."* Both impulses have their roots in the same culturally-determined image, the awful picture of what a highly technological society would be like in stagnation. And both suggest the same remedy, a linear accretion of goods or experiences, so that one never passes the same point twice. This is called "progress."

A group like the Tana Commune will come to realize, however, that it need not follow that all systems are "a kind of death-in-life" when stable simply because a superrationalized industrial environment would so be. Systems organized around the imperatives of life, rather than of technology, will be vital even when stable. But this vitality may be difficult for industrialized eyes to perceive, since its deeper geometries resemble circles, rather than straight lines. Other traditions have seen this more clearly. In speaking of the Mandala, for example, Jose and Miriam Arguelles remind us that "The circle is the original sign, the prime symbol of the nothing and the all; the symbol of heaven and the solar eye, the all-encompassing form beyond and through which man finds and loses himself" (1972:33). And Black Elk makes a related point in simpler language, speaking nonetheless to depths of awareness which are inaccessible to those for whom "progress" means restless, linear change:

> You have noticed that everything an Indian does is in a circle, and that is because the Power of the World always works in circles, and everything tries to be round. . . . The sky is round, and I have heard that the earth is round like a ball, and so are all the stars. The wind, in its greatest power, whirls. Birds make their nests in circles, for theirs is the same religion as ours. The sun comes forth and goes down again in a circle. The moon does the same, and both are round. Even the seasons form a great circle in their changing, and always come back again to where they were. The life of a man is a circle from childhood to childhood, and so it is in everything where power moves. . . . (In Neihardt, 1961:198–199)

Communes that have brought technology back under the control of life processes are likely to share these insights, which grow logically from a sense of the organic nature of things. In these cases, definitions of "progress" will inevitably come to imply a growing awareness of such "circles" as the seasons and the repetitive patterns of work. The unforeseen will always be present. No two journeys around the circumference of the seasons, for example, are ever quite the same. And influences from outside the group may shift beyond recognition the orbit of a circle thought to be fully known.

---

* Quoted from a 1972 draft of Jerome, 1974.

But rather than seeking such novelties for their own sake, as our technological culture suggests we should do, these groups can use them to refine
their comprehension of the recurrent. To extend the metaphor to three
dimensions, this is progress as ascending spiral, moving always closer to
more perfect understanding of "the all-encompassing form beyond and
through which man finds and loses himself." If this is out of harmony with
the imperatives of the industrial life style, it is a natural way for a communal group to measure its forward motion.

Attitudes Toward Work. Many of Tana's "circles" involved "work":
preparing food, washing dishes, weeding the garden, making cabinets, cleaning the house. But members hardly thought of these acts as "work" at all,
at least with the joyless connotations the word has acquired in the country
at large. Rather, such functions were taken for granted as an expression
of living. Had they heard of him, commune members would immediately
have understood E. F. Schumacher in his summary of the threefold function
of work in Buddhist philosophy: "to give man a chance to utilize and develop his faculties; to enable him to overcome his ego-centeredness by joining with other people in a common task; and to bring forth the goods and
services needed for a becoming existence" (1971:13). So viewed, work
flows imperceptibly into other life activities with equivalent meaning, ac- ·
tivities that the society outside tends to categorize separately as "play" or
"education" or "culture" or "growth." For groups such as Tana, all of
these are inseparable parts of being, almost a form of prayer.*

What such communes have achieved here is again quite "tribal." In
contemporary society, people's values and life styles have become functions
of their economic roles as workers and consumers: what is good for the
GNP is good for us. But it has not always been so. In earlier times, the
very concept of a distinct "economy" with a reality of its own would have
been unthinkable, not to mention the idea that this "economy" could be
something to which we should subordinate our freedom, our spirit, and
our social relationships. As Karl Polanyi has argued:

> We must rid ourselves of the ingrained notion that the economy is a field
> of experience of which human beings have necessarily always been conscious.
> To employ a metaphor, the facts of the economy were originally embedded

---

* The idea of work as a sacred act flows through many communal environments. See,
for example, Delespesse and Tange (1971:23) on religious communities in France; Spiro
(1970:89) on the kibbutz; Cheikh Hamidou Kane (1969:91) on Africa; or Roszak
(1972:420–421) on community generally.

in situations that were not in themselves of an economic nature, neither the ends nor the means being primarily material. (In Dalton, 1968:119–120)

"Economic" events, in other words, were subordinate to the kinship, social, and religious patterns that were the basic realities of tribal consciousness. And it is this order of priorities that we showed Tana to have adopted. The commune's raison d'être had to do with the spiritual understandings which—or such was the act of faith—would follow from the interpenetrations of its members with each other and their surroundings. The fact of work allowed for survival; the form and resonances of work expressed the kind of survival the commune sought.

Again, such approaches run across the grain of the surrounding culture. In America, work has come to be something one does in order to have money to fill "free time" with objects and diversions. So justified, work may be barely tolerable. Where no money is forthcoming, it becomes a source of active outrage. Speaking of "the politics of housework," for example, New Community Projects notes "the essential fact of housework . . . it stinks" (1972:5). Such attitudes are symptomatic of a deep cultural malaise—how can we say it "stinks" to prepare our meals and maintain our dwellings? Somehow, we have come to view those activities required to sustain ourselves as being fundamentally unpleasant. Only in doing things that are unnecessary can we normally find enjoyment.

Where we do find enjoyment in necessary acts, it is because we have rationalized them as "play," as if they were not really serious or essential. Murray Bookchin, anticipating the spread of small-scale automated agriculture, comments that "relieved of toil by agricultural machines, communitarians will approach food cultivation with the same playful and creative attitude that men so often bring to gardening" (1971:118). All life is to become a hobby, and we are not to put our hand to anything that is simply a difficult task in need of being done.

The alternative to "play," however, is not necessarily drudgery. Members of the Tana Commune find joy in "toil," just as tribal societies have done:

The long line of reapers hurled itself at the field and hewed it down. Wasn't that enough? Wasn't it enough that the rice bowed before these black bodies? They sang and they reaped. Singing in chorus, they reaped, voices and gestures in harmony. They were together!—united by the same task, the same song. It was as if the same soul bound them. (Laye, 1954: 61)

In fact, the Tana people find joy in a wide range of occupations. They too sing in the fields, but they sing also in the kitchen and even in the workshop, turning out standardized household items day after day.

The counterculturists, on the other hand, felt themselves to be a new American aristocracy (although they would not have used the term themselves), elevated by superior understanding above the toiling masses. As such, they adopted more "playful" avocations: crafts and gardening, primarily to grow organic vegetables for sale to others within the aristocracy. Routinized production of tables and kitchen cabinets would have been far too bourgeois an occupation for them to consider. Such standard items constitute the bulk of both work opportunities and purchases for most of the population, however. And if communal living is to be accessible to more than a narrow elite, patterns for making these goods communally must be explored. As our later discussions of communal experiments will indicate, many groups other than Tana have found that such work can be elevating, rather than corrosive, to the spirit.

Approaches to Education. The Tana example stressed group experience and common understandings, in a setting where the various expressions of life—work, play, prayer, love—were integrated into a seamless whole. And the group's approach to the "education" of its children would follow naturally from this. Children would be involved in virtually every aspect of the commune's life, including its work and (to the extent that their attention spans allowed) the meetings where decisions were made and interpersonal raggedness confronted. Along with the technical and academic skills transmitted, one of the primary "lessons" taught would therefore be this: Certain things need to be done together for spiritual, physical, and group survival. Almost subliminally, the message would be passed on that this requires people to be both wholly themselves and selves wholly in tune with each other. With due allowance for the productive machinery such a commune might use, and for its extensive relations with the outside world, this is fundamentally a "tribal" education.

Such an approach is in obvious contrast to American culture, which is busily educating its children in a self-indulgent individualism. In the straight world, this increasingly takes technological forms: one child, one learning machine—and choose your own program, if you feel like it today. The same impulse, with fewer computers, has permeated the counterculture as well. In a book on the free-school movement, Allen Graubard observes:

> In a way, the drug experience, especially the psychedelic "trip," becomes the paradigm for the good learning experience. . . . It is immediate and personal; it takes no preparation, hard work, cultural tradition, study, or knowledge; it seems cosmic in dimension, but it doesn't engage one in the mundane day-to-day processes of the social world. It is absorbing and seems to be self-justifying. And it doesn't implicate a future. (1972:244)

It is all there: the preoccupation with self and rejection of commitment or group ties; the endless search for the new and diverting experience; and the avoidance of application to any path, particularly one that might imply "work." These attitudes would find little sympathy in the Tana Commune, which believes that the millennium is not yet upon us, that there are serious things we have yet to do together, and that we should let our children know this.

The idea that there are things we can teach our children is in itself a departure from a strong current in American educational theory. Graubard points out that one of the dominant assumptions of free-school teachers has been that "nothing interesting can be said because there is no good basis for valuing one piece of learning above another" (Ibid.:230). In less explicit form, such an assumption underlies liberal education in the straight world as well. A group like Tana, however, has a clear basis for the valuation of learning, which is "interesting" if it contributes to the survival of the commune and the common enlightenment of its members. On questions like these, where wisdom grows with experience, communal adults are clearly justified in setting what they have found before their children. And they can feel comfortable in so doing. In contrast to adults in the surrounding culture, they will know that they have achieved something worthy of being passed to a new generation.

A FINAL WORD

Nothing we have said thus far should be taken to imply that entry into communal life styles is easy, a simple matter of shedding superficial habits. For generations, everything in our culture has trained us to be wary of each other, to objectify and deal instrumentally with each other, to wrap the world around ourselves alone. Under the circumstances, it is a wonder that we have any significant social intercourse at all. And it is tempting to see the additional demands of communal living as being entirely out of the question. Commenting on intentional communities in the United States, the Hutterite minister Joseph Hofer has said:

> They all fail, every one of them. The Shakers—*kaput!* Sure! And you want
> to know why? Because it's hard, too hard for most people.... They can't
> do it. They say they want to, but they can't. If you want to live the way
> God intended, you've got to give up a lot of things, and people want to
> hold on. (Quoted in Swan, 1972:91)

That the things we hold on to do to our spirits what cigarettes do to our
lungs makes it no easier to give them up. If we are to achieve it, liberation
will demand much from us that we are unused to giving.

Perhaps the best way to summarize the dilemma lies in the quality of
our relationships, which must be transformed from contractual to sacramental if communalism is to succeed. The "contractual" approach to relationship assumes that we want limited and specific things from our contacts
with others and the world around us—and that the elements and timing
of these should be clearly understood, whether made explicit or implied.
This is the sort of relationship we are accustomed to in this country, and
its dominance is growing. The "alternatives" movements of the 1960s
and 1970s, for example, have relied heavily on a common understanding
that commitments beyond the specific need of the moment are to be avoided
(see Chapters 5 and 6). And the trend in the straight world is to make
even the marriage bond into a parody of corporate alliance:

> THE PARTIES HAVE MADE full disclosure to each other of all properties
> and assets presently owned by each of them, and of the income derived
> therefrom and from all other sources, and AGREE that each party shall have
> sole management, control, and disposition of the property which each
> would have owned as a single person, all as specifically described in EX-
> HIBIT A, which is incorporated by reference and made a part of this [mar-
> riage] CONTRACT. (Cody and Sadis, 1973:102)

Such contracts are a natural extension of the capitalist economic system
which conditions our lives. But one wonders whether the observable impact
of that system is really such that we should wish to construct our interpersonal relationships on the same model.

The communal alternative stresses the sacramental quality of relationships. In this view, fully to connect with someone—or with land, or a
task, or anything else—is an act suffused at once with joy, opportunity, and
obligation. The bonds may rupture, but such an event must not be taken
lightly; we are far too intertwined to be able to afford frivolity in our ties
to the world. By approaching life in this way, we become increasingly attuned to the deeper flows of existence, rather than being limited to the
transitory material and psychological eddies that provide diversion for most

of those in our diverting surroundings. At the same time, we allow ourselves the strength of comradeship in trying new (or are they old?) ways of organizing the totality of our lives. It is not an easy path to follow, but it is worth the effort. The communalist manifesto might well conclude: "Individualists of the world unite. You have nothing to lose but your egos—and you have your selves to gain!"

Part II: Patterns

Chapter 4: America in the Nineteenth Century—Determinants of Communal Success

In Chapter 3, we illustrated some of the changes in attitude that people seeking to create communal work places today should be prepared to accept. Since our primary concern is with the potential for such work places in the United States, we used a group we call "Tana" as an example of a present-day working commune, and placed it in this country. As we note throughout this part of the book, however, many of the same points could be drawn from experiences recorded in other places or other times. For example, the history of the communitarian wave which began in the United States a decade ago—and which is now fading away—provides useful information on how not to succeed. And invaluable lessons can be drawn from study of such groups as the Israeli kibbutzim, Chinese production units, and worker-controlled Yugoslav industries.

But let us begin with the rich communal tradition of the United States, as seen in a myriad of nineteenth-century experiments. With the perspective of time, we can learn much from these groups concerning the determinants of communal success and failure. And the conclusions we draw have applicability *now,* since there has been considerable continuity between American culture a century ago and that of today. In no way is this more evident than in the uncannily precise parallels between the successive communitarian movements of the nineteenth century and those of recent years. In aspiration, rhetoric, structure, and outcome, the communes of the 1960s and the "new communities" of the 1970s were anticipated by the nineteenth-century movements that have come to be identified with Robert Owen and Charles Fourier.

63

OWEN AND THE "COMMUNES"

Robert Owen would no doubt resent being remembered primarily as the father of America's nineteenth-century "hippie communes." As a social critic in England, he wrote 130 tracts covering aspects of reform from education to working conditions (Gatrell, 1969:11). And he expressed many of these ideas in his management of the New Lanark Mills, near Glasgow, which became a model for the Owenite vision of a new social order. For our purposes here, however, Owen enters the stage in late 1824 and early 1825, when he came to America, bought a village in Indiana, and invited the "industrious and well-disposed of all nations" to join him in a communal venture there (Kanter, 1972:122).

New Harmony. In creating the colony of New Harmony, Owen had at least a general idea of what he wanted to accomplish. He had come to believe that in villages of roughly 1,200 people, relative self-sufficiency could be achieved in industry and agriculture, without requiring excessive effort on anyone's part. By eliminating middlemen, proprietors, and landlords, the inhabitants could provide their needs by working three hours a day (Webber, 1959:137). Whatever the specifics of this message, its overtones of a relaxed, new life had immediate appeal. Within six weeks, 800 people had responded to his invitation. By the end of 1825, the population of New Harmony had grown to almost 1,000. To people unsettled by the social dislocations of the early nineteenth century, Owenism had revolutionary force.

Overwhelmed by the enthusiasms springing up around him, however, Owen let his plans give way to simple faith that the energies of his followers would be enough to bring about his vision. What followed was chaos. Although the previous owners of Owen's village had left behind a number of workshops, few of these were put into operation. Inadequate quantities of food were grown. For Owen, who had returned to England, all this seemed at first a natural part of the transition to a new social order. But his subsequent attempts to bring members together around a written constitution resulted only in bitterness and the departure of many people from the group. By 1827, Owen had spent £40,000, the bulk of his personal fortune, in keeping the experiment alive—with little in the way of visible results (Gatrell, 1969:10). Finally, he was forced to sell the property parcel by parcel to individuals who immediately set up private businesses there. New Harmony was dead, after little more than two years.

Commenting several years later on his father's experiment at New Harmony, Robert Dale Owen wrote:

> There was not disinterested industry, there was not mutual confidence, there was not practical experience, there was not unison of action, because there was not unanimity of counsel: and these were the points of difference and dissension—the rocks on which the social bark struck and was wrecked. (Quoted in Noyes, 1966:48–49)

What there was instead was energy, optimism, an extreme anarchism that resisted all attempts at social structuring, and a willingness to live off Owen's money instead of creating the economic base for long-term survival. In all these respects, New Harmony anticipated the counterculture groups of the 1960s, which we describe at length in the following chapter. In this more recent movement as well, people eagerly embraced the communal life style, on the understanding that neither "unanimity of counsel" nor very much "industry" would be required of them. And the communes that resulted had little more success than did Owen's.

The Communal "Movement," 1824–1846. Although New Harmony was exceptional in its size, it had much in common with the large number of communal groups that came together during the same period. And in these too, we see intimations of the communal movement which was to arise almost a century and a half later. Recalling his months in the short-lived Yellow Springs colony, another Owenite group, one participant had this to say:

> The industrious, the skillful and the strong, saw the products of their labor enjoyed by the indolent, the unskilled, and the improvident; and self-love rose against benevolence. A band of musicians insisted that their brassy harmony was as necessary to the common happiness as bread and meat; and declined to enter the harvest field or the work-shop. (Quoted in Noyes, 1966:64–65)

Upon such rocks the Yellow Springs group foundered, as any number of groups were to do during the 1960s. And the conclusions drawn by those involved were often ones of despair. Among the survivors of Yellow Springs, many "rested ever after in the belief that man, though disposed to philanthropy, is essentially selfish; and that a community of social equality and common property is impossible" (Ibid.). As happened with many survivors of the 1960s, they headed for the woods and relentlessly private homesteads of their own.

Owen was the direct inspiration for perhaps a dozen communes formed in the early 1820s. Many other groups, based on similar principles, followed over the next two decades. But by the 1840s, the movement had largely burned itself out. In 1843, John Collins made what was to be one of the final communal efforts of the time, establishing the Skaneateles Community. As had been characteristic of the period, Skaneateles abjured any imposition of either a formal belief system or a formal structure on its members. The only sanction to be applied against truly undesirable residents was to make them feel unwanted, a pattern that was largely to be followed within the counterculture. Although the events of the previous generation should have been fair warning to the contrary, Collins felt that the best way to make people feel "unwanted" was to assign them no work, while continuing to provide them with food and clothing. Surely, they would then leave.

Predictably enough, they did not. Skaneateles was soon afflicted with disproportionate numbers of members who were more than willing to share in the group's resources, but who were considerably less anxious to contribute to them. In 1845, Collins himself wrote of this in terms reminiscent of the more bitter attacks on the counterculture:

> there is floating upon the surface of society, a body of restless, disappointed, jealous, indolent spirits, disgusted with our present social system . . . because they could not render it subservient to their private ends. Experience has convinced us that this class stands ready to mount every new movement that promises ease, abundance, and individual freedom; and that when such an enterprise refuses to interpret license for freedom, and insists that members shall make their strength, skill and talent subservient to the movement, then the cry of tyranny and oppression is raised against those who advocate such industry and self-denial. . . . (Quoted in Noyes, 1966:170)

Collins nonetheless continued to hope for the future of his experiment. But within a year, it succumbed to the same pressures that had destroyed New Harmony twenty years before. An era was over. And perhaps Collins's remarks serve as a fitting epitaph for it. The communards of his day were by no means all "indolent spirits," any more than they were in the 1960s. But in the unstructured spontaneity that dominated the groups of both periods, bad people tended to drive out good, leaving little hope for communal success.

Individualism and Nineteenth-Century "Communes." The wave of communalism which rose and fell between 1824 and 1846 was an attempt to provide people the advantages of group life without impinging on individual interests, which were assumed to be always paramount. Rejecting any possibility of a common belief system, for example, the Skaneateles Community wrote in 1844 of the necessity for "leaving each individual free to think, believe and disbelieve, as he or she may be moved by knowledge, habit, or spontaneous impulses" (quoted in Noyes, 1966:167). There was to be no group We, save that reflecting the accident of temporary residence on the same land. It was an attitude that would be restated, in virtually the same language, in the communes of the 1960s.

And with the same results. It should be self-evident that a group that intends to share space, property, and destiny requires more in terms of bonds than the hope of coincident "spontaneous impulses." But this was a proposition that the communal individualists of the nineteenth century apparently had to test for themselves, in case after case. Generally, the testing proved all too brief. Speaking of the Yellow Springs experiment of 1825, the participant quoted above observed:

> *Individual* happiness was the law of nature, and it could not be obliterated; and before a single year had passed, this law had scattered the members of that society, which had come together so earnestly and under such favorable circumstances, back into the selfish world from which they came. (Quoted in Noyes, 1966:65; emphasis in original)

Gradually, people stopped trying to create Owenite communes. But by this point, a new pattern of individualistic associations had arisen, of which Fourier was the prophet.

FOURIER AND THE "NEW COMMUNITIES"

The Owenite era had been one of exuberant communal energies. But the people who shared in these were ultimately to discover that the interpersonal demands of communal life were more than they were prepared to accept. In the exhaustion and disillusionment that followed, people became more cautious, approaching social organization with sharply limited assumptions as to what it could offer them—and what they should be expected to yield up to it. If they were to be considerably more businesslike in their approach to association than the Owenites had been, however, the communitarians of the 1840s were not prepared to abandon group life entirely. Given demands that were limited and clearly defined, common activities might still feed the individual spirit. What was needed was a model of how such activities might be structured.

Fourier. The model was provided by Charles Fourier, who had begun with an analysis of human passions, ultimately arriving at a description of a social unit, the "phalanx," in which these could best be acted out. According to Fourier, the range of passions was sufficiently great that a community of 1,700 to 1,800 people, equally divided between the sexes, would be needed to ensure representation of all possible character types. To take maximum advantage of this diversity, life would be arranged in such a way that nobody would spend more than an hour a day at work or play with the same group of people. In the intricate pattern of interactions which would result, all those involved would be able to experience their human possibilities to the fullest.

A further advantage lay in the economy of phalanx living. Albert Brisbane, who was largely responsible for introducing Fourier's ideas to the United States, summarized this case in an article published in 1842. As Brisbane saw it, were an individual to contribute $1,000 to the formation of a phalanx, the interest on this investment alone would be sufficient to guarantee "a comfortable room and board" for life, with "whatever he might produce by his labor in addition" (quoted in Noyes, 1966:205). This assumed a degree of cooperation among at least some of the members, so that food might be produced by the phalanx itself and other economies, such as common dining facilities, realized. But through the efficiencies of communitarian living, those who chose to work would need do relatively little. And many, particularly those whose initial investment had been great, would not need to work at all.

In this last statement lies an important departure from the Owenite ideas of common property and relatively equal distribution of communal resources. The phalanx would be "owned" by its shareholders, who would be rewarded according to the magnitude of their investments. With income also dependent on work done or on independent sources of wealth, disparities between members in economic status could be considerable. Such disparities would in part be expressed through the quarters individual families would occupy, since these were to be rented from the phalanx at rates reflecting their degree of desirability. And there would be less material forms of differentiation as well. As Frank Manuel observes, when Fourier "described a typical day's program of work and pleasure for a rich man and for a poor man there turned out to be substantial differences in the refinement of the pleasures available to them" (1962:236). Fourier assumed that the psychic rewards of his system would be sufficiently great for all that these distinctions would hardly be noticed. But they nonetheless constituted a basic retreat from the idealistic principles of the previous communal era.

The "New Communities," 1843–1866. It was precisely a retreat from these principles that the communitarians of the 1840s were seeking, and in Fourier they found a rationale for what they wanted to do. This did not imply strict adherence to the structures that Fourier had so carefully contrived. Like Owen's ideas, Fourier's approach was adapted to the American situation and took on a life of its own. The specifics aside, people found in his writings an appeal for diversity of personal contacts, in a context where the nature of these was defined in precise and limited terms. In the flight from "communes," with their overtones of total sharing and familial bonds, people were moving toward looser "communities," in which relationships were to be more partial and contractual.

As the following two chapters show, the same transition occurred in the American "alternatives" movement in passing from the communes of the 1960s to the "new communities" of the 1970s. According to Manuel, "Fourier's psychology was founded upon the premise that in plurality and complexity there was salvation and happiness. . . . The dangerous relationships were the limited ones, because in exclusivity there lurked disasters . . ." (1962:239). If the premises of the 1970s were the same, the structural conclusions people drew from them in many ways echoed those of Fourier as well. Fourier had called for people to play musical chairs, shifting from one group to another from hour to hour. The alternative-seekers of the 1970s did the same, if on a less rigid schedule, parceling out their days among a variety of work collectives, living cooperatives, political groups, and other "communities." During both of these periods, community-based social situations were an intermediate step between the aspirations of prior communards and the acceptance once more of the patterns of the surrounding society.

In 1843, however, the Fourierist phalanxes were the communitarian answer of the moment, springing up in large numbers in various parts of the country. One, the North American Phalanx, lasted for thirteen years, but most collapsed much sooner. Typically, members worked for salaries in the fields or at the community businesses, paying for their room and board as they went along. From the profits of these operations, dividends were paid to the phalanx's shareholders, who were themselves often nonresidents. Although far more businesslike in tone than earlier communities had been, this structure involved a similar sort of awkward marriage between group living and the assertion of individual prerogatives. When serious crises in financial matters or decision-making arose, group spirit all too often proved inadequate to resolve them without wholesale defections on the part of aggrieved members. With the collapse in 1856 of the North American Phalanx, the period of explicitly Fourierist groups came to an end.

Another decade would pass before the last of the important "new communities" of the era was finally to fade away, however. This was Modern Times, which was founded on Long Island by Josiah Warren in 1851. Warren had earlier created two similar groups, the second of which, Utopia, was largely populated by disillusioned Fourierists. In all of these efforts, Warren was but carrying the principles of the phalanxes to their logical extreme. Where the phalanxes had established individual claims to property and income, Warren did the same with space, scattering his people among separate village homes and their energies among separate projects. Ultimately, Warren hoped to create a permanent form of labor exchange within his colonies, which would allow their economies to function without the use of money. Nothing enduring came of his efforts, and by 1866, Modern Times had become a village much like any other. For secular groups, the nineteenth-century communitarian "movement" was over.

Individualism and Nineteenth-Century "Communities." The most extreme statements of individualism during this period came from Josiah Warren: "TO BE PERFECTLY HARMONIOUS, ALL INTERESTS MUST BE PERFECTLY INDIVIDUAL . . ." (quoted in Krimerman, 1966:317). But a similar current ran through all of these community groups. Commenting on Brook Farm, which had converted to Fourierism three years after its founding in 1841, Wilson Carey McWilliams notes that "it was always, in theory and practice, fiercely individualistic. . . . None of the Brook Farmers seemed prepared to tolerate a check to his will or abide by group decision" (1973:241). Like the earlier Owenite groups, the new communities of the Fourier period took the individualism of the surrounding culture for granted.

In practice, the Fourierists added to Owenism a strong distrust of communal property, which the Brook Farmers called "the grave of liberty" (quoted in Noyes, 1966:174). But this followed less from differences in fundamental attitude than from applying similar attitudes to different situations. Like the communards of the 1960s, the Owenites were primarily interested in the social energies that flowed as a result of assembling large groups of people in the same place. Starting with little wealth of their own, they were prepared to be casual about sharing what was available.

To generate more wealth, while continuing to believe in its equal distribution, would have raised the question of whether equal work was not also required. Since this would have impinged on individual liberties and interrupted the flow of communal energies, the Owenites dealt with the problem by refusing to confront it. As a result, the Owenite communes also resembled those of the 1960s in having particularly short life spans.

The Fourierists dealt with the same problem in a different way. Rather than avoiding work, they abandoned the principle of equal distribution of its returns. Instead, they established "joint-stock" associations where personal effort was clearly related to personal reward. Given the assumptions of individualism, such an arrangement was more conducive to hard work than that of the Owenites had been. The phalanxes, like the "new communities" of the 1970s, tended to last longer as a result. But in all these cases, the underlying individualism of the participants undercut the sense of common destiny needed to make their efforts successful over the long term. To find examples of communal success, we must turn to groups that subordinated individualism to more transcendent principles of social organization.

RELIGIOUS GROUPS

In addition to the waves of secular experiments which we identify with Owen and Fourier, the nineteenth century also saw a considerable movement toward religious communalism. Groups of this nature tended to be less self-conscious than secular ones about their role in creating a new order for society at large. Generally, they were simply searching for a way in which to live out a wholeness of faith which institutionalized churches seemed to deny. In most cases, the elements of this faith were set forth by a strong leader with a claim to particular spiritual enlightenment. Creeds were therefore as diverse as the leaders themselves. But at least one common thread ran through these experiments. At Oneida, members spoke of the "We-spirit" conquering the "I-spirit" (Hayden, 1973:186). However phrased, it was a sentiment that all of the religious groups would have immediately understood. And it sharply distinguished them from the individualistic, secular experiments of the time.

For most of the religious groups, a desire for communalism grew naturally from the example of the early Christian communities. In other cases, the move to intimate groups followed less directly from Christian teachings. The Society of Separatists, for example, arrived in the United States from

Germany with no communal intent, seeking only to preserve their faith. Given the number of old and infirm among them, however, they soon found need for a collective approach to survival. In 1819, they established a common Society. Members pledged themselves to "use all their industry and skill in behalf of the exclusive benefit of the said Separatist Society," which in turn would provide for the needs of its members (quoted in Nordhoff, 1966:105). The desire to preserve a common religion had led to formal creation of a common life. However arrived at, the institutionalized common life was to characterize all of these groups. And this was generally expressed in specific ways that are deserving of brief review here.

Property and Income. Most of the religious communes required people to sign over all personal property to the group upon admission as full members. At least as a matter of policy, this was often held to be an irreversible commitment. In many cases, no records were kept of such transfers. And although practice could prove less rigid, it was often official policy to return nothing of their original contributions to members choosing to leave. In all of this, there was an obvious effort to express in the handling of property the "We-spirit" of the group. Members lived in commonly-owned buildings, often shared by several families. In most cases, they ate in common dining halls. And always, they shared in the benefits that use of the group's assets made possible. To take any other approach, as to retain personal claims on property, would have preserved the "I-spirit" these groups were trying to shed.

For the same reason, the religious communes paid no salaries to their members. Instead, people were provided what they needed regardless of their work. In some cases, as at the Amana colony, this meant creation of a communal "store" where goods for personal use could be obtained. Often, an allowance for such items was established, at a level reflecting the group's degree of affluence. But there was to be no connection between the allowance, or other benefits, and the work an individual member might do. To have maintained such a connection would have encouraged people to think in terms of the relationship between what "I" do and what "I" receive as a result. Better to assume that people are deserving of being cared for by the group simply because they are a part of it.

Work. The assumption within these religious communes that people in fact would work, even though their living did not directly depend on this, proved correct. For one thing, the creeds of such groups placed great value on manual labor. Even the leaders, whose primary duties were of a spiritual nature, were generally expected to spend several hours a day working with their hands, preferably in the fields. In addition, work seldom became burdensome. As Charles Nordhoff observed following a visit with the Shakers,

> Shakers do not toil severely. They are not in haste to be rich; and they have found that for their support, economically as they live, it is not necessary to make labor painful. Many hands make light work; and where all are interested alike, they hold that labor may be made and is made a pleasure. (1966:141–142)

Finally, underlying all this was the operation of the "We-spirit." In the absence of such a feeling, people might continually have worried whether the fruits of their labor were accruing to others. But where there were no "others," only a "we," work was always in one's own interest.

In addition to drawing on the communal spirit, work could also be used to reinforce it. When major tasks were faced, as at the harvest, the entire community would come together to see them through. These were joyous occasions, often involving as much song as work, and they provided a visible affirmation of the group's collective being. Those jobs that could not be done by the group together were often rotated among the members. This practice could keep people from growing unduly attached to particular jobs or work groups at the cost of a sense of the larger community. Alternatively, it could avoid resentments over being tied to intrinsically unpleasant activities, since everyone would have a turn with these. Whether through "harvesting bees" or the rotation of jobs, work was so structured as to recurrently remind people of their involvement with the group as a whole.

Interpersonal Relationships. To maintain a sense of group, the nineteenth-century religious communes went to some lengths to discourage exclusive bonds between their members. The periodic rotation of people between work groups was one expression of this concern. Even more dramatic was the pervasive attempt to diminish the force of the marriage tie. At the Amana villages, Nordhoff found, "matrimony is not regarded as a meritorious act" (1966:36). And he quotes a member of the Separatists to the effect that "marriage is on the whole unfavorable to community life" (Ibid.:108). Where marriage was not done away with altogether, it was therefore discouraged. At Amana, for example, a newly-married couple would immediately be demoted to the lowest grade in the communal church, the "children's order," to reflect their fall from spiritual correctness.

Often, however, more extreme measures were found necessary. Groups such as the Shakers enforced celibacy from the beginning, and other groups either finally adopted this practice (as did the Rappites) or experimented with it at some point in their histories (as did the Separatists). John Humphrey Noyes discovered a different solution for his Oneida Community, where all men were linked to all women in "complex marriage." But this was simply another way of avoiding one-to-one attachments. Speaking of a man who had fallen in love with the woman carrying their child, Noyes warned: "This is an insidious temptation, very apt to attack people under such circumstances; but it must nevertheless be struggled against" (quoted in Nordhoff, 1966:292). For all these groups, romantic love seemed antagonistic to communalism.

In noncelibate groups, similar principles were often applied to the parent-child relationship. At Zoar, for example, the children of the Separatists were removed from their parents' care at the age of three and raised in separate houses thereafter. At Oneida, infants began to spend their days at the "Children's Home" on weaning, with their remaining care then gradually passing from parents to specially trained supervisors. Such measures did not imply a total rupture of family bonds, since parents would continue to spend considerable time with their children. But they emphasized the primacy of the group, into whose collective care the children had been delivered.

If interpersonal caring in these groups was not to become exclusive, as the family unit threatened to do, it was nonetheless encouraged among the membership generally. In addition to routine social contact, which was both extensive and gentle, many religious communes set aside several evenings a week for friendly group activities: prayer, singing, reading newspapers out loud, or simply visiting. And group criticism, despite its forbidding label, was a supportive exercise of such power that it was believed to cure the common cold, as well as graver sins. A circular of the Oneida Association, which used this technique extensively, describes it this way:

> If it is sometimes severe, it is more often gentle. If it pulls down the old life, it delights to heap praise upon the new. It is quick to spy out good, even where the subject does not suspect it, and that it magnifies and enlarges with a will. Sometimes it is as soothing as a mother's touch and as comforting as a mother's love. (Quoted in Robertson, 1970:145)

At least at the level of the group, members of the nineteenth-century religious communes could feel themselves to be in supportive, totally caring environments. If they had sacrificed the nuclear family, they had gained an extended one.

Separation from the Outside World. To preserve this intense communal existence, all of these groups established a variety of boundaries, physical and psychological, between themselves and the world outside. They established their colonies in isolated areas, and often shielded themselves further by placing barns and outhouses between the road and their dwellings. Many groups adopted uniforms to distinguish members from outsiders, even though most members seldom ventured beyond their own territory. When visitors arrived, there were often detailed rules for dealing with them. And at least at Oneida, there was a ritual housecleaning following their departure. Clearly, the outside world was held to be full of contaminations.

If this view seems extreme, we should recall the magnitude of what these groups were trying to accomplish. To create a "We-spirit" within a nation dedicated to the "I-spirit" is an overwhelming task. In their approaches to property, work, and interpersonal relations, the religious communes were running across every grain of American life. Feeling themselves to be spiritual oases, it is little wonder that they tried to guard their perimeters against the encroachments of the surrounding desert. And it worked. In sharp contrast to the Owenite and Fourierist experiments that briefly shared the century with them, a number of these communes lasted for generations. If in the end the larger society nibbled them away, they nevertheless had largely found the formula for communal success.

DETERMINANTS OF SUCCESS

In describing the groups above as "successful" or "unsuccessful," we have relied in part on the simple measure of how long they lasted, a criterion that runs counter to many of the assumptions of our current disposable age. Today, little importance is attached to longevity, even of the groups that are supposed to anticipate a new social order. Thus, in considering the disintegration of one short-lived commune of the 1960s, Judson Jerome comments: "The experience was a thing in itself. It was what it was. That it ended is not failure, but another manifestation of natural process."* And Elia Katz writes of such communes that the

---

* Quoted from a 1972 draft of Jerome, 1974.

> success or longevity of the enterprise itself is of no consequence.... [It] is more correct to think of the communes as they now are as an intermediate stage in the development away . . . from American life . . . and the step itself is incredible and more than outweighs whatever weaknesses any communal experiment may have, and even outweighs the rapid collapse of any or all communal experiments now with us. (1971:202)

We disagree. Basically, such approaches hold that the fate of specific communes is "of no consequence" so long as those passing through them accumulate new experiences as a result. But of the wide variety of possible new experiences, some emerge only with the passage of time. To experience a person deeply requires knowing that person in a number of moods and situations. To experience land deeply requires walking it in the subtle change of many seasons. To experience a group deeply requires being part of that group through a wide range of its ebbs and flows. Given continuity of people and place, the depth of all such experiences increases over time. This was not an objective for most of the communards of the 1960s, as the following chapter indicates. But it is for us, and a group's longevity is at least a crude index of the extent to which it may have been successful in realizing that objective.

Longevity may indicate the breadth of a group's experiences as well, and this too is important for our purposes here. As we argued in earlier chapters, to overcome the discontents that are built into the structure of American society requires building new social units. Ideally, these should encompass the full range of life activities, from work to play to worship. A group seeking to enfold all these things in a manner consistent with its vision of a transformed social order will need time to accomplish this. And to the extent that it is successful, so that members need not turn to the discontented society outside to meet their needs, the group is likely to last. On both these counts, longevity is again correlated with success.

To agree that we wish our communal groups long life, however, is simply to raise a further question: Under what conditions will they be most likely to achieve this? From the experience of the nineteenth century, several conclusions can be drawn.

Belief Systems. Rosabeth Kanter (1972) has found that success within the nineteenth-century groups we have discussed depended on a series of "commitment mechanisms" which led to communal solidarity: sacrifice, investment, renunciation, communion, mortification, transcendence. In each case, these mechanisms were implemented more fully in religious than in secular groups. Unsurprisingly, all of the lasting groups included in Kanter's sample were religious ones. At least during the nineteenth century, a group's success depended most conspicuously on whether its members shared a system of religious belief.

There are obvious reasons why this should have been true, and should remain true today. Questioned recently about the absence of any kind of pooling of equipment among neighboring farmers, one Hutterite observed: "They'd all want it first when the weather was right, and who would pay for repairs if it broke down when one man was using it? Without religion sharing doesn't work" (quoted in Swan, 1972:92). In communal situations implying even more extensive sharing—of space, income, work, lives—the point is doubly valid. If people find no meaning outside of themselves, their measure of all things will be what they individually receive from these. Where communal groups are drawn from such people, they do not long survive the conflicting perceptions of personal interest which members bring to bear on work, income distribution, and other vital communal functions. Where people can see meaning transcending themselves, however, as in the "We-spirit" that religious groups express, sharing is a routine form of self-expression. And this seems a minimum condition for communal success.

The spiritual base of nineteenth-century religious communes was Christianity, but there are alternative ways in which a sense of transcendent meaning and human purpose can be provided. For many people in China, Maoist principles have the force of religion, allowing for an otherwise inexplicable degree of cooperation within Chinese social units (see Chapter 8). The same has been true of the blend of Zionism and political radicalism out of which grew the Israeli kibbutzim (Chapter 7). This does not imply that all "movements" are at root religious. The political activism of the 1960s, for example, was grounded in a belief system that was neither comprehensive nor transcendent enough to be so described. But given a touch of the sacred, there is great latitude for the discovery by communal groups of systems of meaning which would provide the "religious" bonds necessary to their survival.

The successful nineteenth-century communes drew a number of organizational conclusions from their religious principles. Particularly with respect to the maintenance of group boundaries, economic arrangements, and interpersonal relationships, there are lessons to be found in these that have considerable meaning for communal groups today.

Boundaries. As noted above, the religious groups of the nineteenth century established a number of boundaries to insulate them from the world outside. This would be more difficult to do today, given the accessibility of communes everywhere to people and mass communication, but some effort in this direction remains necessary. Noting the absence of kibbutzim in Israeli cities, for example, Bruno Bettelheim comments: "Kibbutzim can exist only (it seems) if the group life is not interfered with by meeting non-group members at every step" (1969:283). And interference with such groups can be considerable, even in rural areas. Over one three-week period in its early days, the Downhill Farm commune counted more than ninety visitors, most of whom stayed at least overnight. The job of creating a successful communal group in an anticommunal society is simply too demanding to tolerate these external pressures. To provide the greatest opportunity for survival, such groups may need to avoid urban areas and to establish routine mechanisms for selectively filtering out the distractions of the outside world.

Economics. If the nineteenth-century experience is to be trusted, successful communes are those in which property is held in common, members are simply provided their needs by the group rather than being paid individual salaries, and work is so structured as to emphasize the "groupness" of the communal experience. Support for these principles comes from examination of the successful contemporary groups included in this book: kibbutzim, Chinese production units, and such American communes as Twin Oaks, Grateful Union, and the Bruderhof (Chapter 9). In many of these cases, there is routine provision for periods of working together on particular projects. In most, no salaries are paid; where "salaries" exist, they are only loosely related to individual output. And in all of these groups, productive property is held in common. As we suggested in discussing nineteenth-century religious groups, these practices follow naturally from a "We-spirit." But in a book on communal work, they are worthy of specific mention in themselves.

Interpersonal Relationships. As Rosabeth Kanter points out,

> Groups with any degree of identity or stability face the issue of intimacy and exclusive attachments and set limits on how much and what kinds are permissible or desirable. Exclusive two-person bonds within a larger group, particularly sexual attachments, represent competition for members' emotional energy and loyalty. The cement of solidarity must extend throughout the group. (1972:86)

In the nineteenth century, religious communes tended to deal with this problem through celibacy, an approach that would be uncongenial to most groups today. The current example of the Bruderhof suggests that strong family units can indeed exist within strong groups. But this example also demonstrates the amount of attention that must be given to the "cement of solidarity" to make such a system succeed. At the Bruderhof, the membership as a whole shares most meals and evenings, and people work together throughout the day. Along with the deeply shared faith of the members, this pattern more than compensates for the fact that families retire to their own apartments at day's end. Whether communal groups adopt this solution or find others for themselves, the tension between exclusive attachments and group solidarity is an issue that all will confront.

The ultimate resolution of this issue will depend on whether the "I-spirit" or the "We-spirit" prevails. Special affections can continue to exist within a strong group "we," just as they do in a nuclear family. But neither the "we" nor the group itself can survive an insistence on the exclusive couplings that represent the boundaries of interpersonal committedness in an "I"-oriented culture. As we note time and again, communal success depends on the abandonment of individualism in favor of a sense of the wholeness of the group. This is not a particularly original message, but it is apparently one that is easily ignored. The alternative-seekers of the 1960s and 1970s carried the "I-spirit" with them when they plunged into the job of restructuring American society. And as we shall see in the next two chapters, they did not achieve their goal.

Chapter 5: America in the 1960s—The Counterculture Communes

In the mid-1960s, Americans gradually began to feel a stirring deep within the nation's soul. Beyond the war, and beyond the great urban riots and the assassinations, were far more mysterious events, all the more troublesome for their tendency to appear first in the behavior of one's children. Strange things were happening: group gropes, acid, hippies, flower children, dropping out, crash pads, communes, Dylan, Kesey, The Haight, Taos. Worst of all was the fact that the essence of it was somehow incommunicable to respectable citizens. Said Dylan: "There's something happening here, but you don't know what it is, do you, Mr. Jones?"—and Mr. Jones didn't indeed. Charles Reich found easy explanations that made him rich and famous, but others had more trouble:

> Intellectually, I knew that *it* couldn't be grasped by man's analytical tools, his ologies: *it* was a consciousness totally different from that of analytical modern man, who always differentiated himself from his subject, categorically dividing Man from Nature, the Self from Society. *It* was gestalt, a fresh vision, a . . . but my thoughts began to muddle. (Houriet, 1971:73)

"It" came to be known as the counterculture, something so different as to represent a break with history. Keith Melville quotes a communard who put it this way: "This whole new generation, all these people born since 1943, they've been exposed to entirely new vibes from the universe, creating an entirely new species" (1972:161). For those too old or too obtuse to have absorbed these "vibes" at birth, entry to the new species was difficult but not impossible. One could always convert, an idea that expresses both the felt radicalness of the change and its all-consuming, almost religious nature. But however you got there, yours was a clearer vision, a more honorable posture, a happier life than could even be imagined by those whom fate had left behind in the old culture.

Perhaps. The elements of counterculture consciousness were not quite as ineffable as its adherents have suggested, nor were they quite as revolutionary as was at first supposed. Still, there was a certain heady optimism to it all, a feeling that civilization was back on the track after a lengthy hiatus of dehumanized technology worship. Instead of entropy, the idea that the mechanical universe is running out of energy, people embraced the idea of syntropy, whereby the organic universe is seen to take on fresh vitality as our human energies combine in new ways.* Philosophers and physicists could argue the matter, but argument was quite beside the point. It felt right; and in the prevailing doctrine, good feelings were akin to truth. To paraphrase a slogan of the day, the revolution was over and the counterculture had won. Self-congratulation was so pervasive that it seems almost rude to ask the obvious question: *What* had the counterculture won?

"THE GROUP"**

We never ourselves became card-carrying members of the counterculture. We were born before 1943, if not by much. And we never went through the true conversion to counterculture dogma that might have overcome that handicap. But we were close enough to sample the ambiance. We lived communally in Massachusetts, the Pacific Northwest, and Vermont, and visited dozens of other communes across the country. We smoked dope with freaks around Harvard Square, dropped acid in New York pads, did peyote in the hills behind Palo Alto. We consulted the *I Ching* for important decisions and lived otherwise according to the little signs the cosmos provided us. We dropped out and lived off odd jobs and savings. It was all an integral part of our struggle to grow; and much of it remains with us still, if sometimes only as aspiration.

To the degree that the counterculturists seemed to be doing the same things, we intuitively felt them to be our comrades. But there was an uneasiness in us that we could not define, something that kept us from being

---

* See for example Schaberg and Silha (1972:66); and Wheeler (1972:48).

** In different form, portions of this section originally appeared in the *New York Times Magazine.* (French, 1971).

full participants in their brave new world. We were assailed by doubts: was it simply old-value hang-ups that held us back, the unconscious baggage of comforts and familiar patterns of the straight life? Certainly, many in the counterculture, accustomed to seeing the world as one of sharp contrasts between "new" (them) and "old" (everyone else), were urging this view upon us. If we ultimately decided that what we disliked of the counterculture was its own bondage to negative elements of the past, the doubts persisted in another form. Were we simply playing a then popular game, "More Radical Than Thou," at the cost of our own understanding? Finally, we came to trust our judgments, but hardly with the certainty of which holy writ is born. What we offer below is no more than the best insight we can provide into an enormously complex phenomenon.

Much of our insight coalesced around our experiences within The Group, an urban commune founded in the Pacific Northwest by exiles, both students and faculty members, from a local college. The Group is defunct now, but when we arrived in early 1971 it had more than fifty members, most of whom lived in a dozen houses clumped together on the edges of the city's black ghetto. It was financially a comfortable place. Several of the houses had been bought by members. And in The Group's early, earnest days as an alternative learning-living experiment, it had arranged a sizable foundation grant. People nearby might have been struggling to survive, but not The Group. All members were provided with food, shelter, and a group health plan, without cost or obligation.

Not that people simply lay around and pondered their affluence. For one thing, their academic background surfaced in a number of highly informal "learning groups" reflecting the interests of various members: radical economics, Old English, dance, science fiction, woodworking. And there was much activity of a more casual nature still; people spent endless hours talking about ways to extricate themselves further from the straight environment. Finally, much time was spent outside The Group itself in pursuits ranging from remunerative work (the exceptional case) to staffing the local underground newspaper to pruning trees on an eighty-acre plot of land near town that The Group was thinking of buying for its more bucolic members. The energy expended on all these things was incredibly intense, to the point that we were all fond of observing that a day within The Group was like a month in the world outside. We thought of this as a positive thing.

We had arrived in The Group through Martha's House, and our first evening there was a paradigm of The Group's inner life. Martha was cleaning up the debris left by a group that had been there earlier in the day to talk about radical economics. John was cooking dinner, with help from Cathy. George was bringing in firewood. Linda was on her way out to collect a woman referred to the House for a night's lodging by the local abortion counseling center. Through the evening, other members of The Group dropped in and out, exchanging tales of that day in The Group's life or partaking of the running discussion on women's liberation that lasted into the early hours of the next morning. For us, coming fresh from a too-private California life style and temporary jobs as waitress and school-bus driver, it seemed an exciting change of pace. Left behind were months of wandering in search of some elusive next step in our lives. We were finally home.

Or so it seemed for a few golden days. Then, during one of the marathon women's lib debates at Martha's, we abruptly found ourselves under siege. What we were doing with each other, it turned out, was "coupling." (Images of dogs or railroad cars come to mind, and those were exactly the overtones.) Coupling was any long-term relationship between two people; it necessarily led to stagnation, parochialism, sexism, and other counter-revolutionary activities. Since our move to The Group had been born in part of a desire to confront exactly those questions in a supportive environment, we tried to talk of how a couple might deal with them. It was all in vain; knowing smiles informed us of our naiveté. For the women of the house, it was clear that to avoid the chauvinism required avoiding the males. And the men, absorbed by their guilt, fell willingly into line. No coupling for them either, at least until they had purged themselves of their chauvinist tendencies.

In practice, a pervasive suspicion existed of most forms of human connectedness. Group members were constantly on the go, down to San Francisco, back East, moving in and out of The Group or from house to house within it. This mobility was guarded above all else. Martha, for example, held that her house would be a success if people living there could leave altogether without anyone feeling any special sense of emotional strain. The points of human reference became diluted, through both space and large numbers of people, by all this motion. At one point, we asked Linda how many people she could turn to if her head began to come unglued, how many people would understand what was happening to her. Dozens, she said, scattered all over the world; and we could not explain the difference between an understanding spread among scattered dozens and one evolved over time with a single person, or two or three. Much less could we explain why we valued that more intimate sort of understanding. It was an awkward attempt at intercultural communication, and it did not succeed.

To guard against intimacy demands constant attention. Gradually, we began to see a brittleness in the ways Group members dealt with one another, in the set of their faces, in what they said. Compassion was held to be condescending, implying a degree of togetherness superior to that of the person toward whom one was being compassionate. Favored instead as a basis for interpersonal style was a sort of brutal honesty that forced distances between people, stressed their apartness. Ideological confrontation was valued: "That's a male chauvinist thing to say"; "How can you have such a reactionary attitude?" People broke off conversations to analyze each other's neuroses: "You're just projecting when you say that"; "Why do you have so much self-hatred?" Someone wrote a note in The Group's weekly newsletter, advising "you snivelling, back-stabbing shitheads" (his fellow members) that "I hope you curl up and die." Others laughed, pleased at his directness. It had to do again with preserving mobility. Compassion would have led to involvement, involvement to commitment, and commitment to chains on tomorrow.

The coupling phobia spilled over into attitudes toward work. With relationship not an objective, the idea of relationship around work became irrelevant. Instead, people sought activities that expressed their own special apartness. Crafts were in favor, since they were personal things, done alone. And writers, artists, and other solitaries were overrepresented. As for the work that paid the bills, the same centrifugal forces applied. One person, for example, was economic consultant to a major health plan, someone else worked the graveyard shift as a janitor at a local hotel, a third spent odd hours at a skid-row pawnshop. Most people did not work at all, preferring to live off the foundation money or checks from home. There was no sense that any of this inhibited The Group's development in any way. It began to seem instead that strong group life was not really a Group objective, was rather to be resisted, as if it were simply a multiperson version of coupling—which indeed it is.

It led people inward, to an indifference to the experiences of others. At one point, we found an excellent postmortem of a failed commune. The problems described were hauntingly familiar in The Group context, but several people refused to read it. It was someone else's trip in some other place—what could it possibly have to say to them? Such an approach devalued the more extensive life experiences of The Group's adults to the point where they became almost ashamed to take positions on things. It seemed an unwritten law that they were never to appear to know more about anything than the rawest escapee from some middle-class suburban home. They were permitted to take over the tedious administrative work that younger members did not care to do, however. The allowable role seemed to be that of the Token Adult, the ultimately permissive, useful-to-have-around parent, viewed with the sort of tolerant affection that shaded off into dismissal.

It all took its toll. At any given moment, half The Group was sick, an illness level we had encountered only once before, among the people we knew in Nigeria during the worst of the civil war. The animals were, as always, another sensitive index of environmental vibrations. The Group's dogs, a sobering assortment of neurotic creatures, howled and whined and snapped for attention. (The cats, having a greater instinct for self-preservation, simply ran away.) Worse still, The Group children were brittle, supercharged, alienated. One spoke of himself in the third person as "the computer": "The computer is ready to answer your question now," he would say. They were so peripheral that one five-year-old called his own meeting to complain that The Group offered nothing in which he could participate. Where children and dogs are out of place, beware, beware.

We left The Group the same way we entered it—through Martha's House. One day, we went to the state prison to talk with a group of black inmates about Ethiopian culture. The people we saw were *alive*. Open and eager to communicate, they reached out to establish points of contact with us. We went back to Martha's. People were lying around on the floor as if paralyzed, talking with their customary detachment about women's liberation. It was shattering; here were the imprisoned. What we had originally thought of as The Group's ever-provocative dialogue was instead, we were finally realizing, an elaborate mechanism of self-defense. Alone behind their walls of words, people preserved distances between one another by ceaselessly talking. It had become compulsive. "There's too damned much verbiage around this place," someone once said to John. "You and I had better have a long talk about this," he replied.

We had come to The Group for intimacy, and none was wanted. We had come for communal work, and none was wanted. We had come to build a new culture, and what we found was as alienating as the old. At a meeting the next day, someone said something about "separation." The Group three-year-old, who happened to be passing through, was brought up short. He thought about it for a long minute. And then, to nobody in particular, he said: "Being separated is talking." That sort of insight would be driven out of him before long, we knew; and we feared that the same could happen to us. We packed and left.

THE COUNTERCULTURE

In a number of ways, The Group diverged from the norms for counterculture groups. It had more money than most, for example. But more important, it had a certain driven quality that flowed from its cerebralness. At a time when many counterculturists were trying to get back into their bodies, or into nature or various cosmic harmonies, Group members were relentlessly thinking, stopping only long enough to talk or sleep. And much of their time was spent thinking critically of one another. The countercultural doctrine that everyone should respect everyone else's special trip was beginning to seep slowly into Group life, but intolerance remained alive and well during our stay there. (Lamentably, we contributed our share; something about The Group brought out the worst in everyone.) Some of this reflected a certain lay psychoanalytical taint that expressed itself in the unwillingness of Group members ever to take each other at face value. After an article of ours which dealt in part with The Group appeared in the *New York Times Magazine,* one member wrote us to ask "why you think you wrote the things you did." She assumed we would be unaware of the real reasons.

These peculiarities aside, however, the elements of Group life were uncomfortably similar to things we had seen from rural communes to urban crash pads. Finally, we arrived at an unhappy conclusion: In many ways, The Group was but a caricature of broad tendencies within the counterculture itself. Our months in The Group had simply forced us to acknowledge the pervasiveness of these tendencies and to name them. For a time, we worried about the possibility that our bitterness toward The Group might be overwhelming our perceptions of the counterculture generally. But as time passed and we again passed through communes that radiated joy and serenity, the intensity of our experience within The Group fell into its proper perspective. At least, that is our hope.

Basic Principles: Simplicity and Flight. Although our conclusions about the counterculture will accentùate the negative—in a book stressing the centrality of work to our lives, it could hardly be otherwise—we begin by acknowledging the movement's very real achievements. Foremost among these was the realization by those within the counterculture that the world in which they had been raised was flawed in fundamental ways. This conclusion was much more than one of mere ideology. The young, most of them from middle-class families, saw in the lives of their parents the results of living the American Dream. Lubricating their way through days of apparently senseless motion with pills and alcohol, the adults often were achieving little more than wealth and power and divorces and ulcers, doing untold violence all the while to their children, the environment, the world. At some level, the young may have been aware that their elders were still fighting the specter of the Great Depression, searching for an elusive material security that had been absent in their own youth. But any sympathy that might logically have resulted from such awareness was overwhelmed by a more immediate truth. In the moment now, all the world seemed seized by a fine madness, which poisoned whatever it touched.

And so the counterculture broke free—or so, for a time, it seemed. Leaving promising careers or the finer schools, dozens of thousands of young men and women moved together into urban crash pads or broken-down farmhouses, making do together on savings or welfare or sporadic odd jobs. If nothing else, they proved it possible to break the chain that their parents had assumed to be ordained by God, suburb to prep school to Ivy League college to career to suburb, without being struck down by lightning. It quickly became clear that people did not need tenure or the keys to the executive bathroom to feel self-esteem or pleasure in their life paths. On the contrary, once shed of such old-culture ambitions, people found their surroundings more luminous, their heads less cluttered, their spirits more free to soar. For a large part of the population, it would never again seem inescapable that joy and the search for meaning in one's life should be eternally subordinated to status and material advancement. It was a salutary lesson.

At times, the implications of this revelation in daily life could seem almost magical. As we wandered through rural communes, for example, we often found a relaxed sense of interpersonal ease that had no real counterpart in the seminar rooms or committee meetings that we—and many of the communards we saw—were fleeing. No longer scrambling for position on some institutional ladder, people grew more accepting of one another, more able to let human contact find its own way without a felt need to translate such contact always into formulas functional in the System's terms. Even where there was tension or conflict, this followed not from the competitive struggle to meet System requirements better than somebody else, but rather from the necessity of working out one's

humanness in direct dealings with others: confronting one's attitude toward
sex roles among commune members, say, or testing a theoretical commitment to cooperation against a gut resistance to taking one's turn at washing dishes. Whether in tension or in peacefulness, in other words, people
were dealing with one another primarily in concrete ways around specific
issues of daily life. That this could be a path to personal growth beyond
anything The System could offer was another discovery for which the
counterculture may justly take credit.

Finally, the counterculture rediscovered the joys of pursuits which their
parents had forgotten or ignored. Coming upon a new rural commune
was often like finding a fantasy village constructed from images of simpler times and places. Here would be someone milking goats, there someone else bent over a loom. In this room, someone in intense concentration
upon a mandala or a yoga exercise; in that, someone else baking whole
grain bread in a wood oven. Outside, laughing children would be jumping
naked in and out of a spring-fed pond, while dogs happily chased each
other along its banks. Add a few props—a cloudless sky, an ancient VW
bus painted in day-glo psychedelia, a half-completed geodesic dome on
the edge of a meadow—and you have the classic media image of a hippie
commune. Curiously enough, such places did exist. And those who passed
through them could never forget what they learned there of life and of
joy.

If the places where the counterculture lighted could resemble latter-day
Edens, however, they were cursed with their own versions of Original Sin.
Somehow, in spite of all the apparent beauty and human connectedness,
communes folded as abruptly as they formed. And even while they lasted,
people were forever flowing in and out, never seeming to stay for long.
Only in the rarest cases did communes really come to terms with their
environments, forming units that could survive without a steady flow of
gifts from outside. Stranger still, all too seldom did communards fully
come to terms with one another, massive propaganda to the contrary
notwithstanding. Many more communes went under because the dishes
never got washed than were ever forced out of town by hostile neighbors
or zoning boards. As the 1960s ended, the suspicion grew that the counterculture was ultimately far more concerned with escaping the old world
than in building a new one.

Some people have resisted this skepticism. Ray Mungo, for example,
has argued that "the positive, new, and forward aspects of the life are
coming on strong now, and will exonerate us in the long run, I'm sure,

from any accusation that we merely drew back without pushing upward as well" (1970:79). And Keith Melville pleads for time: "To assume that within a few short years the young could reverse all their parents' most entrenched assumptions, explore the alternatives, and invent a coherent lifestyle is surely to assume too much" (1972:113). But a decade has now passed since the counterculture got started, and such communes as continue to exist still tend to serve as temporary refuges for transients in the process of drawing back from their former lives. There is a role for such places, of course, particularly in a society where there is so much to draw back from. But the counterculture has shown a sharply limited capacity for taking the next steps.

Much of this has followed precisely from the movement's counterness, its first and most obvious quality. At The Group, we came to realize that everyone was in flight, bound together primarily in reaction. Traumatized by courses, assigned readings, and tests, Group members would have learning sessions where nobody had to read anything, or even come. Offended by the authoritarianism of their parents and teachers, members would create an environment where age and experience were disqualifications for being taken seriously. Antagonized beyond reason by the social pressures of the straight world, people would see to it that The Group imposed nothing on its members. Appalled by the empty possessiveness of their parents' marriages, the young would ensure that nobody had any claims on anybody else. The specifics varied from commune to commune, but the tone was one we found everywhere we went. There is little originality in so observing. Among many others, Melville has noted that the counterculture was "a movement that can be defined neither by its tactics nor its goals . . . but by a shared sense of a common enemy" (1972:19).

The enemy was real, of course; and communards were right to flee what they were fleeing. But in simply trying to turn society upside down, they fell victim to a posture of extreme negativism, which became the expected natural way for people—or at least young people—to react to their environment. Talking of her own communal experience, Elaine Sundancer says:

> If I wanted my children to go into the country, I would raise them in the way I was raised. I lived in the city and I want to live in the country. I'm raising my children in the country and they're certainly going to want to live in the city . . . maybe for all of their lives. Can you see I feel a kind of sadness about this. . . . (1972:11)*

---

* See also Davidson, 1970:99.

And sadness there should be, if we see even our own children as a bundle of negative tropisms. Such an attitude reflects an understanding of reality which rests on the idea of flight, an insubstantial foundation for building a new world.

The propensity for flight expressed itself most clearly in the tendency of many counterculturists to deal with problems by running away from them. We noted above that people within communes dealt with each other around concrete issues rather than institutional abstractions, clearly a step forward in itself. But if their capacity for stomaching the abstract had evaporated, their willingness to struggle through concrete difficulties could be little greater. Over the long haul, nothing was worth much of a hassle, whether working through conflicts with fellow communards or figuring out how to pay the bills. As we had seen so clearly in The Group, the natural response to unpleasantness (or simply boredom) was to take off for somewhere else: "Marty had left the farm in Vermont some months earlier, disillusioned with the experiment and embittered with some of the people there. It had just stopped working for him, as it must from time to time for all of us, and of course he had to split" (Mungo, 1970:94–95).

To see countercultural escapism only in these terms, however, would be to miss a critical point. If many communards feared and fled problems within their communes, they often seemed equally to fear and flee any possibility that those communes might turn out to be problem-free. To have one's commune "work" would doubtless imply commitments both to its group life and to the other individuals within that group. And this would pose the greatest threat of all: immersion in the commune at the expense of one's own individuality. Viewed in this way, the characteristic transience of the counterculture was attributable as much to people's attempts to guard the autonomy of their separate beings as to the effort involved at solving interpersonal difficulties. If we accept the commune's dishwashing schedule, in other words, our interests have been subordinated to those of the group; and we might as well then be back in our classrooms or jobs. Better to establish the principle that we wash dishes when we feel like it, even if the commune dissolves in anger as a result.

If communes were thus to be tolerated only as long as they did not become too communal, they still had an important role to play in the life of the counterculture. Talking about "The Free People," Peter Marin noted: "The young soar like birds, but like birds they need somewhere to rest" (1970:50). And communes were for resting, if not for staying. Passing through, one could invariably find some dope to smoke, some records to hear, a place to spend the night before soaring off once more. In a sense, the social life that resulted had a "family" flavor of hearthside warmth and companionship well beyond what most of those in the counterculture had ever found in their own homes; and as far as it went, this was all to the good.

If the counterculture built the comforts of family into its communes, however, it insisted on rejecting the bonds that "family" normally implies. As Ross Speck put it, "Perhaps one advantage of the commune as a life style is more freedom to be individualistic, along with a relief from the restrictiveness that accompanies family myths and traditions" (1972:16). But in seeking such relief, the counterculture risked slipping toward equally familiar, if less elevated, social models. Describing communes he had visited in the Midwest, for example, Ron Roberts spoke of "a sort of fraternity system for nonstraight students" (1971:58); and the phrase rings uncomfortably true. Once inducted into the counterculture, people did find local "chapters" scattered across the country, each with its latter-day equivalent of the keg of beer and the guest room for brothers in town for the weekend. This may have been an improvement on the suburbs, but it remains an open question whether it was the path to a transformed society.

New Values and Old. Clearly, there were many faces to the counterculture; and we form our image of the movement from those we choose to see. Which has more meaning, the serenity of a communal setting or the fact that half of those present are about to split for San Francisco? Who is more representative, the seeker finding spiritual truth in a cap of acid or the person self-destructing on speed for want of any other idea of how to pass the day? What is the correct label for those choosing to abandon pursuits that society considers "productive" in favor of a more leisurely life backed by that society's dole: irresponsible? courageous? parasitic? path-breaking? In a very real sense, all such approaches are "true"; and reasoning through what the counterculture actually meant requires careful definition of the grounds on which we are to measure its achievements.

Perhaps the first of these should be simply this: at heart, was the counterculture really "counter" to the prevailing culture? On the face of it, there is a temptation to suspect that it was not, since genuinely contrary social movements are never fed—as the counterculture claimed to have been—by the abrupt discovery of revolutionary truths by a large portion of the population. Musing on his own Bohemian past, Michael Harrington notes "one of the most crucial and Hegelian of truths about contemporary culture: . . . that a Bohemia that enrolls a good portion of a generation is no longer a Bohemia" (1972:102). Instead, it would seem likely that the "Bohemians" of the 1960s could only have included so much of that decade's youth by not being very Bohemian at all, by remaining firmly grounded in the old culture. Any true revolution in understanding would have been either more limited in numbers or much longer in building.

But to assert the theory is not to prove the case. More to the point is the extent to which specific "new" counterculture values were directly borrowed from the old culture. Foremost among these, of course, was the attempt to assert individuality through a posture of individualism. As Philip Slater has noted,

> There must be continuities between the old and the new, but these cannot extend to the relative weights assigned to core motivational principles. . . . [Nothing] will change until individualism is assigned a subordinate place in the American value system—for individualism lies at the core of the old culture, and a prepotent individualism is not a viable foundation for any society in a nuclear age. (1970:118)

Yet this was precisely the foundation on which the counterculture rested. Although they searched for different kinds of satisfactions—counterculturists chased psychological experience, for example, while their parents chased material goods—young and old alike agreed that these satisfactions were individual ones, to be individually pursued. Groups could be useful to the pursuit; but they were not fundamental to one's life.

The fragmentation of experience which resulted was also a tendency held in common by the two cultures. As we had found in The Group, those within the counterculture parceled out their time among discrete social units (commune, work collective, women's liberation meeting) much as did their parents (office, country club, bridge league). Relationships with such groups in each case were functional and fleeting; one was never to be tied down. Even the ways in which counterculture and straight-world apologists described the nature of this process sounded much the same:

> ALVIN TOFFLER: "Thus it might be said that commitments [in the straight world] are shifting from place-related social structures (city, state, nation or neighborhood) to those (corporation, profession, friendship network) that are themselves mobile, fluid, and, for all practical purposes, place-less." (1970:84)

> CHARLES REICH: "The individuals [of the counterculture] preserve every

bit of their individuality. They simply come together to share a feeling, a moment, or an experience, and thus feel united in a community based on having their heads in the same place at the same time." (1970:272)

The straights could meet at professional conferences, in other words, while their children were at Woodstock. But the interpersonal framework of the two experiences was similar.

If people's ties with groups were tenuous, so were their ties with other people generally. Toffler mentions the psychologist, tongue presumably in cheek, who has suggested something called "The Modular Family" for mobile executives (1970:75). According to this scheme, executives on transfer to new areas would leave behind not only their houses but their families as well. The companies involved would then provide "matching" families at the new locations. Toffler claims that nobody has proposed this seriously—yet. But it sounds hauntingly close to the "Modular Communes" that the executives' children created. In the world of the counterculture, Rosabeth Kanter has pointed out, "people and places are increasingly interchangeable" (1972:172). It is perhaps appropriate that Dan Greenburg found the countercultural watchword—Perls's "I do my thing and you do your thing"—posted prominently on the wall, as "The Swinger's Credo," at his first orgy (1972:250). Where rampant individualism means that we can no longer have expectations of each other, all that is really left to do is to "swing" together—sexually, intellectually, spiritually. The counterculturists got a better press out of their version of this than did the adult "swingers" of the suburbs. But this hardly means that they had traveled far from the drift of the larger society.

Even the countercultural assumption that social good would follow from people doing their own separate things is deeply rooted in American assumptions about reality. During our early years of driving for national economic expansion, this was justified in material terms: If people pursued their individual economic interests, the group as a whole would prosper. Now, liberated by enormous national wealth from such mundane preoccupations, we hasten to convert the old rationalizations for material greed into new ones for psychological self-seeking. If the counterculture asserts the right of all to their particular "trips," the straights have been just as quick to produce such doctrines as the need for "self-actualization." Again, the young and the old are in concert in a fundamental area, in this case having resurrected in a new form one of the most basic of American beliefs.

In other areas as well, we hear echoes of our national past. Albert O. Hirschman has observed that the movement to communes itself was "very much in the American tradition." America was originally settled by people on the run. In the counterculture, "once again dissatisfaction with the surrounding social order leads to flight rather than fight, to withdrawal of the dissatisfied group and to its setting up a separate 'scene' " (1970:108). The countercultural habit of dealing with problems within a commune by fleeing to a new place was simply an extension of this principle.* Basically, people in following this path were simply being true to their culture heritage. There is little wonder that the counterculture occasionally provoked strong feelings of déjà vu.

Clearly, the counterculture embodied a series of tendencies which were wholly consistent with those of the straight world: individualism, fragmentation of lives, flight from difficult situations, the assumption that social good follows from personal self-seeking, and so on. In important ways, it would seem, the counterculture failed its own most basic test—to be "counter." And that in turn undermined it in two critical further respects: the ability to lay the grounds for a new social order and the realization of individual growth for those within the movement. The counterculture's limitations as an agent of social change are discussed in the final section of this chapter. Before turning to this, however, a brief comment on individuality.

Since Chapter 3 considers at some length the social conditions for maximum personal growth, that discussion is not repeated here. But to recall our argument, we maintain that a posture of individualism—whether expressed in terms of the "rugged individualism" dear to the hearts of the straight world, or the counterculture's insistence on "doing your own thing"—leads to social conformity rather than to the achievement of genuine individuality. To a considerable degree, the experience of the counterculture confirmed this, as George Woodcock has noted:

> It has already become a cliché that doing one's own thing really means all doing the same thing.... The counterculture, for all its rhetoric of freedom and spontaneity, in fact imposes a conformity of life style, of language, of patterns of thought.... No doubt there are generational differences among lemmings. But they all live in cosy burrows, and they are all intensely suggestible, all liable to destroy themselves *en masse* through the operation on their wills of forces they do not understand. (1971:16)

---

* Hirschman points out that group loyalities can temper such flightfulness, encouraging people to act within the group to reverse any deterioration in its functioning (see, for example, 1970:78). As we have seen, however, the counterculture avoided such communal allegiances, finding them antagonistic to individual freedom.

Woodcock's is the view from outside, but the same doubts, and even the same metaphor, occurred to such a charter member of the counterculture as Abbie Hoffman, who reacted to the celebrated Woodstock festival as follows: "Were we pilgrims or lemmings? Was this really the beginning of a new civilization or the symptom of a dying one? Were we establishing a liberated zone or entering a detention camp?" (1969:92). And Hoffman can find no ready answer to his own questions.

If "lemmings" is in fact too strong a term to describe those within the movement, it remains true that the counterculture did contain a striking degree of conformity, in precisely the forms Woodcock notes. Finally, the counterculturists proved unable to provide much more real differentiation among themselves than had their elders. Both sides will resist this idea. The straights tended to emphasize their own felt diversity while seeing their rebellious children as basically identical; the counterculture had it just the other way around. But in both cases, these groups had clear and fairly narrow images of who was "one of us," to the total exclusion of true deviants. The arrival of a tie and short hair in a hippie commune would have produced the same degree of paranoia and hostility as the arrival of a beard and hash pipe at a meeting of the board of directors. That the counterculture should fall victim to such tendencies is not all that surprising. It had retained old-society values that necessarily led in that direction, and media and mobility were able rapidly to transmit the fashions of "rebellion" across the country. But it is nonetheless a sad conclusion for the Great American Cultural Revolution.

COUNTERCULTURAL ECONOMICS: THE MOVEMENT AT AN IMPASSE

If degree of "counterness" is one obvious measure of the counterculture, another is the extent to which the movement acted to lay the material base for a new social order. And here were further problems, for the invention of new economic life patterns was inconsistent with the counterculture's style. Thought was the source of headaches and ulcers. According to Hoffman: "When you are involved you don't get paranoid. It's when you sit back and try to figure out what's going on, or what you should do" (1968: 60). Even if you sacrificed yourself and did try to figure things out, it wouldn't lead to much anyway. For Denham Grierson, "there is not time enough to spend working out solutions for questions that will no longer seem relevant when the answers are found" (1971:135). Superficially,

these attitudes seem simple reactions to the hated old order, whose earnestness and rationality were to be avoided. But it is at least equally plausible
that the counterculture was simply acting out the very American value of
pragmatism, of concentration on what "works" right now to the exclusion
of grandiose planning for the future. The counterculture was getting by,
after all; why look beyond today?

When the counterculture did focus on more sweeping projects, these
often tended to verge on the whimsical. Jerry Garcia, for example, mentioned in an interview with *Rolling Stone* that:

> A guy had an idea the other night that was good . . . an idea for hippie
> money. . . . [The] rate of exchange would be something like 1000 hippie
> dollars to $1.00. But then there would be a black market rate which would
> be like one-to-one so that you could have a huge income and then convert
> it the regular straight way not getting taxed and all. (Charles Reich, one
> of the interviewers: "That's pretty good.") (Garcia, 1972:36)

The same tone prevailed in more fully elaborated proposals. Here is Arthur
Shaw speaking of Copionics ("the theory of global sufficiency") in *The
Mother Earth News:*

> [We] take factual and actual data and conditions and assemble the data
> into a flow chart. . . . To be more specific, we know what's produced in
> various areas of the globe. Certainly we know the need . . . in terms of
> two-thirds of the world's people being hungry and 10,000 starving to
> death per day. . . . We note these two series of facts—free availability and
> need—in the [World Economic Organization] computer-programmed
> flow chart and, in the expression of the satisfaction of the need, we demon-
> strate the feasibility of free-flow exchange. (1970:8)

Such views had an imaginative quality that made them fun to read. But in
the realm of thinking through serious alternatives to our present economic
system, they left a great deal to be desired.

As already noted, thoughtlessness about alternatives was a defining feature of the counterculture generally. Rather than reasoning things through,
people in the movement followed their instincts around the edges of the
affluent society. By shaving personal consumption, people could reduce their
needs to a level that could be satisfied without devoting much time or attention to the process. As we had seen in The Group and elsewhere, money
always seemed to be there for the having. There were checks from home,
welfare, food stamps, grants, inheritances, savings, gifts, and (as a last

resort) temporary jobs ranging from newspaper delivery to pickle packing.*
One might have supposed that a "counter" culture would have resented living off the scraps from the parental table. But through a curious psychological process, the reasoning became quite different:

> The girl I am talking to, Marie, is the only person in the house with an
> outside job. She works at Yale. The rest of the group is supported by the
> proceeds from exhibitions and by a small grant the group had this spring
> to give a series of seminars at Yale. The commune lives from hand to
> mouth, but they don't mind *and prefer their freedom to economic depen-
> dence on the system.* (Atcheson, 1971:119; our emphasis)

Useless to point out that such dependence in fact remained total. Somehow, the fact of living "hand to mouth" instead of holding a steady job had become a sufficient measure of personal liberation.

If we acknowledge the degree to which members of the counterculture remained their parents' children, however, the reasons for such an attitude become less obscure. Relieved of economic pressures, after all, what would those middle-class parents have chosen to do? There is a range of possibilities, of course. But it is likely that many would have chosen such pastimes as puttering in the garden, taking classes in dance or handicrafts, setting up part-time retreats in the country, traveling, learning yoga, attending encounter sessions, leading recycling drives, doing good works. As it happened, these were precisely the pursuits (in one form or another) that the counterculturists chose to occupy their time. The young discovered that the price of all these things could be less than their parents had ever dreamed possible, and they rejected material security as a prerequisite for pursuing them. But rather than embodying a rebellion against their parents' most deeply-held wishes, those within the counterculture were simply insisting on acting these out. And if that was what "liberation" was to consist of, it hardly mattered who paid the bill.

Little wonder, then, that work alternatives were last among countercultural concerns. The movement grew out of—and expressed—a culture that attached little value to such thinking. Work might be the path to security or material abundance, but it was increasingly being viewed as having little potential for satisfaction in itself. The whole society had become consumption oriented, viewing production as a necessary evil in this process. Other cultural points of reference reinforced the counterculture's inattention to work as well. To have devoted the time and effort necessary to create alter-

---

* See, for example, Diamond, 1971:122–123.

native work forms would have sharply restricted personal mobility, for example; and considerable reasoning through of the alternatives would have been required. If either of these factors would in itself have been sufficient to antagonize the average counterculturist, there was a further problem that tended to remove work from the agenda altogether. If there were conflicts between a group's need to get a job done and a member's desire to take the day off, the member might be expected to yield to group requirements. And in any case, the group as a whole would have to agree on the underlying values relevant to such situations, a clearly intolerable affront to the controlling ethic of individualism.

As happened to Owenism by the 1840s, the communal wave of the 1960s ultimately foundered on a basic contradiction between the radicalism of its participants' style and the conservatism of their beliefs. But with the beginning of the 1970s came yet another "new" movement, one that delayed the alternative-seekers' return to the straight world just as Fourierism had done in the two decades after 1843. If the commune had been the hallmark of the counterculture, that of the new movement was the "community" in its various guises. Since this is the institutional form within which most attempts at social reformation today are being carried out, it is worth a close look of its own.

Chapter 6: America in the 1970s— Cooperatives and "New Communities"

By the 1970s, evidence of the counterculture's decline began to accumulate. In its newsletter, Boston's New Community Projects reported on a survey it had conducted of area "communes" (April 17, 1972:1). Asked if they shared income, forty-four communes replied that they did not, ten said that income was shared "for some things," and one claimed to be sharing income completely. Asked about their political orientation, thirty-six communes responded that they had none as a group, ten claimed to be "radical," and three saw themselves as "liberal." Significantly, NCP saw nothing strange about lumping together as "communes" a range of groups most of which shared neither income nor ideology. It had become enough to be young and sharing the rent on an urban apartment to be considered a "communard," a debasement of language which reflects the extent to which the counterculture had by this time abandoned substantive change in favor of rhetoric.

In other cases, the retreat from the original countercultural ambiance was more explicit. Early in 1971, the editors of *This Magazine Is About Schools* went through an ideological upheaval that symbolized the shift from the counterculture's original concern with social alternatives. Born in the tumult of the 1960s, the Canadian *This Magazine* had originally given serious thought to alternative educational institutions. And it had fed the communal instincts of its readers with articles on Indian village life and such groups as the Bruderhof. By 1971, however, this no longer seemed appropriate. In their summer issue, the editors announced that *"This Maga-*

zine will not continue its present debate (some would say, romance) with the counterculture" (1971a:10). Instead, "we've been utopian socialists and now we're beginning to try to deal seriously with Marx" (Ibid.:21). In the following issue, the message became more explicit: "If there's anything we've learned over the last six years, it's that there is no alternative to the public schools, and that all our energies must go into changing that system" (1971b:1).

From other sources, the message was the same: radicalism that had survived the 1960s was henceforth to be applied to the system from within, rather than being brought to bear through alternatives outside. In early 1972, members of the Vocations for Social Change collective in Canyon, California, began to have second thoughts about their continuing emphasis on alternatives in such things as education, health, living, and work. More particularly, they found themselves worrying about the expression of these in the basic countercultural unit, the rural commune: "[Communes] can be a cop-out or at least a delusion for those thinking they are doing something radical. . . . We hope you will examine your motives for going to the country" (undated letter to subscribers, 1972). In an exchange of correspondence, the members set forth their own goal: "We decided . . . that in struggling to reach our goal of democratic socialism, we had to expand our outreach to . . . professionals, para-professionals, blue collars and unemployed who are working for social change by creating radical caucuses *within mainstream institutions*" (undated letter, 1972; our emphasis). For those interested in systemic change, the counterculture was seen to be increasingly irrelevant.

If *This Magazine* and Vocations for Social Change at least continued to maintain a theoretical commitment to sweeping social change in some distant future, other movements seemed content simply to make piecemeal changes in the existing order. People began to talk about land trusts, for example, as a means for removing land from the market and making it more readily available for use by those prepared to respect it. A California couple held a series of weekend seminars on living communities for urban professionals. Food and housing cooperatives sprang up across the land, and a national, student-based cooperative organization was formed. A minor flood of written material began to appear on the subject of control of industries by their workers or surrounding communities. The word "realistic" entered the language once more, generally applied to one's particular approach to change as opposed to the "unrealistic" fantasies of those beguiled by the euphorias of the 1960s. The counterculture was behind us now, and sobriety had reasserted itself.

Clearly, the counterculture had failed in its mission; but it is difficult not to see these new developments more as a ratification of that failure than as a transcendence of it. At some level of the spirit, the counterculture had affirmed the possibility of integrating the pieces of life in close association with one's comrades. And if that affirmation was ultimately overwhelmed by deeper, contrary tendencies toward disintegration and individualism, at least the question had been raised. The alternatives movements of the 1970s, on the other hand, hardly addressed the question at all. Rather than acknowledging that the counterculture had demanded too little of its members in challenging old beliefs, those leading the movement into the 1970s appeared to feel that those demands had been too great. Better to accept even greater pieces of the system—in terms of production patterns, living arrangements, forms of cooperation, and distances between people—and try to make do.

This shift in emphasis was epitomized in the swing from "commune" to "community" as the basic social unit. At least symbolically, the commune had been a place for total, intimate experience within a relatively small group of people. In the communities of the 1970s, however, relationships were to be segmented and muted. Thus, there would be communities of work, others in which one would play, and still others for living, buying food, or talking politics. If communes had tended in this direction in practice, it became a matter of principle once more in the 1970s. We were to surround ourselves with institutions that could meet the separate pieces of our human need. We might think of such institutions as "communities" of kindred spirits, and therefore as something progressive. But the structure of life was increasingly reminiscent of American society prior to the convulsions of the 1960s. To what point had all that energy actually led us?

A BASIC "COMMUNITY" MODEL: THE COOPERATIVE

The Co-op Movement. The cooperative movement was born in 1844 on Toad Lane, in the English town of Rochdale, when 28 weavers formed the Rochdale Equitable Pioneers' Society. It was not an easy birth. Tradesmen and unsympathetic young workers from the nearby mills gathered in front of the new store at its grand opening:

> Toad Lane was full of them, running, screaming, jeering, and holding their sides as they pointed at Sam Ashworth, standing white-faced, but plucky, beside his attenuated piles of "flour, butter, sugar and oatmeal." Meanwhile one of the tradesmen roared that if he had brought his wheelbarrow, he could have taken the whole stock away in it. It was a ghastly few minutes.

> A handful of the Pioneers stood trembling in the warehouse, uncertain whether to buy or make a bolt for it....But they knew what it was to be laughed at—these weavers of Rochdale, who had dreamed dreams before— they gave their caps another pull over their eyes, they held their ground, and in the end they bought. (Chase, 1969:5)

Of such stuff are legends made, and the story of Toad Lane has been passed down over the years through a cooperative movement that now extends around the world.

From the outset, the Rochdale weavers established the principles that remain at the core of cooperative beliefs today. Ownership of capital, for example, was to be the source of neither profit nor power. Instead, "profits" were to be returned to the consumers, in the form of patronage refunds. Power was to be shared equally among all members, on the principle of one vote to each, regardlesss of the number of shares they might choose to buy. Further, membership was to be open to all who wished to participate. Elements have been added to the co-op canon since, most notably with regard to the need for continuing education of members in cooperative principles and for cooperation among co-ops themselves. But the fundamental breakthroughs remain those of 1844. To some, these have seemed quite enough. Writing in 1936, the Japanese cooperator Toyohiko Kagawa wrote of "a gradual, inconspicuous, and entirely peaceable revolution" which cooperatives represented, a revolution that would be the "basis for eliminating all the evils of modern capitalism—exploitation, the accumulation of wealth in the hands of the few, and the concentration of capital" (n.d.:6). Plucky Sam Ashworth could hardly have suspected where his vigil by the oatmeal sacks could lead.

The evils of modern capitalism appear to be with us still, in spite of the fact that American co-ops now claim to have fifty million members (U.S. Bureau of the Census, 1972:472, 588). But Kagawa can be excused his effusive rhetoric, for the spirit of cooperation seeemed to be coming alive at the time he wrote. In America, the national credit union movement grew to three million members by 1940 (Margolis, 1972:6). The country's first housing cooperative had been built a mere decade before. Establishment of the Rural Electrification Administration in 1935 foreshadowed the rapid growth of electric cooperatives across the country. Farm co-ops were proliferating. And all of this was happening within the context of a Great Depression which cast considerable doubt on the viability of the existing competitive system. In such an environment, discovery of the cooperative alternative was a revelation. Jack McLanahan describes the experience this

way: "At last!—I had found what I had been looking for—a practical way
to build an economic system based on the Christian ethic of love, sharing
and mutual concern—a sound alternative with which to replace capitalism"
(1972:A–2).

Somewhere along the line, however, the dream began to fade. The 1940s
brought a prosperity in which economic cooperation seemed less essential,
and the 1950s brought a political climate in which it seemed subversive.
Co-ops persisted, but the Christian ethic of love began to dissolve in the
reality of co-ops as big business. By the beginning of the 1970s, five cooperative organizations were listed among *Fortune's* "Top 500." One of these,
Farmland Industries, had 400,000 members and assets approaching $400
million (Margolis, 1972:12). Closer to home, our "local" dairy cooperative grew to include 6,000 producers in seven Northeastern states (*Yankee
Dairy News,* July, 1972). The Cooperative League of the U.S.A. now holds
its biennial congresses at places like the Caribe Hilton in San Juan. Even
the little store on Toad Lane has changed dramatically: membership in the
Rochdale Equitable Pioneers' Society was over 50,000 by 1968, and capital
had grown to £500,000 (Chase, 1969:13). In response to tendencies like
these, the IRA blew up the Belfast Co-op, leaving cooperators to bemoan
the fact that "the 'revolutionaries' should see the Co-op as just another pillar
of the capitalist establishment—just another symbol of tyranny to be over-
thrown" (Briscoe, 1972:5). Rather than forming the "basis for eliminating
all the evils of modern capitalism," many cooperatives appeared to have
succumbed to these evils.

At the same time, however, the cultural upheaval of the 1960s had spun
off its own variant of the cooperative theme, one which seemed to promise
a rejuvenated movement. First to emerge on the scene were the self-de-
scribed "food conspiracies," whose tone grew hardly more moderate as they
came to be known simply as "food cooperatives"; *"A food cooperative is
not an end in itself. . . .* [It] is a small step in a larger process leading toward
the *creation of a truly humane, socialist society"* (Philadelphia Citywide
Co-op Organization, 1972:13; emphasis in original). Especially in contrast
to what the older co-op movement had become, the implications were profound: "Whereas the development of old-world co-ops concentrated on
the economic problems and the financial sector, the new co-ops are concentrating on the wide and all encompassing scope of culture—which includes lifestyle, ideology, education, and consciousness, as well as financial
considerations" (Trotscha, 1971:5). Clearly, this new movement owed a
substantial spiritual debt to the counterculture. But in coming up with ex-

plicit material goals as well, it was taking an added step of some significance.

A concentration on "the wide and all encompassing scope of culture" led the new cooperatives into activities that would never have occurred to their older counterparts. At least in sense of direction, co-ops became as much community centers as buying organizations. The Genesee Co-op in Rochester, New York, for example, was part of a complex that included draft counseling, a free university, an underground paper, a veterans' employment service, an "alternative" telephone information service, and a drug abuse program (Genesee Co-op, 1972:5). The Oakland Co-op in Pittsburgh, Pennsylvania, worked to develop a market information service, a speakers' bureau, cooperative baby-sitting, and study groups on such topics as consumer legislation, health care, and problems of low-income consumers (Oakland Co-op, 1972:10). A number of co-ops also wrestled with the problem of how to reach beyond the university constituencies with which they had typically started. The Mifflin Street Co-op in Madison, Wisconsin, for one, anticipated that if enough campus-based co-ops were created, "a sizeable amount of capital could be generated and used to help low income black and working class co-ops get started" (Winfield, 1970:19). Many of these projects failed to get very far, but they were an integral part of the early spirit of the new cooperatives.

As the movement matured, however, it began to slide in directions that seemed alarmingly like those that had vitiated the earlier cooperative wave. Growth began to take over; the Boston Food Co-op, for example, had signed up more than 4,000 members within two years of its founding in 1970. As a direct result, control over co-op organizations moved further and further from the members of these groups. By 1972, the *Monthly News of Co-op Communities* was talking about the "more effective economic democracy" involved in the interposition of representative councils between members and general membership meetings in ever-expanding co-ops (NASCO, 1972b:1). And those presiding over the movement's expansion became ever more respectable in the System's terms. Board candidates for the North American Student Cooperative Organization were by 1973 listing qualifications such as these: "filed an application with HUD for construction of 40 new garden apartments"; "secretary-treasurer of . . . a nonprofit corporation which is presently constructing a high-rise student residence with the aid of a $3.2 million HUD loan"; "planning coordinator with the architects for a proposed 141 apartment co-op complex" (NASCO, 1973). NASCO was still holding its board meetings in places such as the Student Union building at Boston University, but one wonders whether a move to San Juan is not a distinct possibility for the future.

The Co-op as Model. We dwell here on cooperatives not only because of their importance in the current alternatives movement, but also because of what they exemplify as to the dynamics of the movement as a whole. To begin with, the co-op is an institution that makes highly limited demands on its members, and this is a basic condition of the "communities" that took over the alternatives movement in the 1970s. A newly-established co-op may expect its members to take turns bagging raisins or helping out with the inventory (functions that will be taken over by paid employees as the co-op matures), but it requires nothing more of them in terms of interpersonal involvement or commitment to the organization. Even co-op purchases themselves are true "cooperation" only by the most generous of definitions, since once the raisins are bagged and bought, the raisin-eaters need never again encounter each other. As Martin Buber has pointed out, "the Consumer Cooperative is concerned not with consumption proper but with purchases for consumption," which itself remains individualized (1958:77). We cooperate, in other words, only to feed more efficiently our separate lives, a tendency that is equally true of alternative "communities" other than those concerned with food-buying.

A second characteristic follows from this. If the desire for a continuing relationship between specific people is absent from the co-op ethos, people will feel free to come and go, leaving the co-op structure itself as the basic social reality. As one co-op leader has noted, "A co-op is an institution. . . . This is a very different concept from that of a commune" (Adelman, n.d.: 22). It is a different concept indeed; as with General Motors or the Democratic Party, it is the institution that is fundamental, rather than the people within it. As long as co-op memberships are paid up (cars bought, votes cast), the system is content. Other community groups, notably those organized around living space, are more concerned with the full humanness of their members; but the quality of institutionalization is never wholly absent. Turnover of membership is a feature of all the new community forms—co-op, living unit, work collective. And this is generally tolerated as long as a full range of the institutions desired remains available to those individuals seeking them.

In spite of all this, the tone of relationships among people in the new communities has tended to be appreciably more open and friendly than is the case within institutional equivalents in the straight world. Local co-op distribution centers, for example, have often been places where buyers and staff could feel themselves also to be friends, though they might never see each other outside the center itself, and where the "business" of selling food was less important than the "process" of providing goods desired in a context of cordiality and warmth. Much the same is true of other community groups, but there are clear limits to how far this can go. If the new communitarians place value on bringing openness to all their personal dealings, they at the same time guard their individual autonomy against excessive involvement in any of these by splitting their emotional energies among a number of communities in the course of each day. Far from being in conflict, these two tendencies support each other: openness is possible *because* people know that it is transitory—the parties involved will soon be somewhere else. If lives were not structured in this way, openness could imply commitment and full interdependence, which is precisely what people wish to avoid.

This attitude toward group life implies a further general characteristic of the new community wave, one which is readily visible in the drift of co-ops from small-group idealism to bigness and a drive for "efficiency." If our social groups were organic ones, in which we expected to deal with each other wholly, we would have to limit their scope to that which we could comprehend. Where we surround ourselves with a number of communities, however, each of which is to service only a portion of our beings, we will be primarily concerned with how well they do that particular, limited job. Our food co-op should sell us the cheapest food; our housing community should provide the most comfortable accommodations; our meditation society should have the clout to bring us Baba Ram Dass for the weekend; our land trust should buy the most scenic property at the lowest rent; our community resource center should have the biggest laser laboratory in town. The bigger these institutions, the better they will be able to fulfill such functions. And since we do not wish intimacy and commitment of our institutions in any case, we have no reason to resist their inevitable growth.

Co-ops provide a final lesson that is suggestive for the future of the new communities. As institutions, even "alternative" ones, grow more functional and specialized in orientation, they will increasingly resemble their equivalents in the capitalist world. Thus, Vernon Jeffries worries that "there is a predisposition for co-ops to be just like other consumers out of technological society—except to do it cheaper" (1972:4). And Richard Tilmann points out that "from the individual's point of view, there is small difference between a dependence on the management bureaucracy of an American corporation and that of a large cooperative organization" (1972:24). In such conditions, it is the smallest of steps to return to the system altogether, if that system is able to deliver the services desired at lower cost. Even continued allegiance to alternative structures would hardly seem to matter. This, of course, is precisely the path followed by the cooperative movement from 1844 until the 1960s. But there is considerable pathos in seeing a new generation of cooperators moving so quickly to make the same mistakes.

COMMUNITY LIVING

The cooperative ethos can be seen as well in a wide range of recent attempts, both urban and rural, to establish community living arrangements. In the spectrum of possibilities between suburban nuclear household and tight-knit commune, such arrangements fall somewhere in the middle, trying to break down the isolation of the nuclear family without replacing it with the intimacy and group demands of communal life. As in the case of cooperatives, these "new communities" come together around the provision of certain facilities (space, kitchen, land, child care), the final use of which is likely to be more or less private. Where truly joint activities do take place, such as evenings spent in the community living room or the eating of common meals, it is clearly understood that these activities imply nothing beyond themselves in terms of group obligations. Individuals remain clearly distinct, cooperating only around those specific functions for which the community was formed.

There is a further parallel between the food co-ops and these new living communities. In both cases, the tendency is for cooperation around the provision of items for consumption. Work is generally pursued within more traditional patterns—office, teaching job, writing, workshop—which it is assumed are distinct from the living group. This follows not only from the fact that community living spaces are much easier to create than community work places, but also from the extent to which the new communitarians are products of the surrounding culture. In our consumption-obsessed society, work is seen as the nuisance necessary to finance our purchases. It is simply the path of least psychological resistance, then, for community-builders to be preoccupied with the things they take in from their environment, as opposed to what they produce. Further, to build a community of work would require a degree of group commitment well beyond the paying of rent and the rotation of kitchen chores, which form the boundaries of group responsibility in many communities; and this would impinge on the American sense of individualism. With exceptions to be noted below, these new groups therefore follow the counterculture in being joined around

consumption—whether of goods, services, or experience—rather than production.

Urban Communities. In surveying urban communities, Rosabeth Kanter
has spoken of "the domestication of the counterculture," seeing in the new
groups something approximating "alternative forms of the family" rather
than comprehensive new social structures (1972:174). According to this
approach, the centers of community gravity are such traditional family
points of reference as kitchen, fireplace, washing machine, television set, or
children's room. Our own visits to a number of urban groups confirm this
impression of community domesticity, and written proposals for such groups
reinforce such a view:

> Once a group of neighbors start meeting each other's needs cooperatively,
> they can begin changing from the lonely and costly single-family housing
> system to sensible . . . living. For example . . . one house or apartment may
> become a dormitory, another a cookhouse, another a laundry and bath
> house . . . another a place especially fixed up for children, another an
> infirmary, another a general social and recreational center, and so on ac-
> cording to the agreed desires and needs of the group. (Luckywalla, 1971:
> 41)

This vision is relatively ambitious, but its preoccupation with life's domestic
elements reflects the dominant trend of the community movement.

To the extent that the new communitarians seek to "purchase" alternative
versions of the standard domestic services, it is not unreasonable to fear that
they may follow the food co-ops in becoming caught up in such efficiency-
seeking habits as institutional growth. The advantages of size are implicit
in El Luckywalla's scheme, and they appear more explicitly in the thinking
of others. Thus, John Platt, who sees the widespread development of child-
care and dining communities over the next twenty years, concludes that
"larger communities, with . . . a total of two hundred to five hundred persons, might be able to afford more professional managerial services and a
better teaching staff . . .; and the quality and efficiency of the dining services
would probably be better" (1972:24). Were it to come to that, our "communities" would have become fully institutionalized, and the nature of
people's involvement in them would be roughly that which they now have,
say, with their local diaper services.

Even where urban communities remain relatively small, they serve more
as an accommodation to the existing social structure than as a challenge to
this structure. As Judson Jerome has observed, "the relationships between

people in the intentional community are closer, more neighborly, but more or less in the standard family pattern, and don't raise radical questions in terms of the overall design of society" (1972a:24). Instead, people are simply finding communities to be functional in terms of personal growth, in its individualized American version.

There are those with more visionary aims. Dimitrios Roussopoulos, for example, has developed a model for radical urban groups that integrates consumption, work, and political activity in a highly communal setting (1971:317–327). But the promise of most urban groups is extremely limited. Members may find considerable warmth around the community hearth, and this is indeed an improvement over the ways in which they might otherwise be living. But they are unlikely even in their own lives to make serious inroads into the problems of work, political self-determination, or pervasive alienation that characterize the society as a whole.

Rural Communities. If the rural communes of the 1960s represented the farthest advance of the contemporary alternatives movement, the rural communities of the 1970s come close to symbolizing that movement's ultimate failure. Where people in urban communities at least live in the same houses, their rural counterparts tend to move (as quickly as finances allow) into separate homes. According to Glenn Hovemann, for example, Alpha community in Oregon began with the premise that "each family or individual will have separate quarters (unless desired otherwise), even if merely an A-frame cabin for a single person," such isolation to be based on the assumption that "physical privacy for each individual [is] an elementary right and need." As if to further emphasize the group's continuity with the existing culture, Hovemann stresses that "Alpha, rather than being a special accomplishment, is simply a practical way for some people to rearrange their lives" (1972:21, 23). The pattern is the same with most of the new rural communities we have seen or studied.

Many such groups have formed around land trusts, legal devices for common ownership of property. Once resources are pooled for the purchase of land, ownership is vested in the trust, which then becomes liable for mortgage and tax payments. Generally, funds for these purposes and for development of common facilities are raised through assessments on the members. The popularity of this approach follows from hard experience with earlier communities where land ownership was more concentrated: "[In] practice often only one or two members of a group own the land, put most of the money in the pot, and thereby really control and determine communal life. The cooperative [or land trust], on the other hand, is a legal instrument permitting truly communal ownership" (Margolies, 1972:5). But in substituting a structure that lends itself so readily to "rent" payments on individual homes, those in rural communities come uncomfortably close to traditional housing-development models.

The same social assets and liabilities apply here as appear in co-ops, urban communities, and other "new" social forms of the 1970s. At least in their early stages, all such groups provide a degree of neighborliness and simplicity that is a welcome respite from the confusions and depersonalizations of modern American life. But by retaining such mainstream beliefs as individualism, and by almost universally ignoring problems of work, these groups guarantee that their members will never stray too far from the mainstream. Typically, rural communities—like their urban counterparts—take for granted that self-actualization and the earning of necessary income are individual affairs. The conflict is by now a familiar one. Basic living space, work, and psychospiritual growth are personal, individualized; meals (possibly), washing machines (possibly), and the ownership of land are social. In itself, such an approach leaves untouched the roots of contemporary American life. And for rural communities caught in such patterns, the threat of growth and reabsorption into the system is therefore ever-present.

COMMUNITY WORK

Community work carries the same limitations as does community living or the cooperative purchase of food. Instead of being an integrated part of our lives, both personal and social, community work places simply provide an environment for individuals to engage in activities that are not included in the multitude of other communities in which they take part. Given the pervasive American reluctance to think seriously about work, such environments are far fewer in number than communities of living, buying, or recreation. But there have been some, and movements such as that toward workers' control of industry promise still more.

Collectives and Resource Centers. By the beginning of the 1970s, craft stores, "alternative" auto repair shops and legal groups, organic restaurants, free clinics, encounter centers, and other "work collectives" had appeared on the scene. These were typically short-lived. Often, one or two people had the skills and energy to keep the collective going for a time, while others floated in and out of the group. But for most people, participation was but a temporary means for meeting people, learning a skill, or picking up a little money. With the exception of professionally-based groups such as legal collectives, working communities of necessity were therefore limited to activities whose rudiments could be learned in a matter of days or hours. This was consistent with the prevailing attitude toward skills—professional competence bred status differentials, arrogance, and inequality—but it sharply limited the scope of the collective movement.

Even in the midst of such restlessness, however, there remained truths to be discovered. Volunteers in free clinics or law collectives learned enough about their bodies or about legal method that they would never again be intimidated by the aura of omniscience with which professionals in these areas try to surround themselves. Apprentices in auto repair shops gained knowledge that went far to erode the sense of helplessness that most Americans feel in the face of mechanical disaster. And participants in all kinds of collectives learned things about the possible fluidity of work situations—in hours, salaries, division of labor—that challenged the accepted order of things. Had such insights been allowed to mature, they might have led to the creation of working units of an alternative social order. But this progression was aborted by the communitarian assumptions underlying such collectives. Work communities were always more or less distinct from the other communities in which their members participated, and group involvements were limited by each individual's shifting sense of personal growth needs. This familiar pattern had the usual results: a fragmentation of spirit between separate life activities, continual turnover of membership, and a tendency for collectives to be measured by the efficiency with which they provided services to their members.

Under such conditions, we can hardly be surprised to find a trend toward institutional growth within the collective movement. Early in the movement's history, a number of community work places became larger and more complex, to the point where many can best be described as general resource centers. The prototype for this movement was San Francisco's Project ONE, which established itself in 1970 in an old five-story warehouse. Within a year, some 200 people were involved on a continuing basis with ONE's many activities, which included a school, an ecology press, computer and media centers, a theater, and graphics studios, with numerous individual artists and craftspeople filling in around the edges (People's Yellow Pages Collective, 1971). A comparable blend of activities grew up around other projects of the same sort. Project Artaud and the United Projects building, both in San Francisco, offered between them a house-building project, low-cost auto repair, a free store, training in the martial arts, odd-job referrals, drug rehabilitation, and space for artists. The Loft in New York was home for ecology groups, a theater workshop, and a cryogenics project (Bennett, 1970:32–34). Few of these activities were self-supporting; but they provided an environment of high and volatile energies, qualities on which the new communitarians placed considerable value.

ONE and its successors produced a notable sense of community among their members, especially in the early days when groups were converting the buildings in which they were to be located. But this was "community" of the same sort that the co-ops were providing—individuals came together only to serve distinct pieces of their separate selves. Indeed, the chaotic energies of such groups could hardly have led to any other result. As a ONE member has put it: "Each individual has to make his own values and to understand himself in relation to a process that changes every day" (Baird, 1971:123).

Except for its degree of intensity, this sort of restless individualism was largely patterned on the drift of American society as a whole. And other attitudes were carried over from that society as well. Grounded in urban habits of overconcentrating people within artificial boundaries; indifferent as to sources of income; suspicious of commitment, stability, and continuity; and preoccupied with the New, the Different, the ONEs further acknowledged their spiritual debt to the surrounding culture. They may have avoided some of the more oppressive aspects of that culture's work environments. But by adopting so many of its values, they sharply undercut their ability to build truly comprehensive alternatives to American life.*

Workers' Control of Industry. Steps toward workers' control of major industries have been taken in several European countries, most notably Yugoslavia, where workers' control has been a matter of government policy since 1950 (see Chapter 8). And pressures are building on American industry to move in this direction. Under existing patterns of ownership and management, the workers' sense of powerlessness and lack of job satisfaction has begun to show itself in pathological symptoms ranging from absenteeism to extensive drug-taking. In some quarters, a move to give workers greater control over their environments seems necessary to maintain the smooth functioning of the industrial machine.

---

* For a more sympathetic view of Project ONE, see Mosher, 1973.

In its happiest guise, however, workers' control is presented less as a device for ensuring economic stability than as a process providing the workers a sense of meaning in their labor:

> Here, as for God on the seventh day of Creation . . . contemplation of work as object . . . is compensation for work as toil. . . . The deep root of this satisfaction lies in the fact that this work was done under the worker's control, that the worker did it according to his own norms and choosing his own techniques, perhaps even inventing them. (Bourdet, 1970:142)

In the absence of formal mechanisms which would allow this to happen, workers have sometimes found impromptu means for asserting their views. In an article on his stay in an automobile motor plant, for example, Bill Watson describes an incident where workers, offended by a sloppy management improvisation for the hasty production of a new motor, conspired to "counter-plan" (reduce) its output (1971:1). Although the disruptions of the production line which followed were viewed by management as sabotage, Watson sees them simply as attempts by workers to exercise some influence over the product of their labor. Under existing conditions, such efforts will almost necessarily take negative forms. If a system of workers' councils existed within the factory, however, workers would feel they had influence over all aspects of the production process, and the destructive consequences of alienation would disappear. Or so the theory goes.

There are several problems here. Workers' control can be viewed—as it has, for example, by John Case (1972:206) and Daniel Guérin (1970: 150)—as a transitional device to provide workers the training in skills and attitudes required for the ultimate establishment of popular control over the economic system. But workers' control can just as easily be seen as a safety valve by which those who control the existing system can more easily perpetuate their power. Experiments undertaken to date in the United States tend to support the latter interpretation.

As a case in point, General Foods has established a dog-food factory in Topeka, Kansas, that is organized around small work-teams with relatively broad powers. Members of these teams jointly hire new workers, determine who will carry out each job, decide when to take breaks, and assume a number of other responsibilities normally identified with management (Salpukas, 1973:47). The employees seem pleased by these relative improvements in their work situation. Yet the most striking results seem to lie in the direction of higher company profits—productivity has been estimated at

30 percent higher than in comparable plants lacking such reforms*—and the creation of a congenial climate where radical questions are less likely to be raised about management's retention of its most significant powers: total control over decisions on pricing, product, and distribution of profits. Other companies, including A.T.&T., Polaroid, Corning Glass, and General Electric, are currently experimenting with comparable measures. If it seems reasonable to see such moves as the leading edge of a significant industrial movement, it is equally reasonable to interpret the motives behind these moves as having more to do with preserving the existing system of power than with transforming it.

Even were we to assume that American workers would ultimately force a relatively complete version of workers' self-management—along the Yugoslav model, say—serious problems would still remain. The fact of workers' control, for example, may do little to mitigate conflicts of interest between a factory and its surrounding community. Pollution is the obvious case, since profit-sharing workers would have little more incentive than present-day management to install expensive pollution-control equipment. And within the factory itself, the conflict between a desire for full workers' participation and the economic need for rapid, technically-informed administrative decisions may be irresolvable. Albert Meister has noted that self-management in the French communities of work "allowed the antagonism to continue between manual laborers and intellectuals, between the administrators and the administered" (1958:61; see also Gintis, 1972:136–137); and the Yugoslavs have had similar problems in their factories. "Workers' control," in other words, may not solve even the problem of workers' control, much less that of smoothly blending the factories concerned into their social environment.

Once again, these problems can be traced to the "community" basis of workers' control visions: work places are assumed to be only one of the many communities in which employees participate. It is taken for granted, for example, that there will be no integration of work with family life, or with any other social unit of meaning to those involved. Since the factory is simply the place where people earn their salaries, its function is seen as one of making those salaries as large as possible, regardless of the effect on the surrounding community, or even on the extent to which true workers'

---

* Industry has been astonishingly slow to realize the profit potential of involving workers in their work. Almost thirty years ago, Lebret and Desroches (1946) reported on the extraordinary efficiency of the worker-controlled watchcase factory, Boimondau; but capitalist managers have only begun to absorb this message.

participation in important decisions is maintained. To the degree that this view is accurate—and the Yugoslav experience provides considerable support for it—workers' control is only a variant of the cooperative model discussed above, and contains all the tendencies of that model to mimic the existing social order in most important respects.

Community Development Corporations. One attempt to bridge the gap between work place and community is the community development corporation (CDC). CDCs began to appear in significant numbers toward the end of the 1960s, especially among poorer urban groups trying to establish some degree of community control over productive resources. As Matthew Edel describes it, the CDC in theory "is essentially a cooperative, set up in a neighborhood to run economic and social service programs for the community" (1970:1). In practice, CDCs have been more economic than social in orientation, concentrating on running such traditional facilities as factories, shopping centers, gas stations, and stores.* They have been successful enough at this that President Nixon referred approvingly to CDCs as examples of "community capitalism" (quoted in Hampden-Turner, 1970:95).

The CDCs are even less likely than the new work collectives to break loose from conventional American ways of conducting business. Although they avoid any integration of work with other parts of life, the collectives at least try to build a sense of unity into their productive activities. In the CDCs, no such unity exists. The "community" of a CDC's shareholders, for example, is distinct from both the "community" of workers within that CDC's factory and the geographical "community" that surrounds it. The potential for conflict is great. The local community may wish the factory's prices to be low; shareholders and workers will have an interest in squeezing the highest possible profits out of sales. Employees may press for workers' councils; shareholders will be likely to resist anything that could appear to threaten efficiency.** By avoiding any communal basis for their operations, the CDCs have ensured that they will be subject to the same conflicts between narrowly based interests that characterize industry in the surrounding culture.

Even the fundamental CDC principle, that of community involvement through ownership, seems to rest on the most tenuous grounds. As Rosabeth Kanter has observed:

---

* For profiles of twenty-seven urban CDCs, see Center for Community Economic Development, 1971.

** For thoughts on the conflict between self-management and community ownership, see Case and Hunnius, 1971.

> CDC members are stockholders and voters. These two things by them-
> selves do not constitute meaningful participation; stockholders have the
> most minimal kind of involvement in their organizations and are inter-
> ested only in profit, and the fact that most Americans vote does not seem
> to be decreasing alienation.... (1971:66)

One advocate of CDCs has argued: "The aims of community development corporations can only be met if those corporations become part of an effort to achieve fundamental political and economic change in America" (Edel, 1970:6). Conceived in ways that precisely avoid such change, however, CDCs risk remaining more a part of the old America than of a new one.

CONCLUSION

Between them, the "new communities" of the 1970s encompass most aspects of life: home, work, purchasing, play. But these functions tend to be specialized, with little overlap in specific community organizations. It could hardly be otherwise, since individualism has fully reasserted itself after the abortive moves of the 1960s toward communalism. Communities are therefore being viewed once again in terms of the particular things they can provide to sovereign individuals. People are not an organic part of any single community. Rather, they buy from a wide range of communi-ties that package of services that can best maintain their separate identities. To a considerable degree, this "new" communitarianism is following the precedents set in the Fourierist movement of 1843 to 1866. Our greater mobility allows us to scatter our energies more widely through space than the Fourierists could ever have done. But the ground rules are the same, particularly with regard to the psychological lines that are to be drawn between individuals and their groups.

And so we return to normalcy. As with everything else, the process of social upheaval and collapse moves more rapidly these days. We have compressed into a decade the communal and communitarian movements that spanned forty years in the nineteenth century. Perhaps the best thing that can be said of such acceleration of events is that this time, people may not need another century to gather their energies for the next attempt. And perhaps—just perhaps—the lessons of recent years will then be fresh enough in mind that the same mistakes need not be made again.

Chapter 7: Experiments Abroad

Contemporary American alternative-seekers have tended to present their social experiments as revolutionary new forms of living. As we indicated in Chapter 4, however, such experimentation is hardly new to the United States. This chapter describes attempts to form communal or communitarian groups in recent decades in many other parts of the world. Those involved in the American "movement" have often strongly resisted the idea that their efforts have been anticipated by other groups—the idea that only the "new" can be worthwhile remains deeply rooted in our national life. But there are more positive ways to view the persistence of alternative-building across time and space. These efforts suggest the extent of human need for intimate forms of group life and also provide examples from which conclusions can be drawn as to the requirements for successful communalism.

EUROPE, AFRICA, ASIA

The most notable expression of the communal drive lies in the Israeli kibbutz movement, now in its seventh decade. Before turning to the kibbutzim, however, we touch briefly on experiments in other parts of the world. Although their efforts are less well known, community-builders have long been at work at points from London to Lagos, from Tanzania to Tokyo. In its broadest sense, the search for a "counterculture" is truly a global phenomenon.

Europe. During the late 1960s, Europe had a "hippie" movement of its own. Superficially, the movement seemed largely a copy of its American equivalent. Scattered across the continent were large numbers of young people whose beads, blue jeans, and long hair would have allowed them to blend invisibly into the San Francisco street scene. They took the same drugs and listened to the same music as their American counterparts. They borrowed the jargon: in French as in English, for example, one found the words "hippie," "pot," and "freak" (which became "freakesse" in the feminine). And they went through the same migration from urban crash pads to rural communes. To many Europeans these trends seemed a new and particularly unsettling form of American cultural imperialism.

If infection from abroad was involved, however, some areas of Europe were largely immune. Virtually no communes appeared in Spain or Portugal; the few in Italy were concentrated near Rome and Milan (Valenti, 1972). In France, England, and West Germany, communes appeared in far greater numbers, again clustered typically around large industrial cities. Throughout this period, in other words, susceptibility to the communal virus was strongly correlated with an area's degree of economic development. This is hardly surprising. Development breeds alienation, the deterioration of family structures, and a general depersonalization of life. At the same time, it provides the loose change that allows people fleeing these things to exist at least temporarily in "alternative" ways. These conditions may have taken particularly extreme form in the United States, but they existed within the wealthier European countries as well. However derivative may have been elements of their style, the counterculturists of Europe were responding to a very real cultural disorientation of their own in moving toward communalism.

The similar disorientations of European and American youth led them to similar attitudes toward their communes. In describing its own progress, for example, the Anarchist Commune in Sheffield noted that "the important thing is, that despite a continuously changing membership, the development of the whole has been fairly consistent" (1973:5). Another English group, the HAPT Tribe, cautioned aspiring commune-builders to "build them open from the start. *Build only the kind that everybody can walk away from.* Build them . . . for the basic need of many people not for the particular requirements of individual tribes or groups" (quoted in Fairfield, 1972a:29; emphasis in original). Like their counterparts in the United States, European communards found little need for stability of particular groups or for commitment of members to each other. The results have been the same; in recent years, Europe's counterculture has fallen into decline.

Coincidentally, the 1970s saw the end of another series of experiments in social alternatives, the French "communities of work." Formed around a number of French factories in the early 1940s, twenty-seven such communities were in existence by 1957. At the height of the movement, the factories involved created the Entente Communautaire, which provided assistance to new communities and periodically brought delegates together from all member factories to share information. Over time, however, most of these groups gradually slipped away from their original commitment to workers' control, although they retained a considerable concern for the general welfare of their employees. The most famous of the communities of work, Boimondau, recently passed out of existence altogether.

Boimondau was initially established by Marcel Barbu, a skilled watch-case maker who had a deep commitment to the humanization of factory working conditions. By 1942, Barbu had gathered together in Valence some 200 workers, whose decisions as to the nature of a communitarian work environment were greatly to influence the movement as a whole. Predictably, they agreed that the factory's assets should be owned collectively, and that all participating in the experiment should share in the business's profits. Then came a more daring step. They decided to base the distribution of income on the "human value" of each individual, as measured by that person's total contribution to the community. Given two workers of similar skill and application, for example, one might receive greater compensation for playing the violin or being an especially cheerful person. Workers' wives, who were considered equally deserving of a share in the company's revenues, would be rewarded according to the seriousness with which they approached housekeeping, child rearing, or participation in group activities.

As a framework for judging "human value," those at Boimondau adopted a set of rules of conduct which were held to be applicable to all members. Unable to find a common system of transcendent beliefs which could legitimate these rules, however, they stipulated only that "every member commits himself to develop a religious or philosophic position . . . [and] to instruct himself in his chosen direction" (Rassemblement Communautaire Français, 1946:11). As we have seen, the absence of a shared belief system can be a strong barrier to successful communalism. Boimondau at least found a common approach to the details of daily life, and this was enough to sustain it for three decades. Other communities of work were unable to move even this far. They "failed" considerably sooner, even if some continue to exist as more or less benevolent corporate entities.*

In the search for communal value systems, many Europeans have turned to Christianity, a tradition that remains considerably more potent in Europe than in the United States. Christian service groups are common. In Italy, for example, small groups of young women live together and dedicate their energies to serving the poor. In France, the Emmaus communities help alcoholics and beggars repair and sell old furniture and clothing. In England, groups such as the Cyrene Community help young people with psychological problems. In many of these cases, the core of permanent members is relatively limited; a larger number of volunteers move through the community for a year or two of service. But Europe is also the location for a number of more permanent group work places, some of which have stable memberships of well over a hundred people.

One such group is L'Arche, a community in southern France founded by the philosopher and writer Lanza del Vasto (Pyronnet, 1970). L'Arche is strongly Christian, and its members are committed to nonviolence and sharing. Members grow practically all of their food, weave and sew their own clothing, build homes and furniture for themselves, and run a school for their children. Such relative economic independence provides L'Arche a sense of security which allows it to be vigorously outspoken on political issues. At least as far back as 1957, members were fasting in protest against national policies; similar actions have punctuated the group's history. At a deeper level, the people at L'Arche feel their very existence as a group to be a political act, since they provided both a model and training ground for the establishment of similar groups which could be available to poor people everywhere.

Africa. Africa is the last place we might expect to find a need for "intentional communities," since much of African life has long been grounded in an "unintentional" village communalism. With economic and cultural penetration from the West, however, the fabric of traditional tribal life is steadily being eaten away. Most African states have accepted the resulting social fragmentation, but at least one has tried to lay the grounds for an economically dynamic communalism on a national scale. This is Tanzania, whose president, Julius Nyerere, set forth in 1967 the principles underlying such a process:

---

* For more on Boimondau and the communities of work, see Bishop, 1950; Communauté de travail Marcel Barbu, 1946; Gougaud, 1971; and Lebret and Desroches, 1946.

If every individual is self-reliant the ten-house cell will be self-reliant; if all the cells are self-reliant the whole ward will be self-reliant; and if the wards are self-reliant, the District will be self-reliant. If the Districts are self-reliant, then the Region is self-reliant, and if the Regions are self-reliant, then the whole Nation is self-reliant and this is our aim.

As in China (Chapter 8), national strength here is expected to come from the strength of local associations, whose members will cooperate around work, education, health services, and whatever other functions they can jointly perform. Jobs requiring more general cooperation will be pushed upward to broader associations, but the entire basis of "self-reliance" is that intimate communal units will together meet as many of their own needs as possible (Godding, 1972).

On the other side of the African continent is the Nigerian village of Aiyetoro. Rising on stilts and platforms above the coastal swampland, Aiyetoro was built in 1947 by converts to Christianity in search of a home of their own. By 1951, the village housed some 2,000 people. Today as in the past, life in the village is based on the assumption that "economic problems should be solved by living a communal life, every man and woman working for the community with all profits going into a common purse" (Duckworth, 1951:403). In many ways, Aiyetoro is reminiscent of the American religious communes of the nineteenth century. Great value is placed on manual labor, with fishing and weaving the major village industries. Education is at once extremely practical and extremely religious. And as in the American communes, efforts have been made to differentiate villagers from outsiders; Aiyetoro members shave their heads as a badge of distinctness. If Christianity has generally worked in Africa to erode communal bonds, at Aiyetoro it has been the means for re-creating such bonds in new form.

India. Near the former French enclave of Pondicherry, on the southeast coast of India, 500 people live in the communal settlement of Auroville. Auroville was inaugurated in 1968 in line with a vision of "The Mother," Mira Richard, a disciple of the Indian mystic Sri Aurobindo. Members, who come primarily from Western Europe and the United States, work without salary on the communal farms or at one of Auroville's several small industries. In return, they are provided food, clothing, shelter, and other requirements for a simple but comfortable life. Although Auroville is based on its members' quest to become servants of the "Divine Consciousness," its secular experimentation with advanced town planning has drawn support from the Indian Government, UNESCO, and a number of sympathetic private donors around the world. Given sufficient funding, Auroville hopes ultimately to become a town of 50,000 or more people, collectively serving as a model for a new social order.*

Japan. In 1953, Yamagishi Miyozo founded in Japan what has since become known as the Yamagishi-kai Association. Prospective members take part in a series of encounter-type meetings whose purpose is to rid them of possessiveness and anger. According to the Association, more than 30,000 people have been through at least the initial stages of this process. About 800 of these have become residents at one of the group's twenty-two communes, which support themselves through such pursuits as dairy farming or raising chickens and pigs (Fairfield, 1972b:46). As at Auroville, people in these settlements provide the labor of which they are capable, drawing in return whatever they need from the common store. And as at Auroville, the ultimate purpose is to arrive at higher forms of spiritual understanding and social structure which could bring a better life to all the world's people.

Similar motivations underlie many of the member groups of the Japan Kibbutz Association. Founded in 1962, this organization publishes a newsletter, sponsors conferences for representatives of Japanese agricultural communities, and has sent a number of young Japanese to Israel to study the kibbutz movement there. According to the Association, there were at least fifty large communal settlements in Japan in 1969, an estimate that apparently included the Yamagishi-kai groups as well as local "kibbutzim" (Japan Kibbutz Association, 1969:3). Many of these communes have existed for some time; one group was established more than fifty years ago.** In most cases, the Japanese "kibbutzim" are agricultural, although some have branched out into such industries as publishing or tatami manufacture. But whatever their sources of income, they typically share work, play, living space, and income in true communal fashion.

Conclusions. If it seems reasonable to infer from our cursory look at experiments abroad that the communal urge is a global one, other conclusions must be far more tentative. Nevertheless, a striking correspondence exists between communal success and the sharing by commune members of some system of transcendent values. Lacking shared values, or even a

---

* See, for example, Rangan, 1971:8; and Pinto, 1973.
** For the story of one Japanese commune, see Sugihara and Plath, 1969.

desire to find these, the European countercultural groups failed almost as soon as they formed. In French communities of work, which assumed ultimate values to be a matter of individual choice but which at least sought agreement on many lesser issues, success was considerably greater. Aiyetoro and L'Arche, which are based on deep religious beliefs, have met with even greater success.

From the examples given, we might also conclude that a commune's "transcendent values" need not be religious in nature, at least in any strict sectarian sense. L'Arche, for example, has created its own mixture of Catholicism and Protestantism in keeping with the diverse backgrounds of its members. At Auroville and in the Yamagishi-kai groups, people together seek direct spiritual experience with mystical overtones. In Tanzania, villagers find a basis for communalism in a blend of tribal feeling and nationalistic pride. And in Japan, even secular communes rely on a cultural tradition that finds great intrinsic value in strong group ties.* If successful communes require shared allegiance to something higher than their members' separate perceptions of personal interest, the variety of belief systems to which fealty may be given is considerable.

THE ISRAELI KIBBUTZIM

Nearly 100,000 Israelis live in rural kibbutzim. While in 1970 this accounted for only 3.6 percent of total Jewish population within Israel, those within the kibbutzim make up roughly one-fourth of the rural Jewish population. And remarkably, at a time when rural communities in most industrial nations are depopulating, Israel's kibbutzim have continued to grow, if at a rate (about 1.5 percent annually through the 1960s) well below that of the country as a whole (Barkai, 1971:3). Still, the kibbutz remains a relatively intimate institution. Of some 230 existing kibbutzim, only three have more than 1,000 residents, and some have as few as fifty. The average kibbutz includes roughly 400 people, of which about half are adult members.

All of these groups are organized on rigorously communal principles. Although we will concentrate below on the implications of this in work situations, other aspects of kibbutz life reflect the same high level of group

---

* As Chie Nakane has observed, considerable group feeling is present even in the most modern Japanese industries: "The new employee is . . . received by the company in the same spirit as if he were a newly born family member, a newly adopted son-in-law or a bride come into the husband's household" (1970:14).

commitment. Members eat many of their meals together in the kibbutz dining hall, and they live in apartment blocks rather than separate family homes. More dramatically, they have largely collectivized the care of their children. Historically, babies have been moved to an Infants' House shortly after birth, and they have then continued to live with members of their own age groups all the way through high school. Some of these patterns are now in the process of modification, but communal feeling remains strong. Kibbutz members work for their groups, receiving no salaries for this; their groups in turn assume total responsibility for their maintenance. In terms of quality of life, longevity, and numbers of participants, the kibbutzim are the foremost existing example of a successful communalism.

Evolution and Structure. The first kibbutz dates from 1910, when the ten founders of Degania Aleph decided to organize themselves on semicollective principles. Following the First World War, kibbutz-minded settlers came to what was then Palestine in greater numbers. Many were young Eastern European Zionists in flight from anti-Semitic pogroms in their own countries. Often, their search for security and a Jewish national identity was coupled with other convictions. Socialism was a highly potent force, and European youth movements had led many to reject commercial life styles and urban intellectualism in favor of a return to nature and to manual labor.* The kibbutz was a natural structure for organizing such drives, and energies were increasingly turned in this direction. Degania Aleph was reorganized as a full collective following the war, several other small kibbutzim were formed between 1918 and 1921, and in 1921 Ein Harod became the first attempt at a communal settlement of more than a hundred members. By the early 1920s, the kibbutz movement was fully underway.

The movement was not without birth pains, however. Of forty kibbutzim in existence in 1920, only five survived the decade (Kanovsky, 1966:17). In part, this was due to the predictable problems of establishing radically new sorts of communities under geographical and financial conditions that were far from congenial. And in part, it followed from the ambivalent attitude of the Zionist authorities toward what some called these "Communist experiments"; through the whole of the 1920s, the kibbutzim were only allowed to construct permanent buildings suited to the needs of family

---

* On the eve of the First World War, an educational Jewish youth movement, Hashomer Hatzair, was formed. This organization now operates in twenty-five countries and provides training designed to prepare youth for settlement on Israeli kibbutzim (Leon, 1969:120–123).

farms or small-scale peasant agriculture (Leon, 1969:16). As new kibbutzim continued to be formed, however, their advantages became more apparent. They were drawing cards for the idealistic Jewish youth who were needed to settle large areas of Palestine. They required a smaller initial investment than did less communal forms of settlement. And they were easier to defend from the Arab nationalists who could be expected to resist creation of a Jewish state. With the increasing sense of urgency that accompanied Hitler's rise to power, the Zionist leadership reconsidered its position, and gave its support to the kibbutz movement.

By 1948, when Israel proclaimed its independence, nearly half of the new state's rural Jewish population lived in kibbutzim. But this proportion was steadily to decline in the years to follow. Many of those who might have gravitated toward the kibbutzim had died at the hands of the Nazis. As a result, the flood of immigrants following independence came largely from areas lacking the political traditions that had moved the early "pioneers" to attempt radical experiments in social organization. Increasingly, rural areas came to be dominated by less collective, or even blatantly individualistic, forms of development. The kibbutzim continue to have an influence on Israeli life far beyond their numerical strength, but little remains of their original hope of becoming a model for the society at large.

Throughout their existence, the kibbutzim have consistently adhered to what Dan Leon has called "the basic values of kibbutz society—labor, equality, collectivism, democracy and voluntarism" (1969:97). Let us look briefly at each of these values. *Voluntarism* is expressed in the fact that to belong to a kibbutz is a voluntary act. No one is coerced to join or to remain in any of these organizations. Members are expected to provide the *labor* of which they are capable, although more as self-expression than as sacrifice. Describing the founders of one kibbutz, Melford Spiro has commented: "For them . . . labor itself was viewed as a need—probably man's most important need—the satisfaction of which became an end in itself" (1970:11). In return, members may expect to be dealt with on a basis of *equality*. The material benefits of the kibbutz, for example, are spread equally among all members. And all this is carried out within a framework of *collectivism* in production, consumption, and education.

The question of *democracy* is worth a more extensive look. Policy is set down by the kibbutz in the general assembly, which meets weekly and is made up of all kibbutz members. Responsible to this is the secretariat, the main decision-making body, which also meets weekly and whose central members are the kibbutz's principal officeholders: general secretary, treasurer, and coordinators of economics, labor, and education. Below this are a number of committees which deal on a daily basis with such kibbutz issues as economic or labor affairs, housing, welfare, education, and culture. Finally, there are the teams of workers in a particular productive or service unit, where routine decisions are made about specific tasks.

While at first glance this might seem a highly bureaucratic system, in practice it is both fluid and extremely participatory. For one thing, the extensive network of positions and committees within the kibbutz means that at any given moment, 40 to 50 percent of the members will be part of the formal decision-making process. The principle of job rotation ensures that almost everybody will at some point serve in such a capacity (Barkai, 1971:7). Furthermore, work teams are not organized along strict supervisor-worker lines, but rather reflect the values of the kibbutz at large in being groups where decisions tend to be made on an informal consensus basis. And finally, the entire process remains under continuing review by the membership as a whole, meeting in general assembly. To an extraordinary degree, each kibbutz member has an effective voice in both daily affairs and overall kibbutz policy.

Beyond their own boundaries, the kibbutzim are linked at many points with national agencies and with each other. Kibbutz land, for example, is leased from the Jewish National Fund or the government at nominal fees. The Jewish Agency is an important source of capital. Tnuva, a national marketing cooperative to which the kibbutzim belong, distributes kibbutz produce (Fein, 1971:510–511). Histadrut, the General Federation of Jewish Labor, provides a health insurance plan. Various other national groups help with accounting procedures, the provision of credit, lobbying, well drilling, and other functions. And there are a half-dozen kibbutz federations that provide loans, distribute new recruits among their member groups, channel assistance (in money and labor power) from stronger to weaker kibbutzim, conduct research, and engage in a number of other activities.* Just as individual kibbutzim have prospered from an extraordinary degree of internal cooperation, so have they drawn strength from extensive associations with the larger society.

In the popular image, the kibbutzim are agricultural settlements, responsible for making Israel's swamps bloom and its deserts flower. If this has been historically accurate, however, more recent developments have seen

---

* For more on the kibbutz federations, see Gal, 1971:540–543; and Leon, 1969:158–164.

the increasing industrialization of the kibbutz. In one kibbutz federation, accounting for one-third of total kibbutz population, the percentage of total output attributable to industry increased from 20 percent in 1960 to 40 percent ten years later. In the movement as a whole, the number of industrial plants grew from 108 in 1960 to 185 in 1971 (Leviatan, n.d.:2). For the most part, this has been small-scale industry. Only eighteen plants out of 157 existing in 1968 employed more than 100 workers, and there were fewer than fifty workers in nearly three-fourths of the plants then in existence (Rosner, n.d.:3). But kibbutz industry is increasingly significant within the Israeli economy. By 1972, such operations accounted for 7 percent of Israel's industrial production, and revenues were expected to double over the period 1972–1977.

There are several reasons for this dramatic shift to kibbutz industry. The mechanization of agriculture has freed labor for other pursuits. In addition, the physical demands of farming have left many women and the increasing number of older kibbutz members without "productive" work (as opposed to service occupations, such as education or cooking, to which less prestige is attached).* And there is a general shift in members' preferences toward more technologically sophisticated work. One study of second-generation kibbutz men found that while 59 percent now work as farmers, as opposed to 31 percent in industry or workshops, only 38 percent list farming as their preferred occupation. Thirty-six percent would rather be in industry (Leviatan, n.d.:4). Given the high level of kibbutz education (which has included considerable technical training even for those primarily engaged in agriculture), as well as the wide distribution of managerial skills throughout the kibbutz membership, it has been a relatively uncomplicated process to respond to these forces through a turn to industrial operations.

In embracing complex industries, the kibbutzim have sought to maintain the participatory principles on which management was based in simpler times. As with other productive branches, the kibbutz general assembly makes such major decisions as appointment of a plant's manager and approval of its investment plan, while leaving more mundane questions to those most directly concerned. The plant's assembly of workers, for example, elects most plant officers, determines work arrangements, oversees actions

---

* The need to employ these people has led to shifts in emphasis within the industrial sector itself. Earlier concentration on physically-demanding enterprises, such as machine shops, has given way more recently to greater stress on more mechanized plants, such as those producing plastics (Rosenman, 1971:559).

of the management board,* and decides on production and development plans, subject to approval by the kibbutz assembly. Moreover, other standard kibbutz practices keep lines of authority fluid. In one study of kibbutz industry, Uri Leviatan found job rotation to mean that 60 percent of those in his sample had served in managerial positions over a five-year period. And most officeholders, especially supervisors, continue to take part in production work during their term of office. Even if such practices had not been routinized, it is clear that arbitrary management procedures would be difficult to sustain in the kibbutz environment, where all plant personnel live together as equals and share equally in the proceeds of their group.

As with the kibbutzim generally, industry draws strength from the kibbutz federations and other forms of association. One federation, for example, has both marketing and purchasing organizations to serve plants run by its members. And each federation has a department to promote new industries and provide various services to existing plants. Beyond this, there is a nationwide Kibbutz Industries Organization, which provides financing for new ventures; represents its members in dealings with various governmental, industrial, and educational institutions; and carries out such other activities as the establishment of foreign bureaus to promote export of kibbutz products (Gal, 1971:547–548).

In addition, there are a number of jointly-run kibbutz factories. Originally, these were established either as cooperative services to agriculture (cotton gins, feed factories, and so forth) or as forms of assistance from well-established kibbutz industry to younger kibbutzim in search of an industrial base. More recently, however, joint ventures have become more sweeping in scope. Seven kibbutzim are co-owners of Sefen, a multifactory operation producing adhesives, radiation equipment, and laminates for construction and electronics that did more than $11 million worth of business in 1971. If the kibbutzim are to continue their economic growth, it seems inevitable that there will be more such ventures in the future.

The continuing productivity of kibbutz economies flies in the face of basic Western assumptions about motivation and effective business organization. We tend to assume that workers respond primarily to money, with the promise of more money being the only real incentive to optimum performance. In the kibbutz, on the other hand, nobody receives any salary,

---

* This board typically is made up of the central officeholders in the plant (plant manager, production manager) and in the kibbutz (economic coordinator, treasurer), along with workers' representatives elected by the workers' assembly. For more on decision-making in kibbutz industry, see Rosner, n.d.

much less differentials for exceptional performance. Similarly, where we take for granted the idea that orders should flow from the top of a business down through the ranks, orders in the kibbutz are as likely to flow up as down, and rigid hierarchies are minimized.

Functioning under such conditions, the kibbutzim have produced remarkable economic results. Kibbutz agriculture, in terms of efficiency and yields, has often paced the nation. In a study of industrial efficiency in Israel, Seymour Melman found that kibbutz industries surpassed the performance of comparable capitalist plants in terms of administrative cost, net profit per worker, and productivity of both labor and capital (1970:22). Melman attributes this to "the pervasive motivational and operational effects of cooperation in decision-making and in production" within the plant (Ibid.:33), but this may be too narrow an explanation. More to the point may be the fact that those within the kibbutz share totally a cooperative and common life, a fact that expresses itself in effective performance throughout their range of activities.

To the Western eye, this narrative is likely to call forth images of bees in a hive: could the kibbutzim have achieved so much, while being so communal, without great sacrifice to the character of their members? To assume that individuation is inconsistent with strong group loyalties is an error we have already dealt with (see Chapter 3), but the kibbutz experience provides further evidence on this point. If we can assume, for example, that political leadership requires a capacity for independent action, it is worth noting that in 1965, when the kibbutz population was less than 4 percent of that of the country as a whole, 14 percent of representatives to the Israeli parliament were from kibbutzim (Sturm, 1971:115). Likewise, kibbutz members account for 40 percent of the officers in the army's elite combat units (Stern, 1973:36). And according to Dan Leon, "they play a role quite out of proportion to their numbers in every military action which requires special initiative, staying-power and the readiness to make quick and independent decisions" (1969:141–142). As for less sanguinary pursuits, Leon notes: "In literature, art, dancing, music and drama, the kibbutzim are among the most important centers of creative culture in Israel" (Ibid.:150).

Far from being irreconcilable, kibbutz life and the capacity for independent and creative activity are assumed to run in tandem. From earliest childhood, "There is full recognition of individual differences in talents and abilities. . . . Every child is encouraged to follow his interests and do the best he can in contributing to the group effort" (Rabin, 1965:22). In groups as complex as the kibbutzim, the range of possible contributions is enormous. Given such an environment, children become familiar and comfortable with their own capacities; and the results are the opposite of what an American might predict. Jehuda Messinger has argued that "the kibbutz children in Israel are in fact the most [individualized] group you can find—if you wish to compare groups as to the total personalities . . . of their members" (in Neubauer, 1965:204).* It seems almost too good to be true: strong individuals cooperating fully within a supportive and productive environment.

Problems of the Kibbutzim. In fact, there is a clear danger that kibbutz life may, over the long haul, prove too good to be true. While apparently "necessary," the shift to industrial production and other nonagricultural activities represents a break with kibbutz tradition:

> Essentially what has taken place is a redefining of work. To the founders, any work that was not hard physical labor, preferably in farming, was tainted by the ghetto past and viewed as parasitic, exploitative of others. As the land was reclaimed, and as work became ever more technical to sustain a viable economy in Israel, as even the kibbutzim added small factories, even hotel operations, the notions of what work is important and what exploitative, changed. (Bettelheim, 1969:228–229)

In a society as cohesive as that of the kibbutz, a break with one pivotal element of tradition might be expected to have ramifications in other parts of kibbutz life. And this is what seems to be happening. The move to industry is at least associated with shifts in other kibbutz patterns, and in some cases it is clearly their cause.

The most obvious danger is that the participatory democracy which the kibbutzim have exemplified may find it difficult to survive industrial disciplines. One observer puts the problem this way:

> The essence and character of industrial production are liable to lead to a situation in which the economic institutions of the kibbutz lose effective control. A managerial class arises in industrial enterprises and strives for the autonomy of those enterprises. The character of industrial organization

---

* Bruno Bettelheim has expressed reservations about the degree of individuation that a kibbutz education promotes (1969:289–294). Bettelheim's analysis concentrates on measures of intellectual differentiation, however, rather than on differences in total personalities. Even on these limited grounds, he is sufficiently uncertain of his findings that his conclusions are heavily qualified.

is likewise liable to lead to a situation where a rift occurs between workers and management. Neither of these situations prevails in agriculture, where branch management is in daily touch with current work and with the workers. (Rosenman, 1971:560)

Haim Barkai considers the threat serious enough to proclaim: "The challenge facing the kibbutz in the 1970s is . . . to adapt its social framework to the requirements of manufacturing industry without yielding on its socialist principles" (1971:49). Although it is still too early to judge whether the challenge will be met, existing data already cast shadows on the attempt. In studies begun in 1969 in thirty-four kibbutz plants, Menahem Rosner found that workers' assemblies met as frequently as once a month in only fourteen enterprises. In sixteen others, these assemblies met less than once a month, and in four enterprises they did not meet at all (n.d.:7). As noted above, the workers' assemblies are not the only means by which workers in kibbutz plants make their views known. But any tendency toward atrophy here would seem symptomatic of a more pervasive dilution of democratic kibbutz management.

Other principles have also been modified in the wake of industrialization. The kibbutzim long resisted hiring workers from outside their groups, on the assumption that wage labor is necessarily exploitative. By the late 1960s, however, outside workers accounted for 9 percent of kibbutz employment, primarily as a result of wage labor in kibbutz industry. In 1969, more than half of all workers in kibbutz manufacturing enterprises were hired employees,* as compared with 14 percent in farming and 4 percent in personal service occupations (Barkai, 1971:25–26). Efforts have been made to institutionalize this practice in "legitimate" forms. Speaking of industrial partnerships with nonkibbutz interests, Barkai notes that "an important consideration in favor of establishing such joint ventures has always been legitimation of the engagement of hired labor" (Ibid.:26). Clearly, however, the extensive use of hired labor can only erode the communal basis of kibbutz life; and devices such as joint ventures to avoid confronting this fact directly are far too transparent to work for long.

Finally, changing economic conditions are beginning to have a significant impact on patterns of income distribution within the kibbutz. To oversimplify, the kibbutz has traditionally distributed benefits to its mem-

---

* These workers were disproportionately concentrated in a few plants: 80 percent of all hired workers were in but 18 percent of kibbutz factories. Fully two-thirds of kibbutz enterprises, however, employ at least some outside labor (Leviatan, n.d.:8).

bers in three ways. First, there have been goods and services provided freely and equally to all: examples are education and child care, food, and medical services. Second, there has been housing, where newer and more comfortable accommodations have been allocated on the basis of age and seniority within the kibbutz. Third, there have been various categories of such personal items as clothing, footwear, and cigarettes, within which a limited range of alternatives has been offered to accommodate individual preferences. In their early years, the kibbutzim necessarily devoted most of their income to basic subsistence needs—food, medical care, and housing. Relative poverty sharply limited the availability of goods subject to personal choice. More recently, however, affluence has resulted in a heightened desire for individual consumption.

This seemingly unexceptionable development is leading to a change in kibbutz practice that Americans would take equally for granted. The third category of benefits above, that covering personalized consumption items, has long been handled through the kibbutz's "personal budget." Under this system, each person is entitled, say, to clothing, sound systems, cigarettes, and footwear, with a maximum value of goods allowed in each category. According to current ground rules, unused value in one category cannot be used to procure items of another sort. In place of this, the kibbutzim are now considering establishment of "comprehensive budgets," under which members would receive equal total allowances for personal consumption, with freedom to "spend" these on whatever they choose. While seemingly straightforward, this proposal has become the subject of "one of the most heated debates the kibbutz movement has ever come on" (Barkai, 1971: 40), and with good reason. The whole tendency toward more varied and extensive personalized consumption, a tendency the comprehensive budget would accelerate, seems to some to threaten the basis of kibbutz solidarity. If people begin to concentrate on individualizing themselves through their material possessions, or so the traditionalists argue, their sense of common being and purpose will suffer commensurately.

Taken together, these recent shifts in the kibbutz structure raise serious questions about the future of the movement. One kibbutz member has observed: "Today's kibbutz is based on an integration of communal production, consumption, and education. . . . Now if you take away one of the elements of this triangle, you get some kind of cooperative, moshav, or commune—but not a kibbutz" (Joel Dorkam, personal communication, 1972). Yet all three of these elements are now under assault.

The very fact of industrialization means that kibbutz labor is split among an ever greater number of activities. And communal production within the industries themselves is diluted by extensive hiring of outside labor. The debate over the "comprehensive budget" is perhaps the most fundamental expression of a comparable decommunalizing of consumption, but this trend has taken other forms as well. It is increasingly common, for example, for kibbutz families to take meals in their own apartments, rather than in the communal dining hall. And contrary to long-standing practices of collective child-rearing, parents in some kibbutzim are taking their younger children "home" for the night, rather than leaving them in the communal children's house. In important respects, the kibbutzim may have begun to yield to what Dan Leon calls the "dangerous" tendency "for the centrifugal forces . . . to grow and for the individual to be so occupied with his own work, his own family, his own social circle and his own interests that he loses sight of the organic totality of kibbutz life" (1969:73).*

In the most gloomy view, the kibbutzim are gradually evolving toward less collective forms of living, perhaps at first along the lines of another Israeli social model, the moshav shittufi. These moshavim are settlements where work is done communally while consumption is private, based on the individual family home. Noting the trends we have spoken of above, one member of a kibbutz turned moshav shittufi has this to say: "in my opinion, one of these days almost all kibbutzim will be moshav shittufi. I tell you, I am quite sure of this. . . . Life is already becoming that way in the kibbutz!" (quoted in E. Desroche, 1972:247). Since in many cases the moshav shittufi is itself evolving into something less communal still (the moshav ovdim, where both production and consumption are private), the future of collective settlements in Israel would seem to be unclear. The kibbutzim remain alive and well today; it remains to be seen how long this will continue to be true.

Lessons from the Kibbutz Experience. For Americans concerned with creating communal environments, the central lesson of the kibbutz experience seems to be that even within a predominantly capitalist system, it is possible to maintain productive settlements over a period of generations. There are qualifications, however. To follow the kibbutz model requires collectivizing production, consumption, and child rearing. This in turn sug-

---

* If Melford Spiro is to be believed, individualism has penetrated the deepest recesses of kibbutz consciousness: "the demand for privacy seems to have been recognized as legitimate" (1970:xiii). For a discussion of privacy and its relationship to individualism, see Chapter 3.

gests a degree of dedication and agreement on basic principles that borders, in its force, on the religious. This basis once established, however, there is room for considerable variation both between and within particular groups. Kibbutzim range in their orientations from Orthodox Judaism to militant socialism, for example; and the variety of individual concerns in any given group is comparably great. Even in the realm of "productive" activities, there seems to be a wide range of possibilities. At least up to a point, the kibbutzim have been able to move from agriculture into food processing, industrial and service occupations without altering their basic character.

Other elements of the kibbutz experience are less transferable to the contemporary American context. For one thing, those who created the kibbutzim were impelled by more than just visions of a better life, although this was their starting point. Once relocated from Eastern Europe to the remote deserts of Palestine, they found themselves driven by the necessity of making their experiments work. In the face of difficulty and disappointment, they simply could not pack up and move back to their jobs or homes or schools—or even to other collectives. There is no way to know whether the kibbutzim would exist today if their members had had easy alternatives during the years of crisis, but their success would surely have been more difficult to achieve. This is a sobering thought when applied to current American attempts at collective living, where the imperatives of survival are conspicuous by their absence. People do not *need* to make their groups work here. It is simply too easy for them to move on to something else, and the prospects for their groups are all the more uncertain as a result.

There is a further aspect of the kibbutz picture which is missing in the United States. Beginning with the critical years of the 1930s and 1940s, and extending beyond Independence to the present, there has been extensive support for the kibbutz movement from the Jewish community in Israel and abroad. Collective experiments in the United States, on the other hand, would more likely be subject to indifference, if not outright hostility, on the part of their neighbors. They certainly could not count on the sorts of material and technical assistance from government agencies and labor organizations that have contributed heavily to kibbutz survival. At least for relatively ambitious experiments, the difference between the two environments can be that between success and failure. In 1969 and 1970, for example, one group of seventy-five Jewish families tried to find the resources to create a collective settlement in the United States. They were unsuccessful; and in 1971 they moved together to Israel, where support was more readily available. At last report, they had become well established, and nothing comparable had emerged in America. This is not to say that communal work places cannot succeed here, but it does reaffirm that we live in a social context that is far from supportive.

There are lessons to be drawn from the problems as well as from the successes of the kibbutzim. Recent experience, for example, suggests that an increasing reliance on industry can be a divisive force. The extent to which this is inherent in industrial operations, as opposed to being a function of grafting industry onto an existing agricultural base, is not clear from the kibbutz case. At a minimum, however, it does seem reasonable to conclude that sophisticated enterprises pose serious problems for democratic management. And it is clear that negative consequences have followed from industrial expansion beyond the point where available jobs could be filled by members of the kibbutz work force, leading to extensive use of outside labor. This may not mean that industry and communalism are incompatible, but it does at least suggest that communal groups profit from simplicity and modest pretensions in their economic functions, and that industry offers temptations that may be in conflict with these goals.

Related to this is the broader problem of affluence. With greater wealth comes increasing opportunity for individualized consumption, and the kibbutz experience indicates that this can be damaging to communal solidarity. If there were no more to be said on the matter, the prospects for collective settlements in the United States would seem bleak indeed. If a per capita income level of less than $2,000 a year (Israel in 1970) can threaten communal ventures, what hope would there be for such ventures were per capita income to reach nearly $5,000 a year (United States in 1970) (U.S. Bureau of the Census, 1972:813)? At first glance, the lesson of the kibbutzim would seem to be that the considerable wealth of the overdeveloped countries has immunized them from the communal virus.

The money problem, however, may lie less in the *fact* of affluence than in the *process* of affluence. That is, communal groups may be able to survive even relatively high levels of income, as long as these are not growing rapidly. In such a situation, people would establish stable patterns of consumption, around which communal ties could be built. Disruptions would only occur if incomes were suddenly to increase, forcing people to define anew their consumption patterns and thus their communal relationships. If such rapid growth of income were to continue, as has been the case within the kibbutzim particularly since the onset of industrialization, a communal equilibrium could prove impossible to achieve. And tendencies toward individualism might then prevail. The lesson here, or so we can speculate, might be simply that economic stability, rather than economic impoverishment, is a prerequisite for survival of the communal spirit.

The history of the kibbutz movement provides a wealth of information for Western commune-builders to ponder. "The kibbutz has never pretended to be a commodity for export," Dan Leon notes. But he continues:

> Even so, its own modest and restricted experience in agriculture, in the relationship of town and country, of manual to intellectual work, in human relations and incentives, democracy, equality and education—these may be of interest and importance to people in East and West, in the more and less developed countries, who are searching for answers to the quandaries of our times in relation to the specific reality of their own national and social life. (1969:196)

This last phrase is an appropriate cautionary note on which to conclude. Those who would build communal work places clearly must adapt lessons from the kibbutzim, or from any other source, to their own realities. But if lessons are sought, the kibbutz is one of the first places to look.

Chapter 8: Alternatives for Total Systems— Socialism and Anarchism

Practically all the communal experiments dealt with in the last four chapters were carried out within noncommunal societies. This is an unhealthy situation for such groups, if only because their necessary contacts with the outside world run the risk of undermining their communal principles. As one kibbutz member has commented, "We have to produce in the capitalist system and we have to make a profit—there is no way out of that. But when we succeed, we are increasingly influenced by the capitalist way of thinking" (quoted in Stern, 1973:114). Such dangers will persist as long as communes are minority groups in a much greater social mass attached to antagonistic ideas. It is therefore worth speculating as to what a supportive, wholly communal society might be like.

This problem is worth attention on a second count as well. A society of communes would raise a number of issues which no single commune will need to confront. The process of coordination within a specific group may be carried out informally, for example, on the basis of direct contact between the members. Coordination of the activities of a large number of communes, on the other hand, will require less personal mechanisms for making decisions. Whether such mechanisms can be developed without their relative impersonality seeping back into the inner workings of the communes themselves is very much an open question, one we do not try to resolve conclusively here. The United States is still so far from having even a significant number of communal work places, much less a truly communal society, that to examine such points in any detail would be premature. Nonetheless, we can at least try to include their outlines in this chapter.

Unfortunately, the major theoretical traditions that might have cast light on these issues, Marxism and anarchism, have largely failed to do so. Anarchism had its moments in Republican Spain, but Franco ended these along with the Republic. And Marxism has proved to be largely what Murray Bookchin calls "an ideology of naked power, pragmatic efficiency and social centralization almost indistinguishable from the ideologies of modern state capitalism" (1971:92). It might not have been so. Marx himself spoke on occasion of the need for strong communal units, notably in his writings on the Paris Commune and on the potential for revolutionary village communities in Russia.* And the moral appeal of socialism—its call for equality and widespread participation in economic and political affairs—has always suggested some sort of communitarian social framework. But for Marx, and more so for most of his disciples, communalism was always a less central concern than the overthrow of capitalism; and it was quickly forgotten as revolutionary theory became practice in Russia and Eastern Europe. Fortunately, however, we need not rely on these prototypes alone to consider what a communal socialism might be like. Recent developments in China provide an alternative view.

SOCIALISM—THE CHINESE APPROACH

For a decade following the triumph of Mao and his forces in 1949, Western cold warriors tended to view China as little more than a satellite of the Soviet Union. This illusion became more difficult to sustain with the angry withdrawal from China of all Soviet aid and technicians in 1960, after which Western observers accorded China status of its own as a standard Totalitarian Communist Regime. Through such blinkers, the Cultural Revolution that began in 1966 seemed to be simply a chaotic struggle for power among the small group of party officials who served as masters of China's destiny. This view lingered at least through the period of the Nixon visit to Peking in 1971, which was covered by the mass media at a level of understanding which suggested that the reporters involved had read nothing about China for years except one another's dispatches. As more complete information began to flow out of China, however, it became clear that there was much here to learn about the possibilities for communal social organization.

---

* For a discussion of Marx's attitude on these points, see Buber, 1958:86–94.

Structure. Four out of every five Chinese live in rural "communes," although these are far from what the term implies in the United States. Chinese communes are highly productive, for one thing, and they include thousands of members—as many as 60,000 or more in a few cases. People's energies tend to be centered in more manageable social units, however. "Production teams" of roughly thirty families constitute the basic operating groups, making day-to-day decisions on production and determining the distribution of income between their members.

The teams in turn are grouped into "production brigades," between ten and thirty per commune, which are simply villages within the communal area. Where possible, the brigades strive for self-sufficiency. Some have their own schools, hospitals, grain mills, even factories. And they are considerably more than mere cogs within the larger communal machine. As Klaus Mehnert has observed: "In the brigade, everybody knows everybody else, and that's where life pulsates; people debate, quarrel, and make decisions. . . . Whenever the cadres want to give a concrete picture of the commune's work, they are obliged to refer again and again to what is done in the brigades" (1972:76).

The same tendency toward integrating life within basic socioeconomic units exists in Chinese industry. Rather than being simply places to earn a living, factories are places to live. The Wuhan Iron and Steel Works, for example, supports or provides housing, a college for workers and their families, middle and primary schools, nurseries, theater groups, a library, several clinics, a 400-bed hospital, sports facilities, a farm, a rest sanitarium, and a militia group (Goldwasser and Dowty, 1973:21). This factory is an unusually large one, and its facilities are considerably more extensive than those in more modest enterprises. But the principle is the same everywhere: factories have welfare, political, and educational functions that give them more the character of villages than of the stark economic units we have become accustomed to in the West.

There is more to this than simply maintaining a communitarian base for the economy, although this is unusual enough in itself. In structuring their society, the Chinese are also trying to resolve what socialists have long seen to be one of the most fundamental social contradictions, that between urban industry and rural agriculture. One approach to this is to provide rural areas with industries of their own. Brigades may run noodle factories, while communes make farm tools, milling machines, fertilizer, and tractors. From the other direction, city factories are to become more agricultural. Some own farms that their employees maintain on a rotating basis, while others raise fruits, vegetables, or pigs on land surrounding the factories themselves. Ideally, the communal units that lie at the heart of Chinese social planning will be both highly diversified and relatively self-contained.

The economic activities of all these units are centrally "planned," in the sense that agencies in Peking continue to use simplified input-output procedures to coordinate the distribution of capital and consumer goods across the country. But especially since the Cultural Revolution, many key decisions have been pushed down to the provincial, local, or plant levels. Even the central planning document is revised in draft by individual enterprises before final approval. Firms meet directly in "material-allocation conferences" to negotiate purchases from each other. And provincial officials or plant management are allowed flexibility in making decisions on prices and production.* The planning process in China is still evolving, but there is considerable evidence that it will not be allowed to choke off local responsibility and initiative. Given the values now underlying China's development, the approach could hardly be otherwise.

Values. The adhesive that binds China's 800 million people in pursuit of national goals consists of the exhortations of Mao Tse-tung. The "cult" of Mao has often been ridiculed in the West, in large measure simply because we do not understand it. As Ross Terrill has pointed out: "It is odd to us partly because we have no consciousness of Chinese social modes, and because we read the texts and slogans as sets of English phrases, which is like imbibing wine as frozen ice-blocks" (1972:3).

Reduced to their essentials, however, Mao's teachings are relatively straightforward.** Great emphasis is placed on self-reliance. Initiative and effort are to start with the individual or the production brigade, rather than coming from central agencies. This implies recognition of the importance of each individual, whose best efforts—applied to no matter how mundane a task—are worthy of praise in the common struggle. And this in turn suggests the need for a sense of responsibility toward others engaged in that struggle. These are not necessarily easy lessons to apply. Barry Richman found that key officials in a number of industries were typically devoting a half-day each week to discussion of the implications of Mao's works (1969: 765), and such study has been prevalent throughout Chinese society. But

---

* See Galbraith, 1972; and Richman, 1969:474, 676, 709, 712.

** For a summary of the "three old favorite articles" which represent the popular core of Mao's social thought, see CCAS, 1972:39–45.

far from being inscrutable, these are teachings of undeniable moral force. Mao's statement of them has led an entire society to value the responsible, self-reliant individual, united with others in struggle to make communal socialism succeed.

Over the long run, the success of Mao's teachings will depend on the manner in which future generations are taught; and Maoist experiments have been carried out in both form and content of education. In the aftermath of the Cultural Revolution, secondary school graduates were required to spend at least two years in productive labor before being considered for admission to universities, and such admissions were made contingent upon the recommendation of fellow workers that advanced training was appropriate. Students, professors, and others met together to adapt texts and courses of study to local conditions. Everywhere, schools became places of work as well as of study:

> You wonder at first if you are on a campus at all. Here . . . are people, dressed in conical hats and blue peasant jackets, threshing wheat. . . . In the Middle School attached to Peking Normal University, girls are making chairs. Next door are boys, helped by "veteran workers" from a nearby factory, making semiconductors. In Canton . . . I found professors tending a vegetable garden. . . . (Terrill, 1972 : 120)

To a considerable degree, Chinese education had become a process in which all those concerned were expected to participate fully—and one which was to be intimately related to the needs of the larger society.*

Individual and Group. As John Gurley has pointed out, "The basic, overriding economic fact about China is that for twenty years she has fed, clothed, and housed everyone, has kept them healthy, and has educated most" (1970:31). Given the extent of starvation, disease, and illiteracy in comparable developing areas, this is a staggering achievement. But it follows from a simple fact: the Chinese leadership has built its policies on a concern for the individuals who comprise the society, rather than concentrating on the aggregate economic growth of the society as a whole.** Other nations, capitalist and socialist alike, worship together at the altar of Gross National Product, regardless of the millions who may be left behind by a growing GNP, or even of what sort of production that GNP represents

---

* For more on education in China, see Alley, 1974.
** This message has gained a foothold even in such an implausible location as the World Bank, one of whose economists has pursued the same point; see ul Haq, 1971:13.

—guns or butter, bread or baubles. China, however, has not forgotten that it is a collection of individuals rather than of national statistics.

This bias shows through in the ways China measures its achievements: "Occasional production figures are given, but the most consistent reporting is related to experimentation, innovation . . . and so forth—all due to the efforts of workers themselves or in cooperation with scientists and engineers" (Orleans, 1972:210). At all levels of society, there is what Robert Guillain (1971) calls an "ouvriérisme" (worker-centeredness), which tells the worker that "the enterprise is his and that it expects ideas and innovations from him."

Such an atmosphere is clearly uncongenial to monotonous conformity. As a group of American Asia scholars observed on their return from a month in China: "It was quite obvious to us that in China socialism does not blur personalities, but in fact the contrary seemed true—we constantly saw tremendous encouragement of individual initiative" (CCAS, 1972:53). Observer after observer tells similar stories, and to the same point. China may have an enormously strong collective will, but this is built on the individual self-respect and differentiation of her people.

The same tendency extends to processes of decision-making, which are designed to mobilize the energies of all involved in a given political, residential, or working unit. As a start, the Cultural Revolution brought a general decentralization of power in China, with key decisions to be made by the groups most affected. Further, steps were taken to break down hierarchical structures according to the principle of the "two joins": leaders join in production and workers join in leadership (Goldwasser and Dowty, 1973: 3). To institutionalize this broad participation in leadership, revolutionary committees consisting typically of workers, party cadres, and members of the People's Liberation Army were established in factories, hospitals, communes, schools, and government agencies.*

Workers have other outlets for expression as well. In factories, for example, workers' representative congresses control a number of administrative functions. Workers paste *dazibao* (posters) to walls throughout the plants to bring diverse points of view to general attention. Mass assemblies of all personnel provide a forum for the voicing of opinions. And the day-to-day operation of "three-in-one work teams" (workers, cadres, and technicians)

---

* As the group best able to coordinate the efforts of widely dispersed economic units, the party holds a leading position in many of these committees, as well as having Party Committees of its own. As the Cultural Revolution indicated, however, this role can be sustained only if the party remains responsive to the will of those with whom it works.

allows for informal discussion of pressing issues. The premise is simple: if people are to be all that they can be, they must feel themselves in control of the decisions which affect them.

Clearly, the political culture of China focuses ultimately on the individual. If we have tended to illustrate this with examples from the work place, that is because China is perforce a work-oriented society. At their current income levels, the Chinese have little leeway for self-expression in consumption. Yet even here, personal idiosyncrasies find their outlet. Jan Myrdal, for example, recounts the story of a carpenter who had worked on the homes of a village he is visiting:

> "He wanted each facade to suit its family," said Mau Pei-hsin. "If there is some flower that family is particularly fond of, then he'll make a pattern with just those flowers for them. There must be harmony between a family and the home it is to live in. That's why no two windows are alike here among us." (Myrdal and Kessle, 1970:5)

All this is diametrically opposed to the image of gray spirits under a totalitarian heel that has long dominated our vision of life in communist states. At least for the moment, China has achieved a synthesis of collective will and individual strength on a scale without historical precedent.

Prospects. Since 1949, China has wavered between two polar approaches to building a revolutionary state. The first of these stresses the need for economic "rationality," large-scale industrialization, and the disciplines of the market in order to provide the material basis for building communism. Because of its similarity to the economic preoccupations of the West, this reliance on material output and incentives has been attributed to "capitalist roaders," whose "economist" views tend to sacrifice human needs and social cooperation to the dictates of technology (see CCAS, 1972:86). Opposed to this is the assertion, identified closely with Mao himself, that communist social relationships can—and on moral grounds should—be pursued at once. Greater production will naturally follow, but this should not be the central concern. Of prime importance is inculcating in people generally habits of self-reliance, participation in decision-making, and interpersonal responsibility.

Following the Cultural Revolution of 1966, the Maoist viewpoint appeared to have triumphed. By the early 1970s, however, counterrevolutionary tendencies had begun to appear. Income differentials were increasingly based on the standard of "to each according to his labor," diluting the earlier stress on social responsibility as well as work in determining wages. Strictly academic standards began to edge out political and social requirements for university admissions, while instructors came to focus more on academic "achievers" than on those with proven dedication to Maoism. And the party appeared to be tightening its control over economic decision-making at the expense of workers. This was not unforeseen; as Mao noted in 1967:

> The present Great Proletarian Cultural Revolution is only the first of its kind. In the future such revolutions must take place. . . . All Party members and the population at large must guard against believing . . . that everything will be fine after one, two, three, or four cultural revolutions. We must pay close attention and we must not relax our vigilance. (Quoted in Daubier, 1970:37)

By early 1974, vigilance seemed to be expressing itself in yet another "cultural revolution." In a campaign of attacks on Confucius and Lin Piao, the Chinese leadership appeared to signal a reaffirmation of Maoism. Where the pendulum will finally come to rest is uncertain. From afar, it is easy to fear that "economics" will prevail and that China will follow the United States and the USSR into a barren technological centralism. But as Klaus Mehnert concluded after a visit to China, "anyone who has . . . seen and felt the degree to which the Chinese people have been gripped and changed by Maoism . . . will, I think, refrain from hasty predictions" (1972:178).

Conclusions from the Chinese Experience. As in the kibbutzim, the Chinese have shown that people can find exhilaration and a strong sense of personal worth in striving for common goals. Both experiments have found that this process at its best implies the assertion of individuality by all those involved. As conditions for achieving this, certain patterns appear in both cases. In the kibbutz as in the Chinese production unit, the group is based on a strong common value system. In both countries, communal groups are strongly reinforced by the presence of like-minded organizations in the surrounding culture, although this effect is considerably more potent in China, where the entire society is structured along similar lines. And like the Israelis, the Chinese have found communalism easier to achieve in agricultural villages or small-scale industry than in large industrial operations: human contact and decision-making has consistently been more informal and participatory in Chinese production brigades than in large urban plants.

The Chinese are virtually alone, however, in their attempt to integrate communal units in a total socialist economy. The kibbutzim function within a larger capitalist system, while socialist countries such as the USSR are based on anything but communalism. Only China is trying to reconcile the communal requirement for participatory decision-making with the national requirement for "rational" economic coordination. That China has been at least partially successful in simultaneously meeting both of these needs is a note of encouragement for those who would seek to establish communally-based states. China's recurrent swings between Maoism and the "capitalist road," however, indicate that a final synthesis of these two forces has not yet been arrived at. And the job of finding this will become all the more difficult as the economy develops.

The underlying problem is this: some means of binding together the economy's parts will remain necessary even if the Chinese succeed in their drive for relative self-sufficiency within provincial or subprovincial areas. In the aftermath of the Cultural Revolution, a fair amount of coordination was accomplished simply through personal contact and goodwill between firms and their customers. As the economy becomes more complex, however, this will prove an increasingly shaky basis for economic integration. The logical alternatives present difficulties of their own, however. If central planning prevails, the planners may take over; if there is greater reliance on the market, competition and profit-seeking may win out. The ultimate resolution by China of the question of how to mesh its economic parts remains far from clear. But should a way be discovered to preserve communalism and participatory management while the economy grows, this would be China's greatest contribution of all.

SOCIALISM—THE YUGOSLAV APPROACH

Yugoslavia's version of socialism is sufficiently different from China's that the Chinese have assailed workers' self-management, the economic pivot of the Yugoslav system, as a mere device for legitimizing "bourgeois cooperatives" (Wheelwright and McFarlane, 1970:87). And yet, what has evolved in Yugoslavia over the past quarter-century has so captured the fancy of the American left that no book on alternatives to present socio-economic patterns seems complete without its section on the Yugoslav experiment. To Robert Dahl, for example, "Yugoslavia is the only country in the world where a serious effort has been made to translate the old dream of industrial democracy into reality" (1970:130). The Chinese may be more to the point in their hostility, however, than are Dahl and others in their enthusiasm. Ultimately, the Yugoslav model may simply suggest what decentralist socialism may come to where a strong "Maoist" base of common values is lacking.

Background and Structure. As in China, socialism came to Yugoslavia in the aftermath of the Second World War. In both countries, the USSR served as an early model for organization and planning within a socialist state, and subsequent attempts to break free from Stalinist patterns of centralization ultimately led to ideological rupture with the Soviet Union. The final divorce between Moscow and Peking did not occur until 1960; Belgrade went through the same process much earlier. In 1948, Stalin attacked Yugoslavia for its "revisionist" tendencies, choreographing a series of economic and political moves designed to bring the errant government back into line. But far from capitulating, the Yugoslavs became even more extreme in their revisionism. In July 1950, legislation to transfer control of businesses from central planners to workers' collectives launched the country on a unique experiment in decentralist socialism.

Here the parallels with Chinese experience end, for the Yugoslavs had little that was communal in mind. Agriculture was largely turned over to private farmers. Although 500 "communes" were established, averaging 40,000 inhabitants, their role is sufficiently limited that Branko Horvat (1971) ignores them in a lengthy discussion of key elements of the Yugoslav economic system. While self-government has been attempted in such local groups as universities, hospitals, libraries, and neighborhoods, one observer calls the influence of community groups only "small to moderate" (Hunnius, 1971:162). And instead of tapping moral incentives to organize life generally around a sense of interpersonal responsibility, the Yugoslavs have increasingly found principles of organization in markets, profit-oriented investment banks, and other mechanisms familiar in the capitalist world. Only in the internal organization of the business firm have major efforts been made to create closer, more participatory group bonds.

The Yugoslav experiment in "industrial democracy" is extremely complex, and only its central features can be dealt with here.* At the heart of the system is the workers' council. Each enterprise has such a council, ranging from 15 to 120 members according to the size of the firm involved. The council, which is elected by the work collective (all employees of the firm),

* For more detailed descriptions, see Hunnius, 1971 and 1973, or Adizes, 1971.

meets at intervals of one to two months to deal with basic policy matters: determination of pay schedules and distribution of the firm's income, adoption of an annual economic plan, selection of the director. As its executive organ, the council elects a managing board of no more than eleven members, three-fourths of whom must be production workers. Although major changes in policy may be referred to the entire collective for decision, it is through their representatives on the council and the managing board that workers normally influence actions of the firm as a whole.

To provide for even more direct democracy in daily industrial operations, various subsidiary groups have emerged since this general structure was established. The workers responsible for repairing machinery in many enterprises, for example, have banded together in informal associations, and political and social clubs are legion. The most important new groups, however, are the "work units," usually consisting of between 20 and 100 employees whose activities are separable on technological and economic grounds from other units within the plant. From their relatively humble beginnings in 1959, these groups have become sufficiently independent that they sell services to each other, maintain their own accounts, and control a number of important management functions. The unit itself hires and fires its employees, assigns jobs, and distributes income to its members.

Values. At least on the surface, the Yugoslav attempt at industrial democracy appears to have had a measure of success. In one representative plant, Ichak Adizes calculated that decision-making positions were available to 40 percent of the membership at any given moment. Taking into account rotation among these positions and such other processes as elections and referendums, Adizes concluded that participation over time may have been 100 percent (1971:36). An unusual degree of interest in company affairs resulted. Riding home from work in the company bus, Adizes found that:

> the workers continued the discussions from the meetings concerning the managerial aspects of the company and its financial and marketing policies. The weaver, who had only elementary school training, sat with the accountant, who had a university degree in economics, and the two argued about the present policies. Many workers lived their company's affairs.... (Ibid.: 103)

This in turn has led to a mutual concern of workers for each other's welfare. Several observers, for example, have commented on the reluctance of firms to lay off employees. Where this has to be done, considerable effort has been made to release those with the least need for income or the greatest chance of finding another job.* Up to a point, the emphasis the Yugoslav regime has placed on self-management has led workers to value involvement with the conduct of their firms and the well-being of their fellow employees.

A concurrent desire for private enrichment, however, has sharply diminished both the force and the long-term prospects of these communal values. Gar Alperovitz has noted that an "ethic of individual gain and profit has often taken precedence over the ideal of cooperation" (1972:526). This conflict in priorities follows inevitably from basic assumptions of the Yugoslav leadership. By the mid-1960s, material possession had come to be viewed as "both the purpose and the most powerful incentive for production" (Horvat, 1971:90). Given such attitudes on the part of policymakers, behavior within enterprises has become increasingly linked to the financial rewards it will bring the individuals involved.

Self-management and industrial cooperation remain as values. But money, as it is wont to do, may be nibbling them away. In a study published in 1970, Josip Obradovic found that workers listed high wages, good working conditions, and possibilities for advancement as the most desirable job characterisics; participation in self-management bodies ranked fifth (summarized in Hunnius, 1973:303). As one worker told Adizes: "Let someone else manage; I want good pay" (1971:219). The opportunity to serve, which in China would be at the top of any such ranking, was all but ignored. The Yugoslavs have chosen material rather than moral incentives to propel their economy, and workers are responding accordingly.

Problems. As workers have become more concerned with salaries, there has been a push from below to maximize industrial efficiency. In pursuit of this, workers' management positions have been filled disproportionately by "better-qualified" skilled and white-collar workers; the holders of these positions in turn have relinquished considerable authoriy to trained managerial personnel. As the structure of workers' control is refined on paper, in other words, the actual distribution of power increasingly resembles that in capitalist enterprises, with similar results. Friction develops between individuals over the distribution of profits. Grievances on these and other issues express themselves in strikes, a "capitalist" phenomenon that grew more and more common in Yugoslavia throughout the 1960s.

---

* See, for example, Adizes, 1971:128n; and Hunnius, 1973:303–305.

In the plant's external relationships, the drive for profits expresses itself in what the Yugoslavs call enterprise "particularism," or excessive greed at the expense of the larger society. Here too, both symptoms and remedies are famililar. Large companies have come to dominate their markets, and the government has responded with legislation against combinations in restraint of trade (Sherman, 1972:282). When prices have continued to rise anyway at unacceptable rates, price controls have been instituted. In response, businesses have discovered such stratagems as making small changes in their products, calling them "new," and raising their prices. All in all, Yugoslav industry has developed an aura that led even such a sympathetic observer as Gerry Hunnius to acknowledge that "it might appear that Yugoslavia is on the way to becoming the first country to upset the law of economic development by changing from a Socialist society to a capitalist one" (1973:319). Hunnius believes that such a judgment would as yet be premature; in fact, it may be overdue.

Conclusions from the Yugoslav Experience. The Yugoslavs have attempted decentralization without building a communal base on which the experiment might rest. There is nothing here of the Chinese attempt to fuse political, economic, and social functions in multipurpose collective bodies. And there is as little effort to draw on latent moral incentives to create a dominant ideology of interpersonal involvement and responsibility. Instead, the Yugoslavs have followed the communitarian approach discussed in Chapter 6. Although sovereign individuals are to come together with others at home, factory, club, recreation center, neighborhood, and other "communities" of interest, no necessary correspondence is provided between these separate pieces of life. Given such a structure, people's relationships with specific groups will inevitably be both partial and functional. Factories, for example, are simply where one earns a living; if better wages are attainable at another plant, there is no emotional barrier to moving on. "Of course they would leave, if they can get more money elsewhere," says one worker. "What difference does it make?" (quoted in Blumberg, 1968:225).

Such attitudes make the Yugoslav experiment both comprehensible to American reformers and relatively meaningless in terms of solving the problems to which this book is addressed. Workers' democracy may now be more prevalent in Yugoslavia than in other industrial nations, but this is already becoming less true as the search for profits in an increasingly complex economy appears to dictate larger plants and managerial approaches to decision-making. If what little democracy remains is dedicated principally to higher salaries, there are few barriers to irrational (as long as profitable) production and to the capture of the work process by assembly-line technologies. Any structural embodiment of a sense of organic relationship between people would require a total reversal of priorities. The Yugoslavs may seem more "realistic" in their approach than the Chinese have been in stressing a sense of responsibility for others, communal effort, and other moral incentives as prime forces for cohesion. But in rejecting communalism while accepting money as the central mediator of economic relationships, Yugoslavia indeed illustrates primarily what a system of "bourgeois cooperatives" looks like in practice. That many of the most "radical" current efforts to reform the American work place find inspiration in the Yugoslav experience simply suggests to how little we aspire.

ANARCHISM

In current usage, the term "anarchism" has become associated primarily with random acts of violence or general social chaos. Neither association is accurate. In the late nineteenth century, anarchism was characterized by a period of assassination and "propaganda by the deed," but this was more a symptom of frustration in achieving anarchist goals than an expression of the goals themselves. Far from proposing chaos as a way of life, anarchists see themselves restoring a social balance that existing political systems have eroded. As the French anarchist Anselme Bellegarigue once put it, "Anarchy is order: government is civil war" (quoted in Woodcock, 1962:276). Anarchism comes in many versions: individualist, mutualist, collectivist, communist, syndicalist, pacifist. But its common feature is simply a resistance to "government" as a source of coercion and class exploitation, coupled with a vision of a noncoercive future order.

History. Anarchists find their antecedents in times long past. A French Tolstoyan, Lechartier, declared that "the true founder of anarchy was Jesus Christ and . . . the first anarchist society was that of the apostles" (quoted in Woodcock, 1962:38). The modern anarchist tradition reaches back at least as far as the seventeenth century, when libertarian challenges to state power appeared in the United States and England, where Gerrard Winstanley's Diggers had a brief life. Late in the following century, another Englishman, William Godwin, constructed the first comprehensive theory of anarchism. Godwin's approach was that of a thoroughgoing individualist—"Everything that is usually understood by the term cooperation is to some degree an evil" (quoted in Joll, 1964:34). But in his insistence that society and government should exist only for the convenience of the people who comprise them, he found a theme that anarchists of all tendencies would carry forward to the present.

At least in terms of theoretical writings and political activity, anarchism's Golden Age was the nineteenth century. Pierre-Joseph Proudhon was its prophet. A contemporary of Marx, Proudhon helped establish the socialist critique of capitalism. "Property is theft," he proclaimed in 1840, at least where property represents the appropriation by few of the fruits of labor of many.

But by midcentury, Proudhon had come to view Marxist centralism as a "dictatorial, authoritarian, doctrinaire system" and Marx himself as the "tapeworm of socialism" (quoted in Buber, 1958:30–31). For Proudhon, socialism must be based on small groups of people voluntarily allied for their common good. Such groups, whether economic workshops or geographically-based communes, would federate as necessary to provide organs of coordination. But the power of federal bodies would be always strictly limited. Proudhon had no desire to reintroduce government through the back door: "Free association . . . is the only possible form of society, the only just and the only true one. . . . [The] government of man by man, under whatever name it is disguised, is oppression" (quoted in Joll, 1964: 71). Clearly, Proudhon could have stomached a "dictatorship of the proletariat" no more easily than the dictatorship of capital; and his writings laid the basis for a permanent schism in the socialist movement.

The schism became final reality in 1872, when Marx arranged for the expulsion from the socialist International of the anarchist forces led by Michael Bakunin. Bakunin's anarchism found a basic social unit in the workers' factory collective. In this he was closer to Marx's conception of an organized proletariat than had been Proudhon, who acknowledged such associations only as devices for individuals to pursue their separate interests. But where Marx wished to use workers' movements to seize the state, Bakunin found in them a way to negate the state. Out of the chaos of revolution would come workers' control of the purest sort, with no need for an interim revolutionary dictatorship to bring it to life. The positions were irreconcilable, and anarchists and state socialists were henceforth to go their separate ways. Anarchism continued to be influential. Trade unionism in France, for example, was to be dominated by anarchists until the First World War. But the spectacular triumph of Marxism in Russia in 1917 seemed to vindicate the centralist position, and anarchism fell into a decline from which it has yet to recover.

Even in its waning years, however, anarchism continued to produce provocative theorists, one of whom, Pëtr Kropotkin, is of particular relevance to this book. Like Bakunin, Kropotkin was much influenced by the intimate village life of his native Russia. But Kropotkin drew on this for a vision more radical still than Bakunin's industrial collectivism. "Have the factory and the workshop at the gates of your fields and gardens," he advised (quoted in Joll, 1964:161); and make of the whole a commune in which people live in harmony. The economic expression of this would be communism (goods and services would be freely available to all who wanted them), an approach that earlier anarchists had avoided in favor of the principle "to each according to his work." This in turn would be based on drawing more fully from people their instincts toward "mutual aid":

> In the practice of mutual aid, which we can retrace to the earliest beginnings of evolution, we . . . find the positive and undoubted origin of our ethical conceptions; and we can affirm that in the ethical progress of man, mutual support—not mutual struggle—has had the leading part. In its wide extension, even at the present time, we also see the best guarantee of a still loftier evolution of our race. (Kropotkin:300)

Kropotkin has been described as a "saint," but his anarchism depended less on saintliness than on his conclusions as a scientist as to the innate human capacity for cooperative effort. If this capacity today seems overwhelmed by our tendency to do each other wrong, Kropotkin reminds us that we can reasonably expect better of ourselves.

Anarchism in Practice. Anarchism is fundamentally a doctrine of all or nothing. For anarchism to prevail, the state must be destroyed; if the state remains, anarchism cannot survive. Even so, scattered experiments in practical anarchism have been attempted in the face of state power. Italian anarchists founded a short-lived colony in Brazil during the 1890s, and anarchist communities survived in the French countryside until the 1930s. Anarchist groups even emerged briefly in Russia during the turbulent period following the October Revolution, especially among the sailors of the Kronstadt fortress, and the Ukrainian peasants organized by Nestor Makhno. The efforts in the Ukraine were particularly striking. Anarchist communes were established on liberated land, and production units federated into districts and regions in the Proudhonian manner. The Bolsheviks soon moved to pacify the area, but it was not until August of 1921 that Makhno was driven into exile and anarchism finally suppressed (Guérin, 1970: 98–101).

The most notable series of anarchist experiments, however, took place in Spain during the 1930s. The seeds of the movement had been planted there in 1868, when Giuseppe Fanelli carried Bakunin's teachings to the workers of Barcelona. In the years that followed, anarchists emerged as leaders of the struggle for social change. Much of the struggle had to be carried out clandestinely, but the tradition remained strong. With the abdication of the Spanish king and the proclamation of a Republic in 1931, the moment seemed finally to have come for anarchist action. Over the next five years, attempts were made to establish anarchist communes in various parts of the country. When Franco's revolt against the Republic threw Spain into civil war in 1936, the anarchists seized the opportunity in villages and factories to lay the concrete basis for a new social order.

In rural areas, the process typically began with the burning of tax records and the expulsion or murder of landlords and police. Teams were established to farm the land and to carry out other economic activities. New systems of income distribution were developed, generally based on the needs of specific families. Village assemblies were formed where all could participate in making necessary decisions. Literacy programs were begun. Associations of villages coordinated trade and provided assistance to poorer areas in the form of labor, tools, and money. And it worked. By 1937, Gaston Leval estimated that three million people were living in rural anarchist communities, with food and work available for all (Woodcock, 1962:396).

Anarchist patterns of self-management were also implemented in urban industries and public services, most notably in Barcelona. Many employers fled when war broke out, but workers continued to run their enterprises, meeting in general assembly on policy questions and electing representative committees to carry out routine managerial functions. In these efforts, the workers were assisted by technical personnel and even some former managers, who stayed on in advisory capacities. But it was the workers themselves who kept the factories operating, the lights on, and the trains running. Visiting a Barcelona bus factory in August 1936, Franz Borkenau observed that "it seems to run as smoothly as if nothing had happened. . . . Complete success, then" (1971:505–506). The anarchist dream seemed well on the way to becoming reality.

But it was not to last. The continuing civil war forced the anarchists into alliances with other political groups in the common effort to defeat Franco. By the fall of 1936, anarchist representatives had joined the central government and entered into a joint military command with their communist rivals in Barcelona. The requirements of waging war increasingly forced central direction of the activities the anarchists had sought to decentralize. Steadily, the anarchists yielded ground, particularly to the communists and their Soviet patrons. Their final capitulation was symbolized in a decree of August 1938 placing all war industries, including those which the anarchists had so proudly seized in 1936, under military command. Franco won the war the following year, but Spanish anarchism was by then already dead.

Anarchism in the United States. Expressions of anarchism have appeared throughout American history. In one early manifestation, John Wheelwright challenged the right of colonial authorities to mandate days of fasting. True Christians, he said in 1637, were guided by an inner light and were thus above mere law. In the nineteenth century, the "inner light" and its secular equivalents were to provide the basis for more complete theories justifying America's traditional lawlessness and individualism in anarchist language. Josiah Warren, whom Woodcock calls "the first American anarchist" (1962:456), founded several communities in midcentury based on the moral principle "mind your own business" (quoted in Schuster, 1931–1932:98). In the same period, Thoreau was being jailed for his lonely refusal to accept the power of government to levy taxes. At the turn of the century, foreign-born activists such as Emma Goldman and Alexander Berkman introduced the idea of social solidarity in pursuit of anarchist goals, with particular reference to the labor movement. But the climate was uncongenial. Americans in flight from coercion seek refuge in themselves, and the individualism of Warren and Thoreau was to continue as the approved American variant of the anarchist tradition.

If Americans identify anarchism with individualism, however, our examples of anarchist theory and practice elsewhere should make clear that this is only one of a number of possibilities. And some of these—Kropotkin's communalist anarchism, for example—offer far more hope for social change than does the version Americans have adopted. In an analysis of the "events of May" (1968) in France, the American anarchist Murray Bookchin claims that "whether this sweeping movement would become a complete social revolution depended on one thing—would the workers not only *occupy* the plants, but *work* them," establishing their own mechanisms for decision-making and control (1971:263).* To call that a "complete social revolution," however, is to take for granted the separation of work from other social activities. The individualist must structure life in this fashion to avoid comprehensive group ties. But as we have indicated throughout this book, most recently in talking above of Yugoslavia, the result is inevitably to hold us to the sort of society in which we now live. Anarchism's potential to provide the theoretical basis for genuine social reconstruction will not be realized until its communalist possibilities drive out the individualism that has crippled it.

There are other ways in which anarchism has become distorted in contemporary definition. Recent "anarchist" communes in America have so styled themselves as a result of rejecting not only the disciplines of the state (plus parents, teachers, bosses, or leaders of any sort), but also those of work and self-support. But anarchism has traditionally posed a means of reorganizing work, not abandoning it. The Spanish workers and peasants during the Civil War continued to work not simply from necessity, but also because it would not have occurred to them to do otherwise. They were the heirs of Proudhon and Kropotkin, for whom work had value both as a means of producing the communal necessities of life and (in moderation) for its own sake. This is not the Protestant Ethic in action—anarchists have always sought to reduce toil through modest consumption and the judicious use of machinery. But they assume, as do we in this book, that any solution to social ills must encompass the production of socially necessary goods.

Finally, anarchism has recently come to imply the rejection of reasoned programs for change; it is sufficient just to do one's own things. But George Woodcock offers a contrary view, one that lies much closer to what anarchism has been:

> by no means all who deny authority and fight against it can reasonably be called anarchists. Historically, anarchism is a doctrine which poses a criticism of existing society; a view of a desirable future society; and a means of passing from one to the other. Mere unthinking revolt does not make an anarchist.... (1962:9)

As it happens, Woodcock's definition comes close to describing the line of argument of our book. In fact, anarchist views permeate our approach: a

---

* Similarly, Noam Chomsky states that "one might argue that some form of council communism is the natural form of revolutionary socialism in an industrial society" (Introduction to Guérin, 1970:xvi).

distrust of state power or its equivalents in large-scale industry, a rejection of exploitative patterns of property ownership, a stress on local units of modest size and communal outlook, an acceptance of work as a basic expression of life. Stripped of the false associations which have come to surround it, anarchism could be the most appropriate political tradition in the service of communal work.

Or such at least would seem to be the case for the United States. We have no Mao, and we are unlikely to find one. A nationwide communal movement here would have to start piecemeal from the bottom, rather than being prompted by national leadership. Anarchism is a flawed tradition for this purpose. At least in its dominant, nonreligious versions, anarchism is not clearly of sufficient transcendent force to sustain working communes in times of difficulty. Nor have ground rules for association between anarchist groups been developed in any detail, either theoretically or in practice. Still, anarchism is the nearest we come to having a body of political theory suitable to an American communalism. Implemented along the lines developed in this book, it could be a tradition of considerable force.

Part III: Possibilities

Chapter 9: Anticipations of a New Communalism?—Twin Oaks, Grateful Union, the Bruderhof

Throughout this book we have indicated ways in which American ideology, whether expressed through the dominant culture or through alternative-seekers, makes the development of communal work places extremely difficult. This is not simply a conclusion in the abstract. In a four-year search for such work places, we have found only a handful—and not from want of trying. We have visited several dozen intentional communities across the country, and have interviewed or corresponded with representatives of dozens more. We have attended a number of gatherings of communards and others working to escape from traditional work patterns. We have talked with most of the people conducting serious research into contemporary communalism. We have subscribed to more than twenty of the magazines which deal specifically with the American alternatives movement, and five or six of these have published notes from us describing our interests and our desire to exchange information. We have learned a great deal from all of this; for better or worse, little has had to do with communal work.

Such a search, we found, is more than anything an exercise in frustration. For one thing, communards operate on the (largely correct) assumption that people with nothing better to do than ask them questions should be viewed with suspicion. Commune-building is an endeavor of great seriousness even if little shared work is involved, and it tends to become unrecognizable to the participants when filtered through a computer program or some researcher's methodological bias. Unsurprisingly, the result is a considerable reluctance to be bothered. Even the groups described at length below, all three of which were unusually open and cooperative, showed some rough edges. After answering a number of our questions, for example, one of the Grateful Union people wrote: "Resist use as nutty putty datum to be molded into someone's thesis." Kat Kinkade, one of the founders of Twin Oaks, warns that "no honest person can write anything significant" about a commune without having lived in it (1973:3). And before allowing us to visit, the Bruderhof required us to sign an agreement never to publish anything about them without their advance written permission.* Such resistance to being "researched" is probably healthy, but it does little to facilitate a clear view from outside.

A more serious problem was the mirage effect: communal work place after communal work place shimmered briefly on the horizon, only to vanish at our approach. A Colorado design commune had disbanded in anger by the time we discovered its address. A Massachusetts woodworking commune proved to be an assortment of largely unrelated people sharing a loft full of machinery. A Canadian game-making commune on closer look became husband and wife and some interesting ideas. An Illinois law commune disintegrated just before our letter of inquiry reached it. An elusive Vermont candle-making commune had not produced a candle in five months when we finally tracked it down. A much-publicized commune in upstate New York turned out to be a couple of nonprofit businesses whose workers were also friends. Ultimately, we were forced to conclude that we were chasing something that by and large did not exist.

In part, this sense of futility followed from our own definition of what constitutes a communal work place. In everyday usage, "commune" has come to mean any group of more than two people who are not a nuclear family, who live or work or play or do something together at least part of the time, and who feel at least vaguely countercultural about it all. Had we followed this approach, insisting only that "work" be some part of the formula, we would have had an abundance of models. Our more restrictive definition, however, requires that at least three conditions be met:

> (1) the people involved live together, in the same housing or on the same land; (2) these people earn their income through joint work at a project or projects owned and operated by the commune; and (3) the group is bound together by a shared belief system, religion, or ideology.

---

* Such permission was granted for publication of the section on the Bruderhof which appears below. The group stresses, however, that this "should not be taken to imply approval or agreement with the facts or opinions expressed therein."

Other conditions could plausibly be attached: income should be divided on the basis of need; the group should limit earnings to a level consistent with a modest standard of living, or should at least avoid growth for its own sake; decision-making should be shared by all those concerned; the goods or services produced should be items for which society has a clear need, not luxuries. But these are unnecessary complications. From all experience, the three points cited above provide the minimum boundaries for a unit that can expect to overcome such centrifugal forces as individualism or the allure of the "real world." Unhappily, they exclude in themselves most communes in the United States.

But not all. We estimate that a hundred or so communal work places exist throughout the country, although this is no more than a guess. In four years of looking, we have heard tales of perhaps a dozen places that might have fallen within our definitional framework. Of these, we have confirmed the existence of three, which we have investigated through visits, correspondence, and a search of available literature. These groups make a nice study in contrasts. One is a highly rationalistic rural commune whose major business has been hammock-making. The second is a small urban group, of eclectic spiritual conviction, which deals in basically countercultural wares. And the last is a large Christian community, more than a half-century old, which supports itself by making wooden toys for children. Obviously, we cannot claim that these are a statistically precise sample of existing groups. But each is interesting in its own right. And were the lessons of their experience to be absorbed by others, they might serve to anticipate a broader move toward working communalism in the United States.

TWIN OAKS

The best-known of the communal groups formed in the last decade is Twin Oaks, which now has fifty or so members divided between two farms near Louisa, Virginia. Their fame is to some degree self-propelled. The group has long distributed an excellent newsletter, the first fifteen issues of which were published in book form in 1972. Another Twin Oaks book, by one of the founders, was published in 1973 after excerpts had run in two issues of *Psychology Today*.* The commune hosts an annual conference

---

* The newsletter is called *Leaves of Twin Oaks;* the collected *Leaves* are now available under the title *Journal of a Walden Two Commune. A Walden Two Experiment: The First Five Years of Twin Oaks Community* was written by Kathleen Kinkade. These publications are available from Twin Oaks Community, Louisa, Va. 23093.

for potential community-builders. Individual members have toured the college lecture circuit and participated in a number of intercommunal gatherings and projects. This might represent information overkill were it not
that Twin Oaks has a most unusual story to report. It was the first commune
to be based on the behaviorist model that B. F. Skinner outlined in *Walden
Two*. During a time when communes have been ephemeral, Twin Oaks
has lasted the better part of a decade. And it has become increasingly productive over time, to the point where collective enterprises provide most of
the group's income.

Background. Twin Oaks began in June, 1967, when eight people moved
to the first Louisa farm. The eight had met at a Walden Two conference
in Michigan the previous year. There, they had sensed enough of a common
search that they corresponded, arranged to meet again in Atlanta, and
finally decided to create a Walden Two of their own. Within two years,
the group numbered fifteen. At the end of 1971, there were thirty-six
members. A year later, there were close to fifty. With increased population
came physical growth as well. Two new residence buildings and a children's
house were constructed at the main location (Juniper). In 1972, a nearby
farm (Merion) was purchased and additional living space added. For
Twin Oaks, most of the first seven years were conspicuously ones of rapid
expansion.

Throughout this period, ideological focus has been provided by *Walden
Two*, Skinner's utopian description of a community based on the behaviorist principle of positive reinforcement for socially desirable acts. According to Kathleen Kinkade, "Because we have *Walden Two*, we do not
need a leader or teacher. Cooperation is possible because we have all, before
we even joined, agreed upon the general principles described in that book"
(1973:57). It is possible to make too much of this agreement, however.
Another member talks of Twin Oaks behaviorism in somewhat different
terms:

> Twin Oaks does not require its members to understand behavioral princi-
> ples. But because of the culture that has evolved here, people do tend to
> have at least an intuitive understanding of the principle of positive rein-
> forcement, for example. . . . When we pay greater attention (through
> praise, affection, and other ordinary social conventions) to desirable
> behavior than to undesirable behavior, we are functioning as "behaviorists"
> whether we know it or not. Much of the time we do know it and this, I

suppose, makes Twin Oaks more of a "behaviorist" community than other groups are. (Steven, 1973:2)

In this view, behaviorism has at least provided Twin Oaks a rough set of concepts through which to organize its attitudes toward interpersonal relationships—and this has clearly been important. But it remains an open question whether the result is a common world view sufficiently comprehensive and binding to sustain the group indefinitely.

In practice, Twin Oaks seems to find the essence of behaviorism in a willingness to experiment with techniques for helping individuals realize themselves more fully. Attempts in this direction have ranged from the bizarre (an early, short-lived experiment where members slept for three hours and worked for five around the clock) to the substantial (the work-credit system described below). Somewhere between these extremes, Twin Oaks has held group criticism sessions, employed outside encounter-group facilitators, arranged primal therapy marathons, and encouraged group support for individuals trying to free themselves of such bad habits as excessive smoking. The effect of these efforts on group life is unclear. Pointing out that "the right not to attend is fundamental to Twin Oaks's sense of liberty" (1973:158), for example, Kinkade notes that group criticism worked only for volunteers, who were often those who needed it least. If the concept of positive reinforcement is generally held, in other words, there is often resistance to imposing specific applications of this on the group as a whole.

Work. Twin Oaks has modest financial needs; annual expenditures amount to about $1,200 per person. But to earn even this much has been a struggle. In the commune's first year, almost all funds came from donations. For several years more, most income was earned by individual members in nearby cities. From time to time, attempts were made to generate revenue through projects at Twin Oaks itself: hammock-making, veal production, construction of programming instruments for psychology labs, addressing envelopes for a local business, marketing of wild herbs and organic vegetables, crafts production. Of these, only hammock-making has had any notable success, and that relatively recently. At first, hammocks were made but not actively marketed: "There is something about selling that terrifies us. It is obvious that this is and always has been our problem—no salesmen" (*Leaves* No. 8:7, reprinted in Twin Oaks, 1972). But in 1971, a salesman joined the group. Within a year, hammocks accounted for a third of the commune's income, and have continued to be the mainstay of the Twin Oaks economy.

More recently, Twin Oaks has experimented with home-building, drawing on the considerable knowledge its members have acquired in constructing their own housing. A local businessman contracted with the commune in 1972 to build inexpensive homes nearby, and construction began on the first of these in January, 1973. Over the summer, the most skilled Twin Oaks participant, himself a former contractor, and three others who had worked on the project left the group. Threatened by the potential dissolution of the business, Twin Oaks decided never again to allow such work to become dependent on the energies of a few people who might "wear out" or simply depart. Instead, they broke construction down into its component elements (foundation, framing, roofing, and so on) and established separate work crews for each. By placing greater responsibility on these crews, and by rotating members through them, Twin Oaks hoped to establish a broader base for future efforts. So reorganized, the work continued, and a second house was completed in late 1973.

Organization. Twin Oaks is organized as a nonprofit corporation under Virginia law. The corporation owns most of the group's land, businesses, and other assets, distributing all income received from these equally among the members. Twin Oaks has also established its own Unitarian Universalist Fellowship, which as a tax-exempt organization has become a logical recipient of donations from members or outsiders with significant amounts of cash to give the group. In turn, the Fellowship supports a number of the more "religious" activities of the members, including celebrations and rituals, and provides a subsidy for the Twin Oaks newsletter. Much of this structure is the result of improvisations over time. Particularly with respect to its corporate base, it is far from being wholly satisfactory, as Twin Oaks members are the first to point out. Questions about the corporation's "ownership" and handling of income are raised by the IRS after each set of tax returns, with a final accommodation yet to be achieved. With the possible exception of its handling of the group's Fellowship, Twin Oaks offers little in the way of guidance to communal groups seeking appropriate forms of legal organization.

The group's approach to the process of making decisions has been considerably more imaginative. At first, Twin Oaks assumed that this would take care of itself, since members would presumably see clear needs and respond to them spontaneously. But decisions were avoided, or were made badly, or were not followed up, and the group finally adopted a more formal system modeled on that in *Walden Two*. Now, a loose constitution states general principles: equality, communal ownership of property and care of children, nonviolence, the desirability of experimental approaches to social problems. Within this framework, a board of three "planners" makes policy decisions, subject to veto by two-thirds of the members. The planners choose their own replacements, as well as the "managers" who take day-to-day responsibility for specific community activities. At Twin Oaks, there are managers for virtually everything: gardening, cooking, vehicle maintenance, child care, cattle-raising, publications, labor allocation, and so on. In each case, the person appointed defines jobs, requests labor for them, and sees that they are carried out. Where other communes have foundered on an alleged anarchism requiring no one to do anything in particular, Twin Oaks has evolved a system that ensures that necessary work is accomplished.

In reconciling the needs of the community and the desires of individuals with respect to work, Twin Oaks relies on a system of "labor credits." Each week, members individually rank available jobs according to their desirability. Insofar as possible, work is then allocated according to expressed preferences, although most people will necessarily spend at least some time on jobs they would rather not do. To provide everyone a sense of "psychological equality" in this situation, people are given fewer credits for their favorite work (perhaps 0.9 credits per hour) and more for particularly burdensome tasks (1.5 credits per hour, say, for work near the bottom of a person's preference list). Everyone is required to accumulate the same number of credits each week—most recently thirty-five. But since those stuck with relatively more onerous jobs will work fewer hours for the same number of credits, nobody need feel cheated. This system, originally borrowed from *Walden Two,* has been revised by Twin Oaks over time. In its present form, it represents the commune's most striking contribution to American communal theory.

Individual and Group. The counterculture types who passed through Twin Oaks in its early years tended to be extremely critical of such features as the labor-credit system. Mandatory work was a violation of personal liberties, they said, and the elaborate scheduling system was just as antithetic to spontaneity. But as Twin Oaks points out, the truth is quite different: "*The {labor credit system} is a tool for promoting individual happiness. . . .* By providing a framework for the selection of work, people are able to make many different kinds of choices . . . about how to satisfy themselves" (Steven, 1973a). In the absence of such a system, either jobs would not be carried out (the countercultural pattern) or people would be likely to become fixed in work roles over time. The Twin Oaks system, however, gets things done while allowing individuals abundant opportunity to change jobs, experiment with unfamiliar work, or apprentice themselves to members with special skills.

At first glance, this arrangement would seem symptomatic of a happy synthesis of the members' sense of collective existence and their desire for an individualized form of self-actualization. But these are not forces that can easily be kept in balance, and the people at Twin Oaks to a disturbing degree appear to have clung to the "I-spirit" they brought with them from their former lives. In 1968, for example, when the *Leaves* asked members what they liked about the place, the responses were predominantly egocentric: "I like the fact that the work here promotes my own goals"; "I like the variability of schedule"; "It's nice . . . that I don't have to cook all the time" (*Leaves* No. 7:8–9, reprinted in Twin Oaks, 1972). And Kinkade reports a similar, more recent conversation with someone about his reasons for preferring Twin Oaks to the world outside: "Everything I do here is for myself" (1973:10).

If many of the Twin Oaks people search for points of reference in themselves alone, the group as a whole has taken steps to ensure that they can be alone in the search. As a matter of doctrine, married couples joining the group are carefully treated as if they had no special relationship to each other. When children are born, their "biological mothers" become simply more of the "metas" whose work assignment is child care. Twin Oaks has even enshrined the "need" for privacy as one of the ten points of its Behavioral Code: "INDIVIDUAL ROOMS ARE INVIOLATE. . . . We all need a place to be alone" (Twin Oaks: n.d.).

In line with all this, the people at Twins Oaks are relatively wary of intense commitments, to each other or to the group as a whole. Here is Mary, speaking of several members who have just left the commune:

> Right now I'm feeling a little sad thinking about those people and that I won't ever see them again. . . . But most of the time I don't think about them at all. There's too much else to think about, too much to do. And there are always new people to get to know. . . . (1973:9)

But not necessarily very well. The Twin Oaks structure allows members to go days without seeing one another. Much general communication on communal problems takes the form of extended debates through letters posted on the main bulletin board. At one point, a central intercom system was introduced in many of the buildings, so that members could hear community news without having to gather together. And the creation of a Twin Oaks "branch" at Merion had largely to do with letting a small number of people do their own separate thing in semi-isolation from the group as a whole.

The Twin Oaks experiment, in other words, exists in a state of considerable tension between its communal pretensions and the lingering individualism of its members. The consequences for group life are not healthy. Writing recently about a "heavy bout with loneliness" she had been through, one member noted regretfully that "being lonely here is quite common" (Donna, 1974:4). For this and comparable reasons, turnover has been high throughout the group's history. During 1973, for example, roughly one-third of the membership departed, to be replaced by new people. And transience of personnel in turn has made it difficult to create and maintain economic ventures of any complexity. Twin Oaks has something of a common ideology, and it has its moments of joyful communion. But it apparently needs more of both.

It is not a situation that could indefinitely continue. At some point, Twin Oaks will have to choose between abandoning its communal hopes or exploring in depth the group spirit and ideology it has partially established. Members may resist the latter course out of a vestigial American fear of the loss of personality through true group commitment. But the cases that follow give support to evidence of earlier chapters that such a fear is likely to be groundless.

THE GRATEFUL UNION FAMILY

Until recently, Grateful Union lay in patches around Boston. At the southeast corner of Harvard Square, the Grateful Union Bookstore dealt in esoteric literature, its one small room filled with volumes on Islam, the occult, meditation, alchemy, the cabala, Jung, ancient Egypt, the Tarot, and astrology. A few blocks farther south, near the Charles River, a shop called Earth Guild sold dyes, wax, beads, wool, string, corks, candle molds, and other craft supplies, along with a variety of books on how to use these things. Eight miles to the west, in the town of Newton, was a communal household of ten adults and four children. The Grateful Union Family was all of these—the people foremost, and the rest as an expression of their collective ambition: the pursuit of deeper understanding of what can be done with one's hands and spirit, in a context where work, income, and selves are shared.

The various pieces of the Family's lives, always linked in spirit, by early 1974 were beginning to flow together physically as well. The two stores were consolidated at the Earth Guild location. And a new 150-page catalog, beautifully crafted and illustrated, was the first tentative step toward an even more ambitious move. Were the catalog to generate a sufficient volume of mail-order sales, or such was the dream, the Family could carry itself off to the country. Settled, perhaps into an old mill, they would have a place where others could come and spend the day, working with resident craftspeople or sharing what they knew of weaving, natural dyeing, astrology. Friends would be nearby, running organic foodstores and other small businesses. No longer a series of oases in the city, the Family would have built around itself a community of kindred spirits. It was an ambitious dream, but Grateful Union had both the people and the disciplines to make it seem plausible.

Background. As a working commune, Grateful Union began in the spring of 1970, when four people who had been living together in a Cambridge apartment opened the Grateful Union Bookstore. During the summer, Earth Guild was established. That fall, the group (now six) rented a house together. Over the next several years, at least ten more people passed through the group, lingering for periods ranging from four months to three years. Still others came and stayed, and the group bought a larger house in Newton during the summer of 1972. By the beginning of 1974, Grateful Union had evolved from the original foursome to a complex structure embracing fourteen people, a house, a store, and two separate trusts to maintain ownership of the group's assets.

Work and Organization. Despite their organizational sophistication, the people of Grateful Union are engaged in basically straightforward pursuits: selling goods, raising children, maintaining their house. What makes them extraordinary is that they do all these things together, on a basis of complete equality. All members work in the store four days a week, for example, and devote a fifth day to the house, cleaning, repairing, cooking dinner, and taking care of the children. All share equally in income from their businesses, receiving weekly "salaries" that have ranged from $45 to $135 as business conditions have changed. Such income is hardly "private," however. During much of 1973, when salaries were $60 a week, only $15 of this was retained for personal use. The remainder was paid back into communal accounts to be used for group expenses. From child-care arrangements to financial organization, Grateful Union has structured itself in such a way as to underscore its members' sense of a common life.

At first glance, the legal framework of the Family seems startlingly intricate. A Grateful Union Trust owns Earth Guild, Inc., which in turn runs the store and provides group health care for those working there. In addition, there is a Grateful Union Family Trust to hold the mortgage on the communal house. Alongside, there is a household fund to pay for such common expenses as food, automobiles, insurance, and cigarettes. The creation of a Grateful Union "church," a move the group has contemplated from time to time, would add an additional organizational layer and complicate things even further. It is almost as if Grateful Union had been designed as a case study for fledgling lawyers and accountants.

Each element of this structure, however, meets a clear and specific need. The business was given corporate form, for example, to gain the advantages of limited liability and to establish eligibility for group health care. But to have stopped there would have raised even more difficult issues. Would shares of the house and business be allocated equally, or on the basis of funds originally contributed? If people left the group, would they be able to sell their shares to anyone they might find, or would remaining members be forced to raise the capital to buy out their interests? For at least some of these questions, there would probably have been no satisfactory answers; and the establishment of trusts to own business and house enabled Grateful Union to avoid them. Members are full beneficiaries of the trusts as long as they remain, but questions of "ownership" arise neither when they join nor when they leave. It is through participation and work, rather than through possession, that those in Grateful Union find their place in the group, and their legal arrangements affirm this.

Individual and Group. Even more to the point in explaining Grateful Union's communalism are the direct bonds between the people involved. Two of the four "founders" were sisters, for example, providing a blood tie to anchor the network of relationships that gradually grew around them. Attitudes toward their businesses are generally shared; as one woman told us, "we are all compulsive workers." Most important of all, members seem to have a common sense of spiritual direction. As noted, they have even considered reorganizing as a church. And even though they say that the church's first doctrinal principle would be a rejection of all doctrines, they clearly speak each other's language. For one thing, they read the books they sell and share what they find. More revealing still was their response to a visitor who suggested they convert their home workshop into a meditation room like hers. No, they told her, a better idea yet would be for her to turn her meditation room into a workshop. If the people of Grateful Union are "compulsive workers," it is because through working together they find the truest expression of their common spiritual understandings.

None of this, however, implies a homogeneity of lives or people. Although business policies are established by and for the group as a whole, for example, people over time have carved out their own specialized areas of responsibility within the overall work program. One person maintains the books and keeps track of accounts, another handles advertising and graphics, a third orders books, a fourth pays the bills, and so on. Outside of work, individual interests range from locksmithing to electronics to learning to play the banjo. There is no weakening of personalities here. On the contrary, those who comprise Grateful Union have found that an unusual degree of personal strength flows from their group bonds. Like the Bruderhof and other cases examined in this book, the Grateful Union experience supports the proposition that individual differentiation in communal environments is wholly consistent with a strong feeling of commitment to the group.

THE BRUDERHOF

One of the most remarkable expressions of the communal drive is the Society of Brothers, or Bruderhof.* Now more than a half-century old, the Bruderhof has grown to embrace more than 900 people in the United States alone, distributed more or less equally among communities in Rifton, New York; Norfolk, Connecticut; and Farmington, Pennsylvania. And the Bruderhof is extremely "productive." In addition to running a publishing house, the Society does a highly successful business in the manufacture and sale of wood toys for children.

The Bruderhof vividly illustrates the interdependence between deep religious faith and successful communal living. If it is difficult to imagine the Society's persistence through time in the absence of the faith its members have been given, it is equally difficult to imagine that faith as having had any social expression other than a communal one. In a society end-

---

* "Bruderhof" is the German word for "a place where brothers live." Strictly speaking, it therefore refers to any of the several communities established by the Society of Brothers. In line with popular usage, however, we here use "Bruderhof" to refer to the Society as a whole.

lessly trapped in this year's fads, the Bruderhof seems to some an anachronism. But it has more to teach of the sources of communal experience than do any number of the countercultural groups on which the media have lavished such attention in recent years.

Background. Immediately after World War I, in Berlin, what was to become the Bruderhof began to coalesce around Eberhard and Emmy Arnold. The Arnolds had dedicated their lives to joint Christian witness on their marriage in 1909; the horrors of the war drove them all the more urgently to find a form of living which could embody faith within a confused and demoralized society. In a series of meetings with others following similar paths, they gradually concluded, as Eberhard Arnold wrote later, that "voluntary associations of working people—who do not want to have anything to do with self-will, with separate existence, and with anything that is private any more—become signposts pointing to that final, ultimate unity of all men" (1967:14). In 1920, insight became reality as a small group moved together to a farm in the village of Sannerz. Six years later, the group had grown to include more than forty people, and larger quarters were found in the nearby Rhön Mountains. The Bruderhof had begun.

These beginnings were always held to be of greater-than-human inspiration. "Community can never be founded," according to Emmy Arnold; "it can only be given as a gift of the Spirit" (1964:46). Accounts of the Bruderhof's formative years are alive with testimony to the presence of the Spirit within the members: "Many times something broke through among us and gave an answer . . . which placed everything in a far higher light" (Ibid.:173). At critical moments, personal differences would be resolved, money would appear to stave off imminent bankruptcy, or a sense of direction would emerge from uncertainty. Recalling the time of her marriage to Eberhard, Emmy Arnold says simply: "We . . . wanted to put our common life entirely on the basis of faith. This faith has never let us down in any sphere of our lives" (Ibid.:15).

Faith was required in abundance in those years. In early 1934, Nazi insistence on a "proper" education for the Bruderhof children forced the group to send the children first to Switzerland and then to Lichtenstein. As conscription threatened the young men, they too left for Lichtenstein. When that refuge began to appear uncertain, an exodus to England began. In 1937, the Nazis closed down the Rhön Bruderhof, and the remaining members left for England. With the outbreak of war, however, England proved no sanctuary for a largely German group, and the Bruderhof was on the move again, this time to Paraguay. Through all this, other difficulties were rampant: Eberhard Arnold died in November, 1935; funds were forever inadequate to keep the group properly fed; disease (especially in Paraguay) took many lives. Not until 1954, with the opening of the first American *hof* (in Rifton), was the Bruderhof able finally to move toward the relative stability that it enjoys today.

Life and Work. One of the Bruderhof's founding texts is Acts 4:32, which reports that the early followers of Christ had "all things common." Even on the briefest visit to the Society, it becomes clear that it is not only "things" that are had in common there, but lives as well. The family group is extremely strong. But families live in common dwellings, their children spend large parts of the day together from the age of six weeks, and adults share work, play, meals, ideas, joys, and sorrows. At first glance, the emotional intensity that results is expressed most clearly in art and music. Rooms are bright with drawings, especially by the children. People sing at meals and meetings. The sounds of choral and chamber groups fill the evenings. This sense of joyful common experience is deepened by a closer look at daily life. Members apply the same care to work as to painting, and they bring the same concentration to casual conversations as to the playing of a string quartet. For the Bruderhof, faith is expressed in every part of life, by people acting together.

Under such conditions, to single out "work" for special attention—as we necessarily do here—is to risk a distorted picture of the Bruderhof.*
But if work is no more important than other aspects of the Bruderhof, neither is it less so; and the Society's approach to life permeates its two commercial ventures, the Plough Publishing House and Community Playthings. The Plough, for example, continues a tradition dating from the Bruderhof's earliest days of publishing works of Christian testimony. Today, many of these consist of the works of Eberhard and Emmy Arnold, or earlier writers such as Johann and Christoph Blumhardt, leavened by editions of songs and poetry for children. Work is distributed between Rifton (editing, design, distribution) and Farmington (where type is set by hand and

---

* In other ways as well, we have seen the Bruderhof primarily from outside and therefore have different—and considerably more limited—perceptions of it than do the members themselves. The Plough Publishing House has available a number of works which express the view from within. Their catalog is available on request from the Society of Brothers, Rifton, N.Y. 12471.

the books printed). Everything, from original stories to illustrations to translations of German texts, is the product of members of the Society. It is a truly communal enterprise, growing from the Bruderhof's deepest beliefs.

Other expressions of the Bruderhof way of life appear in the operation of Community Playthings, to which (male) visitors are normally assigned for work. Community Playthings produces a wide range of wood toys for children—blocks, chairs, trucks, tables, trains, gas stations, slides. At Rifton, roughly thirty people devote full time to this, dividing the work among themselves: initial cutting of the wood, planing, varnishing, assembly, inspection, shipping. Some of these jobs are highly skilled, with the same person always responsible for a particular task. Others are periodically rotated among the remaining workers. Although in structure this is close to an assembly-line operation, the objects that result are of a quality that is normally associated with crafts production. Sturdily and carefully made, the community's playthings are as pleasurable to the adult hand as they must be to that of a child.

If one's instinct is to say that the Bruderhof takes pride in this work, one would be missing an important truth. For "pride" is too self-important a feeling to reconcile with the sense of humility that the members try to bring to all their acts. People work with caring, as they live with caring, simply because that is Christ's way. And this assumption that the individual is in service to a higher cause takes other forms as well. The toy-makers are assigned their jobs as the community requires—nobody would assume the right to experiment with the planer, for example, in the interests of mere self-fulfillment. For one thing, fulfillment should come as readily from putting hoses on toy gas-pumps as from mastering a sophisticated piece of machinery, since both tasks are equally essential to completion of the job. For another, it is not the work that is fundamental in any case, but rather the heart of the worker.

This attitude toward work distinguishes the Bruderhof from such communal groups as the kibbutzim, where production is imbued with a sacred quality of its own. On our first visit to the Society several years ago, we found the machines untended and the workers all on the softball field. Spring had come that day, and everyone had decided it was far too beautiful to stay indoors. At a deeper level of meaning, the Bruderhof decided in the mid-1960s to cut back on its toy production rather than be tempted to hire outside workers and grow in wealth. In both cases, the same principle was operating: simplicity and joyousness of spirit take precedence over the merely material.* Work has to be done, and it will therefore be done right. But neither work nor the goods it allows the Bruderhof to buy are permitted to dominate life in the manner that the larger society has come to take for granted.

Organization. To present a legal face to the outside world, the Rifton group is registered in New York as a "membership corporation" with the stated intent of leading a Christian life and spreading the teachings of Jesus. For commercial purposes, the Bruderhof becomes "The Society of Brothers, Inc., d.b.a. [doing business as] Community Playthings." At tax time, the group encounters the IRS as a "non-profit organization with a common purse." The Bruderhof itself thus pays no taxes, except on its land. Instead, members file family returns each year, reporting income as if revenues had been distributed equally through the community. In all of this, the Bruderhof has found corners of the capitalist legal system that correspond surprisingly well to its own inner realities. It *is* an organization defined by its membership and common purpose. And if the Society in fact pays no salaries to its workers, it *does* provide them—and everyone else in the group—a more or less equal share of the food, shelter, clothing, and other goods it has available.

In form, the Bruderhof has a relatively complex internal structure. Housemothers allocate rooms and such personal supplies as toys, candy, toothpaste, and clothing. Work distributors assign jobs. One or more Servants of the Word provide spiritual guidance at each community, with a special role in both decision-making and the resolution of interpersonal problems among the members. An Elder, usually resident in Rifton, serves as first among the Servants of all the communities. This structure is deceptive, however. In practice, many issues are dealt with simply through informal discussion at the many points where people meet: work, meals, meetings, recreation. And important decisions are ultimately made by unanimous approval of the entire membership, which gathers for this purpose several evenings each week. If authority is recognized as legitimate for many purposes, in other words, it is not assumed that truth is the monopoly of those holding authoritative positions. For truth is ultimately a gift of the

---

* This deemphasis of the material is pervasive. Members dress simply, often in second-hand clothes bought in quantity by the community. Much of the machinery which Community Playthings uses was purchased used. Objects are functional, in other words; the Bruderhof feels little need to have shinier equipment or more fashionable clothing than its neighbors.

Spirit, which may act through anyone. Everyone therefore bears a responsibility for being open to this gift and for carrying its message to others.

The Individual. One basic fact about the Bruderhof communicates itself immediately to the visitor: people there are extremely alive, full individuals.* Creativity is one measure of this; and a disproportionate number of members are musicians, poets, composers. The range of a group's interests is another index. During our last visit we found ourselves in lively, informed discussions about such topics as European influence on Ethiopian religion, an American Indian demonstration then in the news, the Ra expeditions, conscientious objectors during World War II, and the writings of Chinua Achebe. More subjective still is simply the gut sense one has of people at first meeting. Our impressions were very much of strong personalities, whose distinctness has remained vivid in memory with the passage of time. For all their unity of purpose, those at the Bruderhof are anything but cut from the same cloth.

In part, this is the result of conscious effort to avoid the sort of insularity that could leave members withdrawn and passive. All children are sent to the local high school, for example, and most are then required to spend time living in the world outside before making the choice to become full members. But more basic still is the point that recurs throughout this book: where a common struggle of the spirit is felt deeply enough, individuals will find inner strength, rather than conformist oppression, in a genuinely communal group. Now in their sixth decade of living this condition, members of the Bruderhof would take this for granted. For most of us, it is a lesson yet to be learned.

CONCLUSION

One obvious characteristic of all these groups is an acknowledgement that "business" activities can be legitimate communal functions. Such a belief seems unexceptionable, but it is not. In the early unwillingness of Twin Oaks members actively to sell their hammocks, there is at least a hint of feeling that salesmanship is an unseemly quality for nice people to develop. Comparable attitudes have been prevalent among other alternative-seekers. When we asked if Vocations for Social Change would print a description of our research in their newsletter, for example, they wrote back that our

---

* For a similar view through another eye, see Paulus, 1969:75, 80.

inclusion of "conventional business oriented issues" (how to determine whether a given project will be viable, for example) gave an aura of "hip capitalism" to the blurb. In further correspondence and conversations, this proved a fixation. There was simply no way, it seemed, to justify a conscious desire to create a self-supporting commune. The groups described in this chapter have taken their enterprises more seriously, and their willingness to confront real business issues is as important as it is unusual.

Each of these groups has also come to terms with the need to have clear patterns of internal organization, and this again is a departure from recent communal norms. Keith Melville notes accurately that "most of the communes are experiments in leaderlessness, in erasing boundaries and eliminating rules" (1972:126). But as Kat Kinkade points out with equal accuracy, this does not in fact mean freedom from structure:

> Carefully analyzed, there is no such thing as an unstructured commune. . . . A group that chooses to have no government is not thereby going to do without one. It is merely going to deliver government into the hands of . . . those people who just naturally rise to the top. . . . Furthermore, there is no such thing as an unstructured division of labor. . . . An "unstructured" situation will quickly evolve into a structured one where certain people accept a role as workers and do the bulk of the work, while others do very little or avoid it entirely. . . . What the structured commune does is make a decision to do its structuring deliberately. (1973:23)

For a commune, the difference between the two approaches can be that between success and failure. Intentional communities with "structured" structures can last; groups with "unstructured" structures by and large cannot. By no real coincidence, the communal work places dealt with above all fall into the former category.

It is not enough simply to last, however. Just as important is to keep the imperatives of organization from choking off the commune's original ebullience. Most communards assume the choking to be inherent in the organization, and many social theorists agree: "As any . . . group develops a structure to carry out its goals, its original élan tends to deteriorate, and the routines set up by the structures tend to take over" (Oppenheimer, 1971: 274). In the most stark terms, communes might appear to face what Henri Desroche has called the choice between dying of effervescence and dying of organization. But this is to overstate the problem. While death by effervescence is almost immediate, death by organization can at least be long postponed. All three of our groups are pretty lively places, and the oldest is comfortably past its golden anniversary. Together, they seem to indicate that organization, while as inevitable as death, is not its equivalent.

It may be that the more corrosive effects of organization are at least partially avoided through a strong common value system. If few values are shared, the organizational structure must bear the full weight of the group's existence. Elan will then give way to procedures. Common aspirations, however, relieve the burden that formal organization would otherwise have to carry: where people act through shared dedication instead of institutional necessity, organization can express élan rather than having to serve in its stead as an integrative force. The groups studied seem to bear this out. Twin Oaks, with limited common values, has an organizational structure considerably more obtrusive than that of the Bruderhof, which has eighteen times as many people— and a deeply felt common religion.

These groups illustrate one final point, which by now should need little emphasis: individuality is more likely to flourish than wither in a close communal setting. Given a strong enough sense of common purpose, the individual need fear oppression from neither the group nor the patterns of organization it establishes to conduct its business. But to accept all this is not the final battle. There still remain a variety of technical, economic, and legal issues which must be resolved before a communal work place can take form. These are the subjects of the next two chapters.

Chapter 10: Communal Work—Examples, Technologies, Attributes

In the fall of 1971, the *New York Times Magazine* published an account of our adventures in the counterculture (French, 1971). In that article, we criticized the extent to which the counterculture had retained old-culture assumptions, and we suggested a need for people to develop a genuinely alternative "*counter* 'counterculture' culture" that would be rooted in communal work. Of the dozens of letters we received in response, a large proportion were from people who wanted to know more about this hypothetical next step. Most of the writers were established in traditional careers, many had children, and all were reluctant to enter what they saw to be the "hippie commune" syndrome: subsistence living, rootlessness, financial carelessness based on the assumption that money would "manifest" through welfare or donations as needed. But, they wanted to know, what was the alternative? If they detached themselves from the System, what work would they then do? At the time, we had little specific to say; now, we are at least marginally better able to respond.

Here as elsewhere in this book, we are primarily concerned with the small-scale communal work place. There is no particular theoretical reason not to extend this approach to the entire society, great economic units as well as small. As China demonstrates, a considerable degree of communalism can be built into even the most elaborate industrial operations. But to speculate at this point about the transformation of a General Motors assembly plant along communal lines would be an exercise in self-indulgence. We would like to see such a thing happen, and we believe that workers would in all ways be better off for it. But it is not an event of great imminence, and it seems preferable here to deal on a scale appropriate to smaller groups of people who may now be poised for experiments in communal work. We hope that General Motors and its equivalents will follow in time.

Restricting the discussion in this way still leaves complex, if not obvious, issues to be considered. Frazier, the central figure of B. F. Skinner's *Walden Two,* announces at one point that "the economics of a community are child's play," requiring little serious attention (1948:63). We have heard this sentiment from a number of those involved in the contemporary alternatives movement. But the reality is somewhat different. As anyone who has actually attempted to place an economic base under a communal group knows, several questions immediately arise. What work will the group do? Are technologies appropriate to communal work places available? Are some work processes more "communal" than others? Will the project selected be "profitable" enough to provide its members a living? Within what legal framework would this best be carried out? The first three questions occupy us in this chapter; the last two are the subject of Chapter 11. And in no case are their answers "child's play."

ALTERNATIVE WORK POSSIBILITIES

Although few have done it communally, dozens of thousands of people over the last few years have tried to break free from the constraints of traditional careers. Some have sought to apply their professional skills in more creative ways; others have abandoned their training in favor of new pursuits. These attempts have been just the beginning. With a little imagination, the range of work that could be made communal seems enormous.

Attempts. We have mentioned a variety of work experiments in previous chapters, and brief descriptions of a number of others follow. We have already registered at length our doubts about both the intrinsic value and the long-term viability of such experiments in the absence of a strong communal tie between their participants. Few of the projects described have had such ties, and many no longer exist for precisely that reason. Nonetheless, they represent first attempts at creating small-group work situations of greater human meaning than is generally available through "normal" careers. As ideas, all could be adopted by communal groups seeking an economic base.

The Ant Farm (Sausalito, California). Ant Farm described itself as a "commune/network" of people interested in environmental design, with an emphasis on technological experimentation. Among their projects were domes, air buildings, "nomadic hardware," and a "new age software." The Farm also published the *Inflatocookbook*, a handbook on how to apply their various design ideas. (Heathcote Community)

Behavior Research Institute (Providence, Rhode Island). The BRI intended to create an experimental community generally based on Skinner's *Walden Two*. Income was to be generated by providing a communitarian environment in which treatment could be given to delinquent, emotionally disturbed, or autistic children. At least two such children were placed by state institutions with BRI in its early stages.

Cumbres (Dublin, New Hampshire). Cumbres was founded in 1969 by Cesareo Palaez, who wished to create an environment conducive to personal growth among both permanent members and those who would pay for periods of instruction. Encounter sessions were held, lectures were provided on psychology and religion, and lessons were given in body awareness, Zen meditation, and T'ai Chi Chuan. Work, meals, and spiritual exercises were shared. Income was never sufficient to maintain the group, however, and it closed after two years of operation. (Kanter, 1972:196–198)

East Street Gallery (Grinnell, Iowa). The Gallery started as a cooperative attempt to start "a new culture based on the application of experimental psychology to social relations in hopes of finding more humane and meaningful relations and ways for people to live together." Money came from publishing, free-lance photography, and commercial production of print washing equipment. (East Street Gallery, 1973)

Family Pastimes (Perth, Ontario). From a small nucleus of people, Family Pastimes hoped to grow into a village dedicated to exploring the implications of Krishnamurti's teachings in daily life. In the interim, they survived in part by selling herb tea and a series of games they had invented: "Family" (a card game), "Community" (board game), and "Zen Blocks." All these games were noncompetitive, depending instead on cooperation among the players to achieve a mutual goal.

The Group (Greers Ferry, Arkansas).* The Group, sixty-five adults and twenty-five children in 1973, lived in Texas and California before moving to Arkansas. In Greers Ferry, they had a construction company, managed three motels, owned a bakery and butcher shop, published a weekly newspaper, and ran a school for their children. Most members lived in a converted commercial building, and all shared both resources and income. (Reed, 1973; Bevier, 1971)

---

* Not to be confused with "The Group" discussed in Chapter 5.

Heathcote Center (Freeland, Maryland). The Heathcote Center is a "school of living," oriented especially to homesteading skills. Seminars are held at the Center during the year on such subjects as health, carpentry, organic farming, canning, crafts, and construction methods. The Center also sponsors conferences on life alternatives and publishes a magazine, *The Green Revolution.*

Koinonia Partners (Americus, Georgia). In 1942, Clarence Jordan helped start a Christian community called Koinonia Farm. In the years since, Koinonia has assisted local farmers in establishing partnerships in farming and small industry, often on Koinonia land. Much of this is financed by Koinonia's donation-fed "Fund for Humanity." The core Koinonia group has long survived by raising pecans and selling pecan products through the mail.

KTAO (Los Gatos, California). KTAO was an "alternative" radio station, broadcasting eighteen to twenty-two hours a day to the southern reaches of the San Francisco Bay area. Operating with relatively little structure and a great deal of volunteer help, KTAO provided music (classical, folk, ethnic), an extensive schedule of interviews on controversial subjects, and live coverage of such community events as meetings of the San Jose City Council. (Fessenden Educational Fund, 1973:19)

The Lama Foundation (San Cristobal, New Mexico). The Foundation was established in 1966 as a place for work, meditation, and the study of spiritual disciplines. Early on, it put out *The Dome Cookbook,* a building manual. Later it published *Be Here Now,* an account of the transformation of Harvard psychologist Richard Alpert into Baba Ram Dass. Ram Dass continued to be associated with the Foundation and the spiritual "school" it ran to bring in additional money. (Greenfield, 1972)

The Law Commune (Palo Alto, California). Not really a "commune" (members did not necessarily live together), the Law Commune was established by ten lawyers and legal workers interested in reshaping the way law is practiced in America. Participants set out to handle such alternative legal work as political cases, challenges to local "anticommune" laws, and drug arrests. And this was to be done in an alternative way; salaries were based on need and decisions were made collectively. (Anderson)

Mad Brook Farm (Island Pond, Vermont). The Farmers made a variety of craft items, especially high-quality leather goods. They were also responsible for the *Green Mountain Trading Post,* a newspaper circulating throughout Vermont's Northeast Kingdom to advertise items for sale or barter.

New Alchemy Institute—East (Woods Hole, Massachusetts). The New Alchemists came together to conduct research and education designed to create a "greener, kinder world." Projects included testing varieties of lettuce for pest resistance, raising tropical fish for food, making wind generators from old auto parts, and building a hand-operated washing machine. Some money was raised through selling memberships in the Institute. (New Alchemy Institute—East, n.d.; Zilles, 1973:3)

New Vrindaban (Moundsville, West Virginia). In 1972, New Vrindaban was a collection of three farms and about sixty-five people seeking to live the teachings of His Divine Grace A. C. Bhaktivedanta Swami Prabhupada. In addition to accepting donations, the group earned some of its money through the production of Spiritual Sky incense, which was distributed through the temples of the International Society for Krishna Consciousness. New Vrindaban also hoped to establish an Institute for Vedic Culture, an art and music center, and a press. (Wheeler, 1972)

A Pinch of Love (Putney, Vermont). This group settled on a farm in the Green Mountains of Vermont and began to produce baked goods using "natural" ingredients. At first dependent on sales to organic foods stores, especially in the Boston area, A Pinch of Love later moved to sell primarily to food co-ops. While the bakery brought in most of the "earned" income, members sought through farming to establish roots in the soil as well. (Pinch of Love, 1972)

Symbas Experimental School (San Francisco, California). A part of Project ONE (see Chapter 6), the Symbas School provided "nongraded" education for students aged 13 to 18. The students themselves were to define their own activities with the assistance of staff members. Much learning was expected to take place through participation in the various organizations resident at ONE.

Synergic Design (Cambridge, Massachusetts). Closely related to a nine-member commune in Franklin, New Hampshire, Synergic Design was involved in the construction of yurts, the sod-roofed shelters native to Mongolia. Members of the group traveled as far afield as Mississippi to school others in the art of yurt-building. At one point, they built six yurts to be used for craft demonstrations and sales at the Glen Echo amusement park outside Washington, D.C. (Conroy, 1972: K1)

Vocations for Social Change (Canyon, California). The VSC collective was formed in 1967 to collect and disseminate ideas on how to use work to forge a new society. Although at first concerned with "work" outside the System (political collectives, free schools, the radical media, and so on), VSC later focused on direct attempts to restructure corporate society from within. Never particularly interested in self-supporting communes, the collective nonetheless managed to support its own members through fees from lecture tours and donations for its magazine, *WorkForce*.

Walden Three (Providence, Rhode Island). Walden Three was yet another Skinner-derived community. Its major business was typesetting. Using relatively sophisticated equipment, it worked on textbooks as well as such publications as the *Collected Leaves of Twin Oaks* and *Communitarian,* a magazine briefly put out by Walden Three itself. The group also planned to establish a foundry for nonferrous metal working.

Walrus Woodworking Collective (Roxbury, Massachusetts). The Walrus group shared tools, knowledge, and workspace. Among their products were beds, tables, potters' wheels, and looms. Income was distributed equally. Walrus had a loose association with another woodworking group, New Hamburger, whose shop was one floor up in the same Roxbury warehouse.

Wayfarer (Portland, Oregon). The Wayfarer was a natural foods restaurant operated by a small group of people, some of whom also lived together. Jobs in the restaurant were rotated, and money was pooled to support those working there. Efforts were made to create a cooperative atmosphere in which workers and customers would feel themselves to be joining together around the act of eating. (Cascade Collective, 1972:7)

Wood Heap Garage (Brattleboro, Vermont). Wood Heap was a two-car garage and a bunch of tools. The owners fixed cars, especially Volkswagens, at rates that were negotiated with their customers. People were encouraged to use Wood Heap's facilities to do their own repair work, with the owners available to help with the jobs or to provide instruction on how to do them. (Vermont News Service, 1973:19–20)

Proposals. The projects listed above—restaurants, crafts, free schools, repair shops, woodworking, professional collectives, and so on—are broadly representative of the vast majority of alternative work experiments carried on in the last decade. As discussed below, however, their scope is somewhat limited. Other recent proposals by alternative-seekers do little to expand the sense of possibilities for communal work. From four years of *The Mother Earth News,* for example, come such suggestions as the following: running a lemonade stand (billed as "An Ideal Fun Way for a Commune to Make Heavy Bread") (May 1970:28), fruit picking, being a forest fire lookout or a ranch hand, home typing, maple sugaring, selling sod to racetracks, fly-tying, raising earthworms, knitting, and growing tulips. *Mother's* major concern is with homesteading and subsistence farming, and its readers may in fact be interested only in marginal sources of income to support the simple rural life. Nonetheless, there is a disconcerting lack of weight to such ideas.

This impression is reinforced on reading *Mother's* offspring, *Lifestyle!,* a magazine ostensibly written for the entire range of alternative-seekers. *Lifestyle!* hasn't been around long, but in its first year it seemed to be on a similar tack: features on work suggested window-washing, summer jobs in the suburbs, running a used bookstore, substitute teaching, scissors-sharpening, art shows, and short-term employment in factories. The tone is the same elsewhere. In *How to Live in the New America,* William Kaysing proposes a number of "do-it-yourself ideas that are appropriate for *anyone!*": wine-making, tree trimming, poster printing, advertising by mail, bottle collecting, furniture refinishing, running a remnant store, being a tourist guide, painting curbs, and operating carnival concessions (1972: 17–32). And John D. Martin, in *The Home Income Guide,* weighs in with "Over Six Hundred Ways to Make Money at Home," including making feather flowers or log sculptures, running a secondhand toy shop or a watermelon stand, cleaning carpets, operating a pet cemetery, growing watercress or fuschias, customizing slipcovers, turtle farming, tax consulting, and rock painting (1969b).

More technologically ambitious proposals have come from groups like the Aquarius Project, originally of Berkeley. Aquarius put considerable effort into theoretical study of "postscarcity communes," which would be highly automated for provision of both immediate communal needs (food, clothing, tools) and commodity production for sales outside. Much of the group's attention was devoted to the internal affairs of such projects, which would be organized along "council communist" lines. But Aquarius also gave thought to what might logically be produced there. One early idea, for example, was manufacture of ferroconcrete boats for floating communes, an activity Aquarius estimated would have a return to labor of almost $10 per hour. To supply land-based communes, computer systems could be developed and sold to run "controlled environment" inflatable dome greenhouses. Aquarius also saw potential markets for such devices as "real-time, performance interfaced moog synthesizers," Kirlian photography rigs, and myoelectric biofeedback systems. The group also proposed manufacture of methane converters, a popular suggestion of which more will be said in the "energy" section below.

Critique. Some inspiration follows from looking at alternative work experiments proposed or carried out in recent years, but not a great deal. From the communal standpoint, the "spare change" approach of Kaysing, Martin, and *The Mother Earth News* is perhaps most disappointing, and doubly so because of what this reflects of widespread attitudes among alternative-seekers. All the countercultural qualities we noted in Chapter 5 are there. Many of the jobs are seasonal (fire lookout, fruit-picking, maple sugaring), ensuring that commitments of time are limited. Virtually all are quickly learned, so that one can avoid becoming deeply involved with the task or being significantly changed through doing it. Few could seriously be thought of as ways to make a living (raising earthworms? collecting bottles?), serving instead simply as ways to tide oneself over between checks from somewhere else. Nor are most of these jobs that any significant number of people would do together; they are geared rather to the solitary individual floating through time and space. They are more hobby than work, in other words, and communes in search of an occupation have little to learn from them.

Even the more serious of the jobs mentioned above pose problems of their own. Disproportionately, they involve the provision of services rather than goods. And while this may be natural in an increasingly service-oriented economy, the limited market they tend to meet raises basic questions. Legal services, auto repair, care of children who would otherwise be in institutions, community-oriented radio: these involve work that potentially can serve everyone. But much of the rest represents a closed system where upper-middle-class alternative-seekers serve only each other. There are no laundromats or gas stations here. Instead, there are encounter centers, organic restaurants, underground magazines, and designers of inflatable domes. The same pattern holds in the more limited number of cases where people have turned to production of goods. Organic bread, handicrafts, incense, ferro-concrete boats, and Kirlian photography systems tend to be on the shopping lists only of the relatively affluent.

Many of these goods and services are useful, even elevating—to those who can afford them. But they are symptomatic of a tendency for "dropouts" to carry their class background with them, perpetuating in "alternative" ways the gulf that isolates them from the bulk of society. Given the education and training that most dropouts have had, much of this is inevitable. It should also be possible, however, to work communally around products that meet more widespread human needs. Groups seeking to take such an approach will find few ideas in the work experiments of the last decade. But this is as much a function of the experimenters' predispositions as it is of any difficulties in pursuing a broader range of alternatives.

Occupations for the Communal Work Place. In fact, the range of jobs communes could undertake is almost without limit. Useful service occupations tend to be inherently small-scale, and the same is true to a surprising degree in manufacturing as well. Attempts at auto-making, steel manufacture, or petrochemical production would be too ambitious for most groups. But much production is carried on within working units of considerably smaller size. Roughly 60 percent of all manufacturing units in the United States have fewer than twenty employees, and almost 80 percent have fewer than fifty. A relatively few larger units tend to absorb a disproportionate share of the labor force. But 40 percent of all manufacturing workers are in units of fewer than 250 employees (Stein, 1971:49). Many such units exist within the organizational framework of larger corporations or conglomerates, but there is no overriding reason why this should have to be so. If you seek ideas for communal production, in other words, look at the goods and services you consume. More than likely, a communal work place of manageable size could supply them.

In practice, some items may be more appropriate than others for communal output. As we illustrate in the following chapter, for example, the efficiencies of communal living make it possible for people to survive at a "wage" level far below that required by workers in the surrounding culture. Communes therefore have a competitive advantage in the production of goods and services for which labor payments are a relatively large proportion of total costs. The list of such inherently "labor-intensive" goods is lengthy, including lumber and furniture, apparel, textile-mill products, printing, leather goods, and machinery, in addition to the standard communal craft items (Eisenmenger, 1967:80). The provision of most services has the same bias. Paul Goodman proposed that alternative work experiments in rural areas might include "a better life for people with welfare checks, places for the primary education of children, havens for the aged and the harmless 'insane' . . . real vacations instead of the ersatz vacations of summer resorts" (Introduction to Nearing and Nearing, 1970:xii–xiii). In addition to their intrinsic value, such occupations are obviously quite labor-intensive, making them especially suitable for communal work.

Goodman's proposals are responsive to another communal tendency, that toward settlement in rural areas. As we suggested in Chapter 4, some such move may be desirable to protect groups from the strongly disintegrative forces of the city. But this step imposes limitations of its own on the range of things a commune may easily do. If the city provides the primary markets for the group's products or is the source of its raw materials, firms based closer by will have lower transport costs and thus a competitive edge over the rural commune. Lower labor costs within the communal work place may partially offset this factor. But a more important step to minimize its impact would be to concentrate on production of goods for which transportation expenses are only a small part of total price. A commune selling sophisticated electronic components in the Boston market would suffer little penalty by moving to northern Vermont, in other words. But it could be in considerably more trouble if it were making bathtubs or steel filing cabinets.

Whatever the work finally chosen, various sources offer further guidance. The Department of Commerce has published a series of "Urban Business Profiles" which provide basic information on such activities as dry cleaners, furniture stores, machine shop job work, and industrial linen supply operations. The Small Business Administration produces bibliographies of publications relevant to particular businesses, including restaurants, job printing, woodworking, bakery products, radio and television shops, and bookstores. Trade journals and associations provide information and services; suppliers of manufacturing machinery can deliver useful data as well. If a group in formation needs to acquire new skills, help will be available from sources ranging from the local high school's evening vocational program to a wide variety of written material.* Once a communal group finds its work, technical assistance of a very substantial sort is there for the asking.

TECHNOLOGY FOR THE COMMUNAL WORK PLACE

To establish a communal work place reflects a desire to become disentangled from the social and economic patterns of the surrounding culture. The disentanglement can never become total, but many alternative-seekers would like to push it as far as possible. In terms of alternative work groups, this would take the form of "liberation" from such things as the use of dehumanizing technologies within the work place and dependence on regional power grids outside. Independence and simplification are the watchwords of this school of thought, and considerable effort in recent years has gone into finding the technologies that would allow people to live according to such precepts. A number of the ideas which have emerged from this search might be adapted by communal work groups to their own needs. And an even larger proportion represents goods these groups might themselves consider producing.

Energy. Most recent work on alternative technologies has concentrated

---

* See, for example, the U.S. Office of Education's *Vocational Instructional Materials for Trade and Industrial Occupations Available from Federal Agencies* (1972).

on new sources of energy. Energy gained currency as an urgent issue as far back as late 1971, when *Scientific American,* MIT's *Technology Review,* and *Science and Public Affairs* all gave special attention to the issue. At about the same time, a new magazine, *Alternative Sources of Energy,* emerged from the energy "underground." Through 1972 and early 1973, small groups held energy conferences in such scattered locations as New Mexico, Wisconsin, Maryland, and Vermont. Simultaneously, research into alternative energy sources was underway within both traditional institutions (Oregon State University, the National Science Foundation, McGill University) and various renegade groups (the New Alchemy Institute, New Mexico's Zomeworks). Awareness of these concerns remained largely limited to the cognoscenti until mid-1973, however, when the energy crisis brought them to the center of American consciousness.

At the national policy level, thought about new power sources tends to focus on tidal, nuclear, and geothermal energy, along with large-scale capture of solar power. Such approaches also draw attention from people seeking alternative life styles. But for this latter group, relatively modest proposals are of even more immediate concern. At a School of Living conference in April, 1973, for example, people were distracted from discussion of a participant's solar-heated house only by a visit to a neighboring farm where electricity was provided by an old waterwheel (School of Living, 1973:9).* And at any such gathering, stories are swapped about people who run their homes on windpower or their cars on methane gas produced from chicken manure. For alternative-seekers, logically enough, any revolution in energy use should begin at home.

All of this interest has produced considerable research into small-scale energy technologies. *The Mother Earth News* has published articles in at least six separate issues reviewing in considerable detail experiments in converting manure, garbage, and other organic wastes into methane gas. Windpower has received extensive attention from magazines like *Undercurrents* (MacKillop, 1972) and *Alternative Sources of Energy,* which devoted much of its issue of January, 1973, to the subject. Although its primary audience consists of the people of "less-developed" countries, McGill University's Brace Research Institute has conducted a number of wind and solar power studies whose results could be applied in the overdeveloped world as well (Brace Research Institute, 1972, 1973). Enough other groups are moving along the same lines that, should you choose to abandon your

---

* For a more complete description of a "solar house," see Steve Baer, 1973:8.

local utility company in favor of "natural" power, there will be many ready to show you the way.

"Home Technologies." All these efforts are but the most visible expression of current interest among alternative-seekers in what might be called "home technology." According to the British technologists Robin and Janine Clarke, the basis for such technology is that

> it should enable its practitioners to adopt a life style which is satisfying and ecologically sound; which is in harmony and close contact with nature; and which provides better ways of satisfying basic wants at greatly reduced capital cost and at a labour cost which is compatible with the values of the new life style. (1972)

For the Clarkes, this implies a broad measure of self-sufficiency within the home, or perhaps a cluster of homes. And this in turn suggests development of technologies which would allow such living units to provide their own food and water, as well as energy. To create these technologies, the Clarkes and friends in late 1972 established Biotechnic Research and Development, a residential collective in Wales.

Comparable thinking is reflected in experiments elsewhere. A civil engineer in England, for example, is in the process of converting his home into a "complete living system." Solar energy will be used in the production of heat and electricity, rainwater will be collected and recycled, sewage and wastes will be composted or used to make gas, and food will be grown through hydroponics. In a similar vein, three Manchester architects have designed what they call an "eco-unit" in which little would be drawn from the world outside save rainfall, wind, sunshine, and stray insects. With these as raw material, and with creative use of land and wastes, the eco-unit would be able to provide its inhabitants with food, clothing, power, and water (Wood, Eastman, and Carden, 1972). Closer to home, *The Mother Earth News* plans establishment of a research center which would investigate many of these same problems (*Mother Earth News,* n.d.).

The "closed-system home" approach has influenced more ambitious projects as well. Prior to the military seizure of power in Chile, for example, the University of Lancaster's Peace and Conflict Research Programme had proposed creation of a "self-organizing, ecologically viable" community in the southern part of that country. Although the population of this community was projected at 500 people, its basic technological elements were largely extensions of the family-scale plans already mentioned: wind and solar power, methane production, waste recycling, provision of food, and so on (Peace and Conflict Research Programme, 1973). And two California groups—Communitarian Village and the Pahana Town Forum—were moving in similar directions, even though the "alternative" communities they hoped to create were to have memberships, respectively, of "several hundred" and 2,500 people (Communitarian Village, n.d.; Pahana Town Forum, 1972). All of these groups have given token attention to possible output of goods. But the primary focus of their creative energies clearly lies elsewhere, in the "home technologies" of food, water, and power.

Critique. Robin Clarke sees the thrust of these alternative technologies as leading to something like this:

> a countryside dotted with windmills and solar houses, studded with intensively but organically worked plots of land; food production systems dependent on the integration of many different species, with timber, fish, animals and plants playing mutually dependent roles, with wilderness areas plentifully available . . . ; a lifestyle for men and women which involved hard physical work but not over-excessively long hours or in a tediously repetitive way; an architecture which sought to free men from external services. . . . (1973:75)

Clarke calls this a "new Utopia," and it has much to recommend it. Local production of power from abundant energy sources such as sun and wind has obvious merit. Efforts to become less dependent on industrial society in such matters as food are at the very least not uncongenial to the spirit of communal groups. And there is considerable allure in the idea of a total life-system that would require minimal expenditure of money and not much more work—except tilling the soil, which alternative-seekers view as more self-actualizing than laborious.

Such thinking, however, raises as many questions as it answers. The "home technologists" will be using a rich assortment of store-bought goods in all these endeavors, at least at the outset: light bulbs, wire, cooking utensils, glass, pens, hammers, generators, nails, paper, plumbing fixtures, and much more. Where is the money to come from to pay for such things? Traditional jobs or savings, presumably, with the assumption that these would no longer be necessary once the truly "ecological home" was built. But expenses continue—phonograph records, replacement parts, land taxes —and these require a continuing source of income, however small. What is to supply this? When posed at all, the question is generally pushed off into the dim future. First things first, and these are the technologies of the home. In many ways, the home technologists are thus a more imaginative extension of the counterculture. That movement also sought to reduce its cost of living,* growing some of its own food and cutting back on consumption generally. It too was willing to fudge the rest through odd jobs, savings, or gifts. And most important of all, it also took for granted that somebody out there in the straight world would always be producing the nails and utensils it needed. The home technologists are serious people. But in retaining such assumptions, they sharply diminish their ability to create genuine alternatives. Experiments in creative homemaking are surely important, but so are attempts at creative production of the whole range of socially needed goods and services. In choosing to fight only half this battle, those pursuing the technologies of energy, water, and food are being all too con-

istent with the antiproduction bias of the counterculture.

There are lessons here for communal work places nonetheless. Although limited in scope, such new technology has considerable merit in its own terms; and working communes would do well to examine its relevance to their own domestic needs. Beyond that, the generators, windmills, and other paraphernalia involved might be well suited to communal production. There have already been groups trafficking in such equipment. In Massachusetts, Earth Move sold conversion kits for running cars on fuels other than gasoline. And in England, two editors of the *Ecologist* established Low Impact Technology Ltd. to provide waterwheels, solar heat generators, and "organic farming equipment," as well as consulting services on how to use these. The next step would be for alternative groups to make, as well as sell, such products.

Intermediate Production Technologies. Should a communal work place decide to make these goods or others, however, there is a further technological issue it is likely to confront. On a number of counts, such groups may wish to avoid production methods that rely on elaborate machinery. Money may simply be lacking to invest in expensive equipment, for example. Further, a communal work place has the advantages noted above in applying its low-cost labor to more labor-intensive production patterns. If located in a rural area, the group will face limitations on the availability of cheap electricity to run power-hungry equipment. And most communal groups will

---

* Two well-publicized books of the period were *How to Live on Nothing* (Shortney, 1971) and *Secrets of Saving Money* (McLean, 1970).

seek to keep jobs as creative as possible, avoiding work processes that leave little to do but push buttons on the console of a sophisticated machine. For all of these reasons, there is considerable incentive to find simpler, "intermediate" technologies for communal production.

But where are these to come from? If many American manufacturing units are small in terms of numbers of employees, they often rely on facilities that would be hardly transferable to most communal ventures. In 1967, for example, the average corporate maker of apparel or other fabricated textile products had depreciable assets worth nearly $130,000. In the furniture and fixtures business, the average was more than $240,000; in leather and leather products, as well as in printing, publishing, and allied industries, over $300,000 (U.S. Internal Revenue Service, 1971b:38–42). And these are relatively labor-intensive industries; the averages are even higher for capital-intensive products. These figures can be misleading, since in each case a few large corporations raise the average considerably. But they are indicative of a tendency for American businesses to be heavily capitalized, using sophisticated machinery to maintain productivity at high levels. Examples of intermediate production technologies are not likely to be found here. And as already noted, the "home technologists" have done little research in this area.

There remains one place where research into small-scale technology might logically be expected to be underway: the "less-developed" world. In such overdeveloped areas as the United States, Western Europe, and Japan, capital tends to be relatively abundant, labor scarce, and populations docilely adjusted to large-scale, depersonalized production methods. In other areas, however, the situation is reversed. And the need is great there for the discovery of technologies which are relatively inexpensive, labor-intensive, and not overly disruptive of the communal basis of traditional social patterns.

To date, however, most research along these lines has been limited to the sort of "home technologies" discussed above. In its *Village Technology Handbook* (1970), for example, Volunteers for International Technical Assistance concentrates on such topics as water resources, health, agriculture, simple construction methods, and such "home improvement" items as solar water heaters, stoves, and bedding. Although it has recently moved to prepare a series of industrial profiles, E. F. Schumacher's Intermediate Technology Development Group has largely confined its research to the same kinds of problems. When the Massachusetts Institute of Technology received a grant to study adaptations of technology for developing countries, the project proved to have more to do with energy, water resources, and housing than with small industry (Reinhold, 1971; and MIT, n.d.). Private groups such as World Neighbors, Technoserve, and Partnership for Productivity—all of which provide technical assistance to rural projects abroad —edge away from comparable concerns only to the extent of providing some management assistance to small businesses.

Productive intermediate technology remains a matter of live concern. But as Mahbub ul Haq has queried,

> where does it exist? I found very little evidence of it in the developed countries.... There are no great improvisations going on in the developing countries themselves and no major research institutes devoting their energies to the development of intermediate technology. The only place where I found something resembling intermediate technology was in mainland China, but there has not been much transfer of it to the developing countries.... (1971:10; see also Jackson, 1972:23)

This is not from want of talk, as a gabble of conferences has been held on the subject.* But the conferences have tended to be short on specifics and long on assertion of principles, sometimes of a suspiciously conventional sort: "it was necessary to keep in mind the main object . . . which was to transform developing countries into modern industrial/agrarian States" (United Nations, 1972b:18). In a couple of cases, groups have endorsed the idea of establishing an international inventory of available technologies from which small-scale businesses could draw ideas (McRobie, 1971:70; United Nations, 1972a:20). But even this modest proposal has seen little in the way of implementation.

It would seem that in the area of intermediate technologies, communal work places will have to make their own discoveries. Bert F. Hoselitz, among others, argues that already "for all but a handful of industrial processes there exist varying technologies calling for varying plant sizes and for varying ratios between labor and capital" (1971:61). Hoselitz further maintains that equipment suppliers in some countries, notably Italy and

---

* See, for example: German Foundation for Developing Countries, *Development and Dissemination of Appropriate Technologies in Rural Areas* (workshop report), 1972; Intermediate Technology Development Group, "Conference on . . . Appropriate Technologies for . . . Developing Countries," 1968; U.N. Department of Economic and Social Affairs, *Transfer of Operative Technology at the Enterprise Level* (report of expert group), 1972b, and *Appropriate Technology and Research for Industrial Development*, 1972a; Catholic Rural Life, "Populorum Progressio . . .: A Symposium on Intermediate Technology," 1968; Hawthorne, *The Transfer of Technology* (based on OECD Istanbul seminar), 1971.

Japan, have already come up with creative adaptations of machinery to the needs of relatively labor-intensive projects.* Over the long haul, research groups may catalog these or make discoveries of their own, most likely intended for the use of small-scale business in developing countries. But progress is likely to be slow. If existing technologies prove too rich for the blood of communal groups, they are largely on their own in finding alternatives.

WHAT WORK IS "COMMUNAL"?

We dealt with the search for alternatives to sophisticated technology primarily because relatively poor, simplicity-seeking communal work places will need modest capital equipment. But there are other issues here as well, the most important for our purposes being that capital-intensive processes appear to destroy human interconnections between workers, rather than creating a sense of collective endeavor among them. That is, work as now organized seems inherently "uncommunal." In response, seekers after alternative life styles have instinctively tended to abandon industrial pursuits in favor of things like vegetable gardening, where the human touch is more apparent. Little genuine communalism has resulted, however, raising the question in turn of whether these activities are themselves truly "communal." And if they are not, what work *is* communal?

There are at least two problems in dealing with this question. First, little research has been carried out to relate specific work activities to the social interactions among workers engaged in them. What has been done tends to take modern industrial processes as given, and seeks only to discover what kinds of social arrangements will best serve these.** Communal work, in other words, has been foremost among nobody's research priorities. Thus, our conclusions here will necessarily be highly speculative.

Second, production methods are in themselves only a partial determinant of the social structure of the work place. In an analysis of work among "nonindustrial" peoples, Stanley Udy asserts that certain aspects of social

---

* See, for example, *Guidebook for Rural Cottage and Small Industries,* a Japanese catalog of tools and machine specifications (CeCoCo, n.d.).

** Much modern organization theory, with its T-groups and "work-enrichment" programs, is of this sort. More tragically, the same bias is applied to situations which are already communal, as in developing countries, and where communal realities are ignored or viewed as an obstacle to "progress" which must be quickly overcome. See, for example, the articles on social aspects of economic development by Hoselitz and Nash in Finkle and Gable, 1966.

solidarity can be generally predicted from technology alone (1959:126). But in industrial systems, the problem is more complex. Factories producing the same goods, for example, may be highly communal on Israeli kibbutzim and riven with interpersonal alienation in America. Nonetheless, various sorts of work are likely at least to embody tendencies conducive or antagonistic to communalism. And it is worthwhile to speculate as to what some of these might be.

Simplicity versus Complexity. For the counterculture, much of the appeal of gardening lay in its apparent simplicity: "The kinds of jobs to be done around the land often require no special skills and provide an opportunity for everyone to work equally—even the children—rather than undermining the brotherhood with excessive specialization" (Kanter, 1972:53). But there are also forces in such simple operations that may in fact work to undermine the group. Labor so unskilled that "even the children" can do it rapidly becomes boring, and people may simply walk away from it. At the beginning, Twin Oaks exempted gardening from its labor credit system on the assumption that people would do this work for the sheer communal zest of it. But one chore after another lost its savor and was added to the labor system to ensure that the work was both done and spread among the group (Kinkade, 1973:41). In less structured communes, the process more typically ended with a handful of people assuming responsibility through most of the growing season, the group as a whole coming together only for the harvest. In either case, gardening tended to be more divisive than cohesive. Perhaps such simple tasks should be viewed with suspicion by groups in search of communal work.

If gardening (to have a few organic vegetables in the fall) is simple, farming (to make a living) poses a contrary problem. Since it involves a wide range of complex skills, from tractor maintenance to soil preparation, the danger of "excessive specialization" in farming is very real. Someone can become the resident mechanic, others can develop a proprietary interest in the fruit trees, a marketing "expert" can appear, vegetables can become the purview of a still separate group—and the commune can end up a loose association of only partially overlapping interests. While this tendency is even more apparent in large manufacturing operations, agriculture can clearly fall victim to it as well. When they moved to the United States, for example, the Bruderhof chose to abandon farming as a way to make a living, having found through lengthy experience that such work separated people both physically (in different fields or orchards) and psychologically (as specializations arose).* If too little specialization is anticommunal, in other words, so may be too much.

If not carried too far, a certain complexity of work structure seems functional for communal work places, since preserving challenge and variety in the midst of unity is one important objective of such groups. At least in a group's early stages, however, complexity might profitably be minimized. Communal ties are then most tenuous, people most in need of activities that reinforce their sense of being together. If people feel that they are sharing in one another's work, or at least that they clearly understand it, a greater sense of wholeness will emerge than if specialized tasks are shrouded in mystery. And people will then feel more competent to enter into the consensus-based decision-making process to which most such groups aspire. As communal bonds grow stronger, greater complexity can presumably be tolerated. But it should be handled gingerly at every stage.

Variety and Uncertainty. A work structure that provides variety of effort, rather than sameness, also seems to feed communalism. The Bruderhof has been highly successful in spite of minimizing work rotation, but it has achieved in other ways a degree of common dedication that can sustain people in doing the same work day after day. Most groups forming now, however, will confront the sort of desire for variety of which Gordon Yaswen speaks in recalling his days at the Sunrise Hill Commune:

> Community offered me a far more diverse gamut of roles than I ever incurred elsewhere. Here—in a single day—I could be a farmer, mechanic, carpenter, driver, accountant, writer, dishwasher, laborer, and committeeman, and never feel "stuck" in any one of these. . . . For once I felt whole: my life was balanced, and my growth even. (1971:24)

And if such individual gratification is advantageous in building group loyalty, there are other helpful factors at work as well:

> Job rotation can be extremely effective as a communion mechanism, for it increases the area of the individual's responsibility to the group rather than limiting it to one task, and it emphasizes that the member is ready to perform any service the community may require of him. . . . (Kanter, 1972: 96)

---

* Separations due to job specialization can take complex forms. In a study of several industries, Paul Lawrence and Jay Lorsch found, for example, that members of different departments tended to have sharply different orientations to time—sales people looked to the short term, researchers to the long (1967:34). Such differential attitudes can flow imperceptibly into nonwork relationships, feeding divisiveness, the sources of which are not clearly recognized by those involved.

On a number of counts, a little variety in communal work would seem to be a good thing.

If true, this conclusion would dovetail neatly with the arguments above for relative simplicity of tasks. If people are to change their work with any frequency, each job should be simple enough that no long period of training is required. But just as too much simplicity can lead to boredom, too much variety can lead to chaos. The Sunrise Hill Commune lasted only a few months, in part because people were so busy exploring a "diverse gamut of roles" that jobs requiring sustained effort, like building living quarters for the winter, were never completed. To create a working commune will require that certain things get done, and this in turn may require some limitations on job rotation. But the possibility of such variety, even if not fully realized, is probably worth guarding.

Change in communal work patterns may come about in other ways, with effects that are more ambiguous. Demand for a product may sharply fall, doubts may arise as to the best way of producing it, supply may be affected by external forces like raw material shortages or poor weather. Such uncertainty can teach humility: "a farmer . . . is not altogether in control. That too is very good; there are gods" (Goodman, 1972:34). Complacency and routine may be broken down, releasing energies otherwise unused. And of particular importance here, people may be drawn together by crisis, transcending whatever grievances and interpersonal games might be afflicting them. Some occupations are especially open to these forces: farming, education (where new teaching methods must continually be reviewed), urban retail outlets (a competing store may open next door at any time), and so on. At first look, communes engaged in such work might appear to be fortunate.

As usual, however, there is a conflicting aspect to the story. In his study of nineteenth-century communal groups, John Humphrey Noyes attributed many of their difficulties to an undue "fondness for land," since farming "is the kind of labor in which there is the most uncertainty as to modes and theories, and of course the largest chance for disputes and discords in such complex bodies" (1966:19). Uncertainty, in other words, can be a mixed blessing. But there is a distinction to be made here. Noyes is speaking of confusions as to "modes and theories" arising within the group, an obvious source of divisiveness to which such other occupations as education are also prey. Given the possible fragility of their initial ties, communal groups might do well scrupulously to avoid this kind of work, where egos are recurrently thrown into uncertain combat. Short of calamity, however, confusions arising from outside may have the more salutary effects outlined above; and communal work places have less to fear from them.

Inwardness and Outwardness. Many communes have tried to generate items for their own consumption, particularly food. Up to a point, this seems a sound path to follow. If members are providing concrete goods for common consumption, a visible link between work and survival is provided around a process in which all can share. And such a concentration on activities that start and finish within the group can help establish the boundaries around it that may be needed to ward off the centrifugal tendencies of the society outside. Any search for total self-sufficiency would be chimerical, of course. Land taxes and other cash expenses will intrude into the most utopian retreat, and some product will have to be sold in the world beyond the commune's gates in order to pay these bills. But if "inwardness" is valued, much of it can be preserved even so by relying on mail-order sales, say, in the manner of Twin Oaks or the Bruderhof.

Again, however, there are qualifications to be added. In studying industrial organization, Paul Lawrence and Jay Lorsch began with the idea that sales personnel, who are "accustomed to being concerned about customer relations, would be expected to care more [than other personnel] about fostering positive social relationships among their co-workers" (1967:33). Their data confirmed this expectation, and something of the same tendency emerges from the groups we reviewed in Chapter 9. At least to the casual eye, Grateful Union, whose members deal daily with a wide variety of customers, seems to have a somewhat more intimate group life than prevails within Twin Oaks or the Bruderhof, which sell primarily through the mail. And this seems to come naturally to the Grateful Union people, where the other groups appear to rely more on formal mechanisms to facilitate interaction. This may not be the whole story, since other important variables are at work here as well. But there may nonetheless be something valuable for communal groups in the idea of maintaining a measure of routine contact with people outside.

Summary. Together, the criteria above can cast at least some light on the degree of "communalness" of specific work possibilities. A woodworking operation such as that of the Tana Commune (Chapter 3), for example, may be inherently communal. Production methods are sufficiently demanding to be a challenge to those participating, but most tasks remain within reach of anyone choosing to learn them. A certain variety of jobs can thus be built into each person's work schedule. While enough external uncertainty exists to keep the group on its toes (will the cabinet-making contract be renewed?), production methods themselves are sufficiently standard that people need not spend endless hours arguing bitterly over philosophy or technique. And while routine contact is provided with others through retail sales, geographical isolation maintains certain boundaries that help the group define itself.

Other kinds of work may be relatively uncommunal. For example, printing and publishing, one of the standard "new culture" aspirations, involves discrete skills of considerable sophistication: design, illustration, typesetting, running the press. In this situation, people are most likely to carve out separate areas of expertise, with little common participation in any single task. So far as work requirements are concerned, in fact, there is no reason why the various jobs involved could not be scattered across the country; the United States postal service could serve as the prime integrating mechanism. Even if everyone is in the same location, job rotation may be minimal, with changes in the work situation more likely introduced through events from outside—and possibly calamitous ones (after months of work on a book, nobody wants to buy it). Work contacts within the group may disproportionately center on such thorny questions as what to publish next, questions which may bring people's egos into sharp conflict. And contacts outside may be both spasmodic and limited to whoever is negotiating the next distribution contract. For a commune, there are probably better things to do.

All of this is to be taken with a grain of salt, of course—no absolute principles are involved. If an assortment of printers decided to form a commune, they would clearly be better off at printing than at woodworking. The same would probably be true of a group of people who *thought* they wanted to be printers. In the latter case, however, the group might do well to inquire of itself whether the appeal of printing lay in part in its very "uncommunalness," in the separations it embodies. If the group's motives proved genuinely communal, it might then wish to give serious attention to developing integrating mechanisms to overcome such separations. The point is simply that some jobs are more communal than others, and no commune in search of work can afford to ignore the factors that make this so.

Chapter 11: Making Communal Work Work
—Economics and Law

Having agreed at least tentatively on the venture that will provide its economic base, a communal group's work has only begun. Some determination must be made in advance as to the project's financial viability. Patterns for distributing income among members of the group must be arrived at. Decisions must be made as to the legal forms within which land will be owned, commercial assets held, and business conducted. Account must be taken of governmental requirements with respect to licensing, zoning, sales taxes, unemployment compensation, income tax withholding, and Social Security payments. And accounting procedures must be established. Only when all of these things have in some way been dealt with can the commune begin the serious business of earning its living.

THE ECONOMICS OF THE COMMUNAL WORK PLACE

The basic tool for determining whether a given project will succeed or fail is the "feasibility study," an analysis of a business's markets, technical processes, capital requirements, and projected costs and revenues over time. Although it may seem obvious that some such study must be conducted before resources are invested in a project, the recent history of communal groups is replete with instances where the obvious was ignored. The cost of ignorance can be high; Twin Oaks, for example, lost $1,500 at one point buying and feeding cows who were to have been used for nursing calves in a veal production program. Unfortunately, nobody thought to check in advance whether newborn calves were available for purchase in the area. They were not available, or at least not in sufficient numbers to justify the investment, and the project failed (*Leaves* No. 13:1–2, in Twin Oaks, 1972). Given adequate feasibility analysis in advance, this project and many similar ones might have turned out differently.

This is not to say that all business contingencies can be foreseen, or even that they should be. Were a communal group able to anticipate with perfect accuracy all that would befall its business—the periods of struggling to survive, the unexpected loss of vital contracts, the breakdown of machinery—it might never push forward with the venture at all. But groups tend not to anticipate such periods of adversity, and that is often to their advantage. Albert O. Hirschman, who speaks of the forces which limit our foreknowledge of events as "the Hiding Hand," summarizes the workings of the principle this way:

> since we necessarily underestimate our creativity, it is desirable that we underestimate to a roughly similar extent the difficulties of the tasks we face so as to be tricked by these two offsetting underestimates into undertaking tasks that we can, but otherwise would not dare, tackle. (1967:13)

At least within limits, we are blessed by our lack of precognitive powers.

Communal groups need not add to these blessings, however, by pursuing ignorance where knowledge is possible. Most "new-culture" experiments of the last decade have simply happened, without feasibility studies or financial analysis, generally around the energies of somebody with a particular skill or driving interest. In some cases, like that of the Grateful Union Family (Chapter 9), the result has been a fairly solid economic enterprise. But more typically, such groups either have long since gone under or have run continuing deficits requiring work outside the group or the support of some financial angel. For people with more serious aspirations to communal success over the long haul, giving thought in advance to economic problems is an effort well worth making.

Feasibility Studies for Communal Businesses. Businesspeople invest money in order to make more money. In practice, this means that they will consider the range of available investments according to the after-tax returns that can be realized from each, allocating funds to the most profitable. According to the textbooks, this process is the driving force behind the capitalist system, the source of our national greatness. In some respects, communal ventures of the sort we have been discussing must share the concerns of the traditional investor, at least to the extent of ensuring that as much money comes into the business as goes out. But at significant points, their sense of economic reality may lead them to approaches far from the textbook examples. To illustrate this, we outline the kind of feasibility study the Tana Commune (Chapter 3) might have carried out before setting forth on its woodworking venture.

To recall: the Tana Commune began with ten people in the summer of 1968. From the beginning, the group chose to build its financial future around woodworking, which seemed a way to meet real consumer needs and promised to provide satisfying work for those participating. Of equal importance, several members of the commune brought considerable woodworking skills with them. As a start, the group planned to establish a relatively limited line of salable products: desks, tables, bookcases. Other work, such as subcontracting on construction jobs or assisting neighbors in their building projects, could eventually be introduced. But these projects were left to the future; the first task was to determine whether the commune could live off its core group of products.

Commune members first surveyed the market for these goods, talking at length with furniture and department stores in Boston and New York to determine demand and prices. Satisfied that the market indeed was there, several people then checked with other woodworking operations to refine their sense of the equipment and technical processes their project would involve. At the same time, others were contacting hardware manufacturers and lumberyards to check availability and prices of raw materials. Information was collected at auctions and through catalogs on the cost and specifications of needed equipment. Finally, an estimate was made of the cost of converting one of the commune's farm buildings into an adequate workshop. All these things done, the group sat down together to see whether they had a viable enterprise in view.

To begin with, the Tana people calculated the investment that would be required to establish their business. Here, the primary concern was simply whether their pooled resources—less than $10,000 available for this purpose—would be adequate to cover the initial outlay. To everyone's great relief, anticipated investment costs came to only $7,920, broken down as follows:

Physical Plant		$1400
renovation of outbuilding (including heat, insulation, wiring, lighting)	$1250	
preparation of "clean room" for finishing	150	
Office Supplies		605
typewriter	350	
file cabinet	80	
furniture	75	
desk calculator	50	
letterhead stationery	50	
Brochure (for sales promotion)	100	100
Pickup Truck	1500	1500
Equipment		3565
12" table saw	300	
12–14" radial arm saw	300	
36" band saw	450	
saw blades	400	
circular saw set	50	
single-surface planer	450	
6" belt sanders (2)	350	
flat table belt sander	100	
lathe	250	
router	125	
miscellaneous hand tools	500	
tool grinder	40	
bench and vises	150	
vacuum cleaner	100	
Legal Fees	250	250
Contingency Fund	500	500
Total Investment		$7920

Once assured that the workshop could be fixed up and equipped, the group turned to a projection of costs and revenues resulting from the business's operation. For their first full year of production (1969), they assumed that commune membership would have grown to about twenty-five, of whom perhaps ten would be working in the shop. By the second year (1970), membership would have reached its anticipated peak of fifty, with twenty people in the shop. Not until the third year (1971), however, would markets be consolidated, people fully trained, and production problems solved, allowing for maximum output. At this point, the group would be producing each year 350 desks, to be sold at $120 f.o.b.; 600 tables at $75; and 600 bookcases at $35. Subsequent years were expected to follow the 1971 pattern. Given these assumptions, the income picture looked like this:

	1969 (25 people)	1970 (50 people)	1971 (50 people)
Revenues			
desks (350 in 1971, at $120)	$18,000	$36,000	$ 42,000
tables (600 in 1971, at $75)	18,750	37,500	45,000
bookcases (600 in 1971, at $35)	8,750	17,500	21,000
Total Revenues	$45,500	$91,000	$108,000
Expenditures			
wood, fittings, finishes, glue	$12,000	$24,000	$ 27,250
sharpening of carbide blades	20	40	40
saw blades (replacements)	150	300	300
sanding belts (replacements)	50	100	100
office supplies and postage	50	50	50
telephone	400	600	600
"rent" (share of commune's mortgage payment and land taxes)	1,000	1,000	1,000
repairs to building	100	100	100
heat and electricity	1,000	1,400	1,400
maintenance of vehicle	750	1,000	1,000
insurance	1,000	1,000	1,000
depreciation	950	950	950
Total Expenditures	$17,470	$30,540	$ 33,790
Income (revenues less expenses)	$28,030	$60,460	$ 74,210
less taxes*	$ 0	$ 0	$ 0
Available for Living	$28,030	$60,460	$ 74,210

One final piece of information was now required before deciding whether to go ahead with the project: the cost of keeping the commune members alive. Independently, an estimate was made of this:

	1969 (25 people)	1970 (50 people)	1971 (50 people)
food	$12,000	$24,000	$ 24,000
clothing	2,500	5,000	5,000
electricity and heat (excluding woodshop)	2,000	2,500	2,500
telephone (excluding woodshop)	800	1,500	1,500
books and records	500	1,000	1,000
maintenance of cars (excluding woodshop pickup)	2,000	4,000	4,000
auto insurance (excluding woodshop pickup)	750	1,000	1,000
health insurance	2,500	5,000	5,000
property insurance (excluding woodshop)	2,000	2,000	2,000

* For at least the first three years of the project's life, the commune assumes that all income will be paid out for basic living expenses. No "profit" will accrue to the woodworking operation, and it will therefore pay no taxes. For the IRS, revenues allocated for living expenses will be handled as if they had been paid in equal salaries to all workers, who will then pay taxes on these "individual" earnings. This is much the same procedure as that followed by the Society of Brothers (Chapter 9).

mortgage and land taxes	4,000	4,000	4,000
repairs on buildings	400	400	400
school supplies	250	500	500
stationery and postage	150	300	300
personal allowances	4,500	9,000	9,000
income tax (personal)	500	1,000	2,000
contingencies and miscellaneous	5,000	10,000	10,000
Total Living Costs	$39,850	$71,200	$ 72,200
(available for living, from above)	($28,030)	($60,460)	($ 74,210)

For each of the first two years of operation, the shortfall in income apparently would be more than $10,000. But by the third year, the commune would be making more than it needed to live. With a little judicious trimming of expenses, the Tana people decided, the early deficits could be cut back. And later surpluses could be used to repay loans that might be needed in the first two years. It seemed worth the gamble, so they proceeded—and lived happily ever after.

Feasibility, Traditional and Communal. Something like the previous process has been implicit in the decision of many alternative work collectives to establish themselves in business. The example above differs primarily in the care with which data—especially concerning cash flows—were gathered by the Tana people in advance. In the work collectives, intuition and hopefulness have tended to play greater roles. This difference is not unimportant, since careful preinvestment analysis can warn groups away from projects that would only separate them from their money. But this aside, Tana and its counterparts are akin in significant ways that distinguish all of them from the traditional business approach to the analysis of investments.

An example of this is the importance that alternative groups attach to the work process itself. A project is simply not "feasible" unless the tasks involved feel good to do. At a conference on new life styles several years ago, we suggested that groups looking for occupations might consider making standardized products like aspirin, where private brands stand a fair chance of financial success. The reaction was one of horror: who could conceivably want to stand over an aspirin machine all day? Better to make leather belts or something equally creative, even though there would be little hope of surviving off such projects alone. A group like the Tana Commune would be more temperate in its views. But even here, the preference could be for challenging work with limited returns, like woodworking, rather than more alienating work such as aspirin-making where income might be greater.

The same reversal of traditional priorities holds in judging the product itself and the people it is designed to reach. The conferees at our life style meeting were insistent that consumption of aspirin was simply a symptom of a society so sick that it gave people headaches, and they held that to produce aspirin would be to endorse that underlying sickness. Wearing leather belts, on the other hand, seemed an index of health, and that was a market they were willing to satisfy. Again, a Tana Commune would be less doctrinaire, but it would no doubt still be sensitive to the fact that many of its goods were priced out of reach of all but the relatively affluent. In response, it might move over time to develop a more modestly-priced line. Or as woodworking groups like Boston's New Hamburger have in fact done, it could devote a significant portion of its time to low-paid or voluntary community projects. In either case, to produce useful goods and to make these available to the people most in need of them would be concerns at least as great as the profits accruing from the work.

Traditional businesspeople might argue that they too seek to produce truly necessary goods and to devote an important part of their cash and energies to useful civic endeavors. The most cursory glance at the shelves of any store, or at representative corporate income statements, should show this to be false. But there is a deeper level at which many alternative work places differ unarguably from traditional businesses. In the example above, the Tana people decided to go ahead with their wood shop on the reasonable promise that they could cover minimal living costs from its proceeds. Such an approach would appall the average corporate executive, who feels that investments must be made in the activities yielding the highest profit, and that the prospect of realizing only "minimal living costs" should be no grounds for investing at all.

A traditional look at the prospects of the Tana wood shop would have had quite different results. Revenues would have been taken as given in the estimates above. Expenses would have been adjusted to include an item for salaries.* For each year of operation, expenditures would be subtracted from revenues, giving that year's income. Taxes would then be deducted and depreciation allowances added back in, resulting in the net cash flow for the year. Since the standard approach insists that future net cash flows from business operations must together be greater than the initial invest-

---

* The Tana people appear willing to work for $1.80 per hour, which yields the $72,000 that the commune requires on the assumption that twenty workers are each putting in 2,000 hours of labor per year. This would mean adding to the expenditures listed above $36,000 in salaries for 1969 and $72,000 in all subsequent years.

ment, we would then be almost ready to calculate the advisability of the wood-shop investment according to traditional criteria.

There is one more refinement to be added, however. In general, we assume that the promise of receiving $1 next year is worth less to us than the reality of having $1 today. And the promise of $1 two years from now would be worth still less. In interpreting a business's financial estimates, we must therefore discount future cash flows at some rate that reflects our preference for present money over future money, say 8 percent compounded each year. It is the sum of these discounted cash flows over time which must exceed our present investment in the project—and by as much as possible. Using this approach the Tana investment looks like this, projected over ten years:

Year	Revenue	less Expense	equals Income	less tax	plus depre-ciation	equals Net Cash Flow	times DF*	equals Discounted Cash Flow
1969	$ 45,500	$ 53,470	− $ 7,970	$0	$950	− $ 7,020	.926	− $6,501
1970	91,000	102,540	− 11,540	0	950	− 10,590	.857	− 9,076
1971	108,000	105,790	2,210	0	950	3,160	.794	2,509
1972	108,000	105,790	2,210	0	950	3,160	.735	2,323
1973	108,000	105,790	2,210	0	950	3,160	.681	2,152
1974	108,000	105,790	2,210	0	950	3,160	.630	1,991
1975	108,000	105,790	2,210	0	950	3,160	.583	1,842
1976	108,000	105,790	2,210	0	950	3,160	.540	1,706
1977	108,000	105,790	2,210	0	950	3,160	.500	1,580
1978	108,000	105,790	2,210	0	950	3,160	.463	1,463

Total Discounted Cash Flow, 1969–1978   − $ 11
(versus original investment in 1968 of $7,920)

Clearly, this investment is far too unprofitable to be justified in conventional business terms. For the Tana Commune, however, profitability is not the relevant measure. For a limited outlay, the commune's fifty members could embark on a worthwhile project that would enable them to live indefinitely at a comfortable standard of living. This is no way to get rich, but most alternative groups would be satisfied just to comfortably survive. In the spring of 1970, for example, Twin Oaks opened a small grocery store to serve the neighboring community. Seeing no reason to make more than $1.50 to $2.00 per hour from their labor, they set prices at a level

---

* DF = discount factor, at 8 percent. Tables giving discount factors at a wide range of rates are available, among other places, in Financial Publishing Company, n.d.

designed to yield returns of this magnitude. As it happened, income never even approached the low point of the projected salary range, and the store was abandoned (*Leaves* No. 12:2–3; in Twin Oaks, 1972). But to live comfortably and happily would have been quite sufficient for them—as for the Tana people. And why should it be otherwise?

Continuing Issues. Once a commune establishes its business, a further range of issues must be dealt with that will continue through its lifetime. As a start, an accounting system is needed. This will be most obviously essential at tax time, when various levels of government will show interest in the business's affairs. But it is equally necessary to provide a clear financial picture for those making decisions from day to day. Beyond that, the keeping of accurate accounts can make comprehensible to all members the continuing state of their business, and thus the efforts they should expect of themselves to sustain it. Hints for establishing an accounting system can be gleaned from such publications as the Small Business Administration's "Financial Recordkeeping for Small Stores." But for many groups, the hiring of an accountant to set up their books would be money well spent.

Less predictable as to timing, but equally a part of any business's operations, is the periodic crisis. This can arise as a need to finance new equipment, as a problem in marketing a product, or in any of a thousand other forms. In many cases, guidance could be provided by congenial groups that had already dealt with such problems. Other sources of help include the Small Business Administration, which provides various management services to small businesses. Among its other offerings, the SBA sponsors SCORE (The Service Corps of Retired Executives), which was established to help groups unable to afford professional consultants. At least in their early stages, communal work places are likely to fall squarely into this category. For them to arrange a visit to their commune in time of need by a retired executive could well prove illuminating for everyone concerned.

Prescriptions for dealing with the issues above are much the same for both traditional and communal work places. There is a further problem, however, which communes are likely to want to deal with in a manner all their own: the distribution of business income. Convention has it that salaries are set by the workings of the labor market; highly skilled workers are paid more than are those with less to offer. Profits remaining after salaries and other expenses have been met are then paid to the owner. It is a neat and tidy system, at least on paper, and it is much revered in free-enterprise rhetoric. But it ignores and often violates such principles as justice, social solidarity, and responsiveness to individual need, principles that communards are likely to consider overriding.

Difficulties immediately arise, however, in proposing systems for distributing business income that would be responsive to these principles. The capitalist system takes for granted that money is passed out according to certain economic laws designed to foster effort and efficiency. If the resulting pattern of income distribution is judged to be somehow "unjust," that is not the economist's problem. Others may wish to fiddle with this, redistributing a pinch of money here and there around the edges of the system. But it is clearly understood that they cannot tinker too much with the iron laws of economics, lest incentives evaporate and the system break down. At best, social and economic considerations can maintain an uneasy truce as distinct, often conflicting, concerns.

We are taught to take this state of affairs for granted, but it has not always been so. In an extraordinary body of work, the economist Karl Polanyi sought to demonstrate that our current analytical separation of economic and social questions is an isolated historical phenomenon. As George Dalton has summarized the case, Polanyi showed that in most societies through history, "the institutions through which goods were produced and distributed were 'embedded' in—a subordinate part of—social institutions: that the 'economy' functioned as a by-product of kinship, political and religious obligation" (Dalton, 1968:xii). Instead of "free-market" mechanisms as the basis for distributing income, most societies have relied on patterns that reflected such obligations: "reciprocity" (the systematic exchange of gifts between relatives and friends) or "redistribution" (collection of money or goods in a central fund for redistribution among the people as a whole).*

Serious communes have typically rejected the "market" system of income distribution. The underlying rationale for this rejection has been expressed by Max Delespesse: "As soon as people are rewarded according to some evaluation . . . of their kind of work, of their contributions or their 'responsibilities,' . . . we enter into the abstractions of the capitalist system" (1972: 5). Less abstract and more personal is "redistribution" of goods by the community to its members, and adoption of such a system has been a general characteristic of successful communal groups. In her study of such

---

* There are elements of "redistribution," of course, in even the most relentlessly market-oriented systems. The United States, for example, redistributes money through welfare and other programs. But this is a negligible part of our total economic activity, where in a redistribution-oriented system it would be dominant.

nineteenth-century groups, for example, Rosabeth Kanter found that they "did not pay wages to members for their labor in the community, either in the form of money or credit, whereas many unsuccessful groups did" (1972:95). Most successful communal enterprises today—the kibbutzim, Grateful Union, the Society of Brothers, Twin Oaks, and others—have likewise tended to minimize salaries or pay none at all, distributing goods instead by community decision.

Polanyi's contribution is to put such tendencies in their rightful historical place as normal expressions of community feeling, rather than as the aberrations most Americans would see them to be. As Michel Sautois has pointed out, "Sharing supposes a 'we,' a common spirit and activity capable of supporting the community in permanent fashion" (1971:53). Lacking a group "we-spirit" or lives in common, most Americans can imagine no way of distributing income other than individual wages. But once communalism is embraced, some system of sharing by group decision becomes not only possible but essential. The communal world-view does not admit of any other solution.

The sharing of goods and income does not imply any rigid, mathematical equality in what people receive. In all communal work places we know of, individual differences in need and personality are accounted for in the allocation of goods. But this can be a complex process, one in which the interdependence of individual and group can find subtle expression. Delespesse puts it this way:

> Every man has the right to have the material goods he needs to live and to grow; they are a necessary extension of himself. The *need* must be evaluated according to a basic criterion, the person himself; but the person not only as seen by himself . . . but as seen also by others. For it is through dialogue with others that I can discover what my real needs are. (1972:2)

Within a commune, the process of income distribution is clearly a metaphor for the communal process as a whole.

At a superficial level, what we have been speaking of here sounds vaguely like the process through which the counterculturists shared the goods they had. As Elia Katz described one northern California commune, for example, "one gives anyone whatever is asked for with the knowledge that after a while equal distribution will have been attained and one can start roaming tent to tent in search of food and dope and they will be provided" (1971:179). But like the counterculture itself, this process was largely without human connectedness, save through the accident of roamers touching briefly on their way to another tent. In the sorts of communal work places this book is about, goods are made available around an intimate flow of caring, knowledge, and interdependence. And the goods involved are those that the common effort of everyone concerned has made available. The one process is profound, the other casual; their respective impacts on the participants will have greatly different meaning.

There is one final point to be made here. The communal sharing of income is likely to be most straightforward when resources are limited and needs clear. A group earning only enough to feed and clothe its members has few decisions to make as to how to distribute resources. The same group with a little affluence is commonly thought to have greater problems—individual preferences for use of its "surplus" might conflict, straining the unity of the group. The success of a group like the Bruderhof in preserving unity in the face of a half-century of increasing wealth, however, indicates that such problems can be solved. Given the comfortable standard of living which at least some communal work places could expect ultimately to achieve, it is worth considering the factors that can keep wealth from becoming a divisive force.

As mentioned in discussing the kibbutzim (Chapter 7), the strains on communal solidarity may be most severe where the growth of income is relatively rapid. When growth is maintained at a more leisurely pace, the daily requirement for individual choices among new material goods is less overwhelming, and the prospect for integrating changing patterns of individual consumption into the communal framework is commensurately greater. Even more important, however, is simply the way in which people within a group tend to define themselves. If egos are large, and if they find validation through possession of material objects, the greater availability of such objects will necessarily be disruptive. It is our assumption here, however, that in communal work places both tendencies will have become largely subordinate to forms of individuation which are both less material and more oriented to personal interaction. Wealth may still cause problems in such a case, which is one reason why those at the Bruderhof have chosen to limit theirs. But there is no a priori reason to consider these problems insurmountable.

COMMUNAL WORK PLACES AND THE LAW

If the total reality of communal work places is not in fact defined by economic and legal concepts, it may sometimes appear so. We have spoken of a wide range of economic issues; the variety of legal questions a commune may confront is at least as complex. Often, a lawyer is the only person qualified to deal with these, a prospect that communes of limited means may find depressing. The recent creation in some states of prepaid legal insurance plans may take the edge off the problem in the future (De Baggio, 1972:45–46). But for the moment, communal work places must count on periodic outlays of money for legal advice. What follows is *not* such advice. We are not professionally qualified to provide it, and the law varies from state to state—or from locality to locality—and from day to day. But it is at least a bare outline of the major issues communal work groups may have to confront.

Communes and "Family Law." Before moving into an area, a communal group should find out something about its zoning laws. In places zoned for single-family residences, ordinances often define "family" in such a way as to limit the number of "unrelated" people who may legally occupy the house, thus excluding communes of any size. If this seems blatantly dis- criminatory, it is unashamedly just that. As a federal judge announced in a 1970 California decision, "given the state's clear interest in preserving the integrity of the biological and/or legal family . . . the court sees no arbi- trariness in limiting the number of unrelated persons . . . while not so limiting the size of the traditional family" (*Palo Alto Tenants Union* v. *Morgan,* 321 F. Supp. 908). Such laws are enforced. Among groups sub- jected to legal action on these grounds over the last several years have been a Catholic workers' collective of priests and lay people in Milwaukee, a therapeutic community in New England, and a multigenerational commune on Long Island (New Community Projects, n.d.:16). It may sometimes be possible for communes to skirt such regulations by calling themselves clubs, churches, or other sorts of organizations, but only your legal counselor will know for sure.

Real Estate Trusts. A root belief of our economic system is that everything must be "owned" by someone. Especially regarding land, whole cultures have managed somehow to survive without this concept. But not our own. Whatever its attitudes toward "private property," any communal group must therefore find a way to "own" its land and common buildings, one which is at once satisfactory to legal convention and responsive to the group's sense of how it relates to its "property." Unfortunately, the usual forms for holding real estate—individual ownership, joint tenancy or tenancy in common, partnerships, for-profit corporations—are primarily designed to define and protect the interests of individuals. Communes may twist these forms (and have done so) to fit their own needs, but it may be an awkward fit. Not only are most of these ownership patterns inherently uncommunal, but they may also pose problems of taxation, legal claims on the property "owned" by individual communards, and admission or departure of members, all of which can strain the fabric of the commune. In their search for appropriate ownership forms, an increasing number of groups have therefore turned to a less common device, the "land trust."

The essentially communal element of the land trust arrangement is that no individual has a separate ownership interest in the land in question. In the most obvious case, the land is held by a fictitious entity called the "trust," which serves for this purpose as a legal expression of the communal unit. Management is carried out by trustees, who may include any or all members of the group, in the interest of the trust's "beneficiaries," who would normally be simply the group itself. This is all done within terms set forth in the trust agreement, or charter, in which the group would presumably wish to define its common sense of purpose. The basic land trust concept can also be implemented through incorporation as a nonprofit organization, of which the communards would be members. This pattern could facilitate sale or purchase of land, for which court approval may be required in the case of a trust.

Land trusts have advantages other than being expressive of communal will. Members may come and go without the need to rewrite the basic legal instrument, as may be the case with partnerships, and without issues arising as to their legal claims on the group's property, as may happen with most other forms of ownership. If members suffer individual legal judgments against themselves, encumbrances cannot be placed on the communal property as a result. Mortgages can be entered into without members themselves having to assume personal liability for these. And to borrow a leaf from the business world, trusts can be used to disguise the true buyers of a piece of land. In its more bourgeois forms, this last device has been used by developers seeking to accumulate large amounts of property parcel by anonymous parcel, thus avoiding payment to small landowners of what their real estate would be worth if all the facts were known.* For communards, such a cloak of anonymity could serve to circumvent the

---

* See, for example, Casey et al., 1971:209, where the point is made somewhat more circumspectly.

objections of real estate agents or sellers of land with unexamined prejudices against the sort of people who live in communes.

Although presented above in terms of communal "land," with the possible implication of a rural setting only, the trust idea has a wide variety of applications. An urban trust called "Landlords End" in Palo Alto, California, for example, held seven houses in 1973 (Kirkland, 1973:18). Communitarian Village, a projected West Coast group of several hundred people, planned to keep village property in a community land trust (Communitarian Village, n.d.:3). And according to at least some observers, even cooperative housing developments like New York City's Morningside Gardens bear a family resemblance to the land trust concept (International Independence Institute, 1972:13–14).

The inclusion of Morningside Gardens as a "land trust" case may be a stretching of definitions. But there is a more basic way in which the idea has recently been expanded (or perhaps narrowed) in contrast to the communal land trust model on which we have concentrated above. As the American Friends Service Committee has put it,

> The land trust and the concept of trusterty assume that all natural resources . . . belong to us all, and that we are to use these resources carefully, with thanks, and with consideration for future generations. Thus only that which comes into existence as a result of human labor is property —all else is trusterty. (1972:12)

According to this concept, all land should ultimately be liberated from private ownership and held in trust, with appropriate guidelines for its use to ensure it is treated with the respect it deserves. In an attempt to propagate this idea, articles on the subject have been published in a number of alternative magazines.* The International Independence Institute (III) published a comprehensive land trust manual in 1972. And efforts have already been made to establish trusts in (at least) Maine, New Hampshire, Vermont, Massachusetts, Rhode Island, Ohio, West Virginia, and California, with most actively attempting to remove as much land as possible from the private market.

The idea of removing land from the universe of things we feel are ours to buy and sell is a valid one. But by itself, it has only limited relevance to the sorts of immediate and personal issues this book is about. The III manual, for example, suggests that the majority of trustees controlling a

---

* In addition to the articles cited, see Bouton, 1973, Swann, 1973, and any issue of the *Maine Land Advocate* (44 Central St., Box 7, Bangor, Maine 04401).

piece of land not be people living there (1972:28), thereby reaffirming that the "community" for whom the land is in trust is all humanity. Much of the manual then deals with leases and other arrangements by which individual residents or businesses can establish their separate claims to use of pieces of the trust property. Formal obeisance once made to humanistic principles, in other words, people will presumably wish to guard their separate lives. As a "movement," the current drive to land trusts thus takes largely for granted the sort of virulent individualism we have criticized at length in earlier chapters. But as an organizational form, the land trust remains available to serve as legal expression of group purpose for those who have more ambitious objectives for personal and communal growth.*

Forms of Business Organization. On paper, we have now got the commune members together, their business chosen, and land or urban space acquired for living and working. The (more or less) final step is then to choose among possible legal forms for organizing the communal business. The simplest of these is the *single proprietorship*. But since one person then owns the business and at least in theory absorbs all the profits, it is obviously the least appropriate for communal ventures. In perhaps only one case would this form logically be adopted. Should an individual wish to start a venture on the assumption that other people would join communally around it, a single proprietorship might initially be formed. If the venture then failed, losses could at least be charged against other income the founder might have, resulting in a possible tax saving. If the venture succeeded, the business could be transformed into one of the organizational forms below as the commune came together. This is unlikely to be a general pattern, however, and thus deserves no further elaboration here.

A more logical communal form is the *partnership*. In a *general partnership*, two or more persons may simply decide to start doing business together. Generally, they will agree on their respective capital contributions and shares of business profit or loss. This agreement need not be in writing, however, nor need it be deposited with the state agency responsible for chartering businesses. Since this form leaves each partner fully liable for any financial obligations of the business, a more restricted form, the *limited partnership*, might also be considered. Here, there must be at least one "general partner,"

---

* In this section, we have bypassed such issues as what to look for in land, especially in the country, and what legal procedures are involved in taking title to it. For discussions of these points, see Moral, 1972, and Boudreau, 1973.

who may again be held personally responsible for all business liabilities. But the other, "limited," partners are protected against financial claims in excess of their original capital contributions. In this case, a written agreement establishing the partnership must be filed with appropriate state officials.

For communes, partnerships have several apparent advantages. In contrast to proprietorships, they clearly indicate the joint authority and responsibility of those participating. In contrast to corporations, they are relatively simple, avoiding a number of the statutory regulations and miscellaneous taxes to which corporations are liable. Further, although the business must report its income each year to the IRS, the partnership itself is not taxed. Taxes are paid individually on each partner's income from the business, thus avoiding the double taxation (on both corporate income and stockholders' dividends) that the corporate form involves. Finally, a commune may simply find magic in the idea of being a "partnership" rather than a "corporation," with all that the latter term implies as to impersonality and overstructuring of basic life processes.

Partnerships have significant disadvantages, however. As noted, all members of a general partnership are fully liable should financial disaster strike, and this could mean loss of both communal property and personal assets as well as of the business itself. Although a limited partnership may ease this problem, it gives the "general partner" greater legal authority over the business than the limited partners have. Finally, an entirely new partnership must be formed each time a member joins or leaves the commune. Members may feel this to accord with their sense that the group in fact is born anew in such cases. But it seems an unnecessary complication to have to reconstitute the legal structure of the business each time along with the group's sense of itself.

These particular problems are largely avoided if the business chooses to organize as a *corporation*. A corporation has continuing legal status of its own, regardless of changes in membership. At least theoretically, the process of adding or subtracting members is an easy one, achieved simply by an exchange of the stock which represents "ownership" in the business. Once created, a corporation can in its own name enter into contracts, buy and sell goods, and carry out all other business functions. In case of financial difficulty, only its own assets are jeopardized. Owner-members can generally lose no more than what they initially supplied as capital when the business was formed. As an added dividend for a communal venture, corporations convey an aura of seriousness and stability, thus at least partially offsetting the opposite image that popularly attaches to communes in themselves.

For communes, however, the corporate form poses problems all its own. Normally, a corporation (commune) pays taxes on its income and then distributes dividends to stockholders (members), who in turn are taxed on these.* A communal business may avoid this "double-taxation" dilemma if all available income can be paid out as salaries to its members, leaving no profits for which it might itself be taxed. But this may not always be possible, and the IRS might take a skeptical view of such a practice. Further, a for-profit corporation can be expensive and complicated to establish, is subject to considerable governmental regulation, and must meet requirements (as for income and unemployment tax withholding) from which partnerships and proprietorships are exempt. Finally, distribution of shares among a commune's members could lead to problems should somebody leave in a mood to cause trouble for the group. A share represents part ownership of the company, and the commune might be forced to choose between buying back the shares from the departing member or seeing these—and an ownership interest—pass outside the group.

A less usual variation on the corporate theme is the *nonprofit corporation,* which is expressly created for purposes of social welfare rather than profit-making. Since such an organization sells no stock and pays no dividends, the double-taxation problem is avoided. Should a commune be eligible to organize in this fashion, it presumably would simply live off what it paid its members in "salaries," with any surplus funds plowed back into the business. With no stock to be distributed, the problem of who is to own this disappears as well. A nonprofit corporation may also qualify for exemption from paying federal and state taxes on corporate income, although members would still be taxed on their individual salaries. If this sounds like an ideal arrangement, however, there is one more thing to be said. Depending on the state in which such a corporation is chartered, it will be limited to carrying out benevolent and charitable, social, recreational, educational, cultural, scientific, religious, or other such functions. Many communal businesses would find difficulty in wedging themselves into any of these categories.

In sum, communal businesses must weigh the advantages and disadvantages of various organizational forms, choosing the ones that seem most appropriate to their circumstances. If they choose a for-profit corporate

---

* So-called "Subchapter S corporations" may elect not to be taxed on their business income. But such groups may have no more than ten stockholders, presumably too few for a commune of any size.

structure, there is a further move that could solve at least the ownership problem. As the Grateful Union Family (Chapter 9) has done, they could form a trust that would hold all corporate stock and thus "own" the business, possibly along with the group's land. As mentioned in the discussion of land trusts, this would mean that "beneficiaries" (members) could arrive and depart without impact on the business's legal framework. This does, however, add yet another level to the organizational structure, while doing nothing to alleviate double-taxation or other problems a corporation may face. As with the basic business form itself, in other words, groups will simply have to weigh the trust instrument in light of their own particular needs.

Miscellaneous Requirements. Whatever form a communal business adopts, it will confront a seemingly endless series of further legal obligations to various governmental bodies. Local zoning regulations must be observed. The IRS must provide an Employer Identification Number. The business's name may have to be registered with local officials. Sales tax procedures must be learned and followed. And depending on whether it is corporation, partnership, or something else, the business must do some or all of the following: withhold income and social security taxes from employees, pay its own social security contributions, and pay federal and state unemployment taxes. In Vermont, our local Small Business Administration office provides a four-page mimeographed summary of such obligations for businesses within the state, and equivalent services are available at SBA offices elsewhere. For further guidance, see your lawyer or accountant.

None of this, we should note, is quite as complex as it seems. Something like twelve million businesses exist in the United States, and they have all come to terms in one way or another with the problems raised in this chapter. A new communal work place can do the same.*

---

* For general information on communal legal questions, see Goldstein, 1974. On organizational forms, see also Casey, 1971, and U.S. Small Business Administration, 1972a, 1972b. On tax questions, see the annual IRS *Tax Guide for Small Business.*

Chapter 12: The Communal Work Place and Social Change

In the chapters above, we have set forth a vision of what communal work places might be like and how they might be created. If this remains as yet largely "vision" in the American context, which powerfully conditions us all to reject moves toward communalism, it is nonetheless far more than mere fantasy. At each point, the image set forth corresponds to realities of the many working communes which have existed in the past, and which persist in many parts of the world today. The fact that such groups *can* exist, however, does not in itself prove that they *should*. To bring together the case for their creation, we summarize below the extent to which such groups in America today would be likely to avoid, at least for themselves, the most pernicious features of the prevailing system. And we speculate briefly as to the initial steps that working communes might take to make a genuine "movement" out of their isolated efforts.

COMMUNAL VERSUS CAPITALISTIC WORK PLACES

In Chapter 1, we outlined a number of problems inherent in the American system: the disconnectedness of people from one another and from their physical environment, the lack of control people have over the institutions and decisions that most affect them, the deadening quality of practically all work, and the pervasive senselessness of both production and consumption of goods and services. In other chapters, we have made the case that American "individualism" is an almost insurmountable barrier to our being fully and freely ourselves. On all these counts, communal work places are likely to be a marked improvement over the present state of affairs.

Ecology: Physical and Human. The American system is rampantly destructive of any sense of the human and environmental "ecology" of which we are a part. People, events, goods, and places flash by at dizzying speed, surpassing our powers to visualize the evolving mosaic into which they fit. Most notably in economic functions, the result is almost total subordination of personal relationships to capitalist abstractions. Our lives are ordered by concepts like "market price," "seniority," and "wage scale," all of which are totally devoid of specific human content. An equivalent process separates us from our physical environment, which becomes comprehensible only as a series of "natural resources" or "factors of production" to be digested by the economic system, or by us for our momentary amusement. In such a situation, we can hardly maintain deep connections with our own being, much less with the physical and human world outside ourselves.

As opposed to this, the communal work place provides its members with an extended primary group of considerable stability and continuity. People here are visibly connected to one another over time around the full range of their life activities. An appreciation of the intricate web of interpenetrations among people becomes not only a possibility, but also a requirement for simply moving effectively through the day. Necessarily, the impersonal distancing criteria of the "market" for judging people and allocating them tasks and resources gives way to more intimate measures of group and individual need. And since this full range of connections takes place within a coherent physical territory, rather than being spread from home to office to school to club to playground, a sense of deep relationship with the territory itself will inevitably grow as well. In no area have communal groups a clearer superiority than in this one, the appreciation they build of relationship with people and environment.

Control. As noted above, the potential chaos of our economic system requires in theory that it be controlled by the "market," just as work places are controlled by flow charts and committees, social decisions by legislatures and the law, and educational processes by computerized schedules and boards of trustees. In other words, none of these things is controlled by *us*. Given the size and complexity of the institutions which surround us, it is inevitable that such mechanisms should have arisen to help coordinate our affairs. But the mechanisms now have a dominant life of their own, and limited groups of authorities, or perhaps just institutional inertia, account for most of the important decisions which affect our lives. In fact, we are doubly victimized, since institutional decisions must be made on the basis of the "average" person to be dealt with: the average auto buyer, the average lawbreaker, the average worker, the average student. Since there is no such "average person," we are all constantly being bent to fit institutional needs. And we can do little more with our protests than bend them to fit the protest-absorbing mechanisms the institutions provide, which will average them out to average conclusions.

At least in its internal affairs, a communal work place is almost totally exempt from these forces. The economic and social issues confronting a group of this size will be comprehensible to all members, and each person can therefore feel competent to render judgment on pressing questions. Such judgments need not be filtered through "representatives" or complex procedural devices, since a meeting of the whole can be readily convened, or people making decisions from day to day can be approached directly. Some compromises will still be necessary to arrive at "average" solutions, as in fixing the length of the working day or setting a policy for vehicle use. But each voice in this process is a proportionately larger part of the whole than would be the case in situations outside, and ears are better attuned to the nuances and intensity of what is said. Finally, "rules" may always be bent to allow for individual circumstances, since people are necessarily aware of and able to adjust to one another's needs.

The Nature of Work. The question of work is a bit more complex. At least since Adam Smith, theorists have recognized the contribution to efficiency of a "division of labor," whereby individuals separately do the pieces of a total job for which they are best qualified. This process has become caricatured in the modern assembly line and business office, where tasks so minor as to be wholly meaningless in themselves must be performed repetitively under the tyranny of the clock. The psychological consequences for workers are by now abundantly clear. Isolated in their respective tediums, people find meaning only in their salary checks—or in drugs ranging from alcohol to heroin.

At least on the surface, communes will find it more difficult to escape this particular social disease than to deal with the others we have mentioned. To bring a number of people together in performing a group task requires organization and division of work in communes as it does in any joint effort. But since a communal work place is presumably formed for purposes other

than making the largest possible profit, a compulsive drive for efficiency—
and thus the worst features of the assembly-line mentality—will be largely
absent. Where routine work must still be done, its impact on workers will
be appreciably different from that within conventional businesses. For one
thing, the work process as a whole is always in sight, so that the contribution
of routine tasks to the overall job is clear. And even more important, the
communal business itself is subsumed within the larger social framework,
so that each of its tasks has immediate visible relationship to the total
process of living—and to the people with whom one lives.

Production and Consumption. Most of the goods and services our economy
produces contribute little to anyone's human growth, or work actively to
thwart such growth. Cigarettes, television shows, candied cereals, police
forces, social science research projects, children's fashions, automobiles, convenience foods, program budgets, advertising campaigns, insurance policies,
input-output models, bombs and bombers: all are deadening, often quite
literally, to the senses. In part, we are able to foist these things on our fellow
citizens because they are used out of our sight, relieving us of the need
to see the results. And in part, we are able to do this because we ourselves
have lost all perspective on what these results are. Numbed by our work,
impotent to control the social forces that afflict us, and bereft of supportive
human community to provide other meaning for our lives, we too scramble
to narcotize ourselves through the endless consumption of economic garbage.

It is conceivable, of course, that a communal work place might choose to
live by packaging TV dinners, or that it might seek to provide a car for
every member. But the odds are strongly against it. Sources of interpersonal
joy and struggle are abundant in such groups, refining the sense of human
possibility and making of "consumerism" an irrelevant concept—even were
there the aimless time to indulge in such a thing. As for what it sells, a
communal group works to express its life, not to make a buck, and it will
want its products to reflect this. Moreover, communal living builds a
heightened awareness of the consequences of one's acts on others, making
even more implausible the sale by these groups of goods they know to
be demeaning to the user. In this area, as with the points above, communal
work places have consistently shown themselves to be superior to their
equivalents in the conventional business world.

Individualism and Individuation. Throughout this book, we have made a
further point that should need only the briefest summary here. In its endless

insistence on "individualism," American culture persuades us from birth to avoid anything like the comprehensive group involvements a communal work place implies. Instead, we are individually to surround ourselves with an assortment of more partial relationships, each built around one of our interests: political group, yoga class, hearth-and-home partners (nuclear family or residential collective), job (career or temporary), food co-op, and so on. Most such groups depend on a closely-defined area of common concern among their members, however. And we quickly grow accustomed, context by context, to dealing only with people of like mind. The social life of an individualistic culture, in other words, *must* be conformist, since there is no other basis for its existence. Since in no situation can we be fully and spontaneously ourselves, we are unlikely ever to discover who we really are.

In a communal work group, people gradually come to think of themselves as "family," a relationship that embraces work, play, loving, learning—indeed the whole range of life activities—for those involved. For each person, of course, the pursuit of these things will not be restricted to the communal group alone. But it will be centered there, and there people will find the greatest latitude for experimenting with their own possibilities. "Families," after all, have almost legendary tolerance for eccentrics and eccentricities. And naturally so, since they have inherited—or, in "intentional families," discovered—bonds that far transcend the fragile ties of "interest" which hold associations together in the culture around us. In addition to all the other things they offer, communal work places present us the opportunity to be fully ourselves.

THE PROCESS OF SOCIAL CHANGE

The salutary effects of communal living are all very well for those few people now within such groups. But there remains the question of whether communal work situations can be extended to any significant part of the population. We would be gratified if this book helped even one group establish its own communal work place. But there are millions of people who feel a pressing desire for an alternative to the way they now live and work. As long as nothing is done in response to that desire, communal work places will remain a fragile parenthesis in the midst of an unhappy and potentially self-destructive society. For those now living communally and for those not yet doing so, it would therefore be desirable for the principles underlying the communal work approach to spread deeply through the society, to the point of bringing fundamental changes in national values and structure. A wide range of social critics would generally agree with these principles—more human work patterns, greater control over our lives, an end to consumerism and senseless production, deeper interpersonal relationships. But is the establishment of communal work places the best way to implement these, particularly given the variety of other approaches available?

The Counterculture and Social Change. A counterculture slogan exclaimed: "The Revolution is over, and we've won!" Most charitably interpreted, this presumably meant that a revolutionary way of life had been discovered that could be adopted by all without further hullabaloo. According to Charles Reich, the "grand strategy" was simple:

> listen to music, dance, seek out nature, laugh, be happy, be beautiful, help others whenever you can, work for them as best you can, take them in, the old and the bitter as well as the young, live fully in each moment, love and cherish each other, love and cherish yourselves, stay together. (1970:376)

Directly or by implication, this approach had a great deal to say about relationship, control of one's life, and more human use of consumable goods. But on issues of work, it was less illuminating: "The hard questions— if by that is meant political and economic organization—are insignificant, even irrelevant" (Ibid.:388).

It is here that the counterculture's inability to create widespread social change most clearly lay. Many have criticized the movement for its more political failures: "From my vantage point—one of being black . . . [the counterculture's] ersatz philosophy evinces a wholesale abdication of responsibility, a pulling-back of commitment to social progress and social justice" (Daniels, 1972:2–3). But the deeper abdication by those involved was of responsibility to *themselves.* In ignoring "hard questions" like the organization of work, and in instead letting the larger society pay the bills, the counterculture expressed its ultimate dependence on that society. In so doing, it closed off any hope that all could join in its postrevolutionary revels. Clearly, a movement that depends on society to generate the largess off which it lives cannot embrace any significant portion of that society, since the largess would simply fade away. For all its many virtues, the counterculture finally offered no hope of social transformation.

The Political Left and Social Change. In the fall of 1970, we briefly took part in a socialist studies group in northern California. Every other week, we would gather with faculty members from the nearby university to discuss the dialectics of the corporate system, or the seizure of state power. After a few meetings, however, we began to notice an unsettling pattern. From their respective private homes in their respective parts of the city, these young professors would converge in their private cars, leaving their private wives behind to take care of their private children. We began to be haunted by visions of the same people, after The Revolution, converging in the same way on their planning bureaus, their wives still at home alone with the children. Somehow, it didn't seem like much of a revolution.*

Such political leftists should have had no theoretical objection to the restructuring of their own lives in imaginative ways—they were, after all, planning the "restructuring" of an entire society. But beginning with Marx, the theory of centralist revolution has been conspicuously silent on the question of how, specifically, people might live differently from day to day. More interesting, and far less demanding in terms of immediate personal effort, is to speculate on how central institutions might ultimately function. In *Socialism,* Michael Harrington dwells at length on proposals like this:

> There should be an Office of the Future in the White House. Each year the President should make a Report on the Future . . . which would be submitted to a Joint Congressional Committee where it would be debated, amended and then presented to the entire Congress for decision. This process should establish the broad priorities of the society and annually monitor the result of past efforts. (1972a:359–360)

Less democratic centralists would streamline this process and have the Office of the Future responsible only to the central party committee. But in neither approach is there any hint of change in the structure of daily existence for people generally. If social change is to involve the decentralization of life to a human scale, as in communal work places, this variety of leftist politics is largely beside the point.

There is another grouping within the political left whose concerns more closely parallel those of this book. These "decentralist" leftists believe that our problems lie with the concentration of power in state institutions. In

---

* Writing in the San Francisco *Good Times* during this period, Steve Engert termed such leftists "bourgeois verbal radicals," who "reproduce the schizophrenia of society in their own political work—which is no more than a hobby, of a leisure-time character" (quoted in Fairfield, 1972a:142).

such a view, neither reform of these institutions nor their seizure by radicals can cure the disease. What is needed instead is to disperse power itself among local units, such as neighborhood committees or worker-controlled industries, which are more directly responsive to their constituencies.* As opposed to the centralist position, this version of leftist politics proposes remedial actions to be taken now. Churches can support self-help projects in their communities, students can claim their rightful share of power within colleges and universities, and so on. Always, the emphasis is on bringing local institutions under local control, or on creating such institutions if they do not already exist.

The problem, however, is that this approach almost invariably takes for granted the continuing dispersal of individual energies among a wide range of distinct institutions: work place, home, neighborhood committee, school, recreation center, meditation class, and more. At root, this is the "community" approach outlined in Chapter 6, and it has all the limitations of that method. Where people have but a limited functional relationship with each of a number of groups, there is an inevitable tendency to want increasingly "efficient" performance of these functions by the groups involved. As the Yugoslav experiment with workers' control makes clear (Chapter 8), the result is likely to be a slide back into greater institutional size and more limited popular participation. Even were this not to happen, the communitarian attempt to guard individual options through avoiding comprehensive primary groups has all the conformist social features we have discussed at length in earlier chapters. The "decentralists," in other words, have uncritically embraced the individualism that is the essence of the culture they wish to transform. In so doing, they have seriously undermined their ability to promote lasting, fundamental social change.

Communal Work Places and Social Change. On however limited a scale, a communal work place in itself is testimony of social change. As opposed to the counterculture communes, it is a self-reliant expression of a principle that could be extended throughout the society. As opposed to the changes that "centralists" envision, it is a restructuring of its participants' immediate lives in a form that anticipates a transformed social order. And as opposed to the political "decentralist" approach, it represents a search that has penetrated to the very core of the belief system that oppresses us, emerging with

---

* See, for example, Raskin, 1971, and Alperovitz, 1972.

new understanding of what gives durability and human fulfillment to relationships and institutions.

For many, the entry into communalism will begin at home, as fragmented family lives are brought more closely together around work and other activities. More limited forms of sharing may then be extended to others, with money pooled or space shared in a larger community of people. And this *may* then lead to a full communal environment. Max Delespesse puts it most optimistically: "In learning within such primary groups to contribute to the community what we have earned and to receive from it what we need, we are striking at the roots of the tree of capitalism. From this will be born communities of production" (1972:8). Perhaps. As we have noted in several contexts above, the "community" form of limited sharing can be a trap, since it leaves untouched the taproot of the capitalist tree—individualism. But if viewed clearly as paths to further development rather than as ends in themselves, communitarian forms of cooperation can still be supplanted by the communal work place.

There, the struggle will continue. People will gradually have to learn to take responsibility for areas of their lives they had always left to parents, teachers, superiors, The System. Unfamiliar capacities will have to be found for self-examination. As George Ineson has noted from a communal context of his own, "It is more difficult to preserve illusions about oneself when living and working with others than if one is alone" (1971:100). In addition, the collective "we" will have to be discovered. For the people involved, this implies personal development of the most profound sort. As a group process, it expresses a form of social change which is equally revolutionary. · A single communal work place is no more than a seed of social regeneration. But it is at least that, and that is a start.

In fact, it is the only possible start. To continue the botanical metaphor, Martin Oppenheimer has pointed out that "we must sow the seeds of the good society within the context of the bad" (1971:277). There is simply no other way to bring about fundamental alterations in the social system. Some, like our socialist friends in California, have hoped for deliverance through revolution. But this is to stand the process on its head. As Martin Buber has said,

> in the social as opposed to the political sphere, revolution is not so much a creative as a delivering force whose function is to set free and authenticate . . . something that has already been foreshadowed in the womb of the pre-revolutionary society; . . . as regards social evolution, the hour

of revolution is not an hour of begetting but an hour of birth—provided there was a begetting beforehand. (1958:44–45)

Murray Bookchin warns of the consequences of ignoring this fact: "if assembly and community are not allowed to emerge organically, if their growth is not matured by the process of demassification, by self-activity and by self-realization, they will remain nothing but forms, like the soviets in postrevolutionary Russia" (1971:46). If the basis of the "postrevolutionary" society we envision is the communal work group, the only genuine form of revolutionary activity is to create such groups.

There is a final trap to be avoided, however. We have stressed above the personal challenges involved in creating a communal work place. These challenges overcome, the group may feel that its job is largely done. One of the Bruderhof members, for example, has written:

> All of us hope for a future of peace, love, and brotherliness. . . . And so we want to make use of our lives to show and shape—now in the present time—the image of the future. We have turned toward the future, changed our direction in the present. And since our existence spans the arch between present and future, we believe that it is history we are living. (Quoted in Zablocki, 1971:145)

But history may need more of a nudge than this. People need to know that the communal alternative exists. They need help in undertaking such projects. And once formed, communal groups will need to experiment with a variety of forms of mutual aid in order to create a viable movement. Fully to realize their potential as agents of social change, in other words, communal groups will have to find ways to reach effectively beyond their own gates.

REACHING OUTWARD

In the early stages of the recent communal movement, a "reaching outward" often seemed the opposite of what the communards wanted. According to Ray Mungo, "We live far from the marketplaces in America by our own volition, and the powerful men left behind . . . do not yet realize that their heirs will refuse to inhabit their hollow cities . . . will run back to the Stone Age if necessary for survival and peace" (1970:17). But the hope of so doing soon proved illusory. As Theodore Roszak countered, "no community today can ever remove itself so far from the urban-industrial network that it can for very long avoid fighting for its privacy, freedom and peace of mind, for fresh air, pure water, self-determination" (1972:427). Beyond such self-protective measures, there were more positive forms of contact that communes found they wanted after all, from finding someone to publish their books to locating suppliers of batteries for storing the power generated by their windmills. In one way or another, all such groups discovered that they were inextricably linked to the larger world outside.

The communal work place will know this from the moment of its formation, and the only real question will be the nature of its outside relationships. In the specific area of working for wider social change, which we assume will be at least one of the commune's objectives, there will be a number of things it might do. It could organize itself around a "product" such as community-based law or medicine, thereby experimenting with new models for delivering such services to those who most can use them. And regardless of what it produces, it might wish to work at the local level for the sorts of "reforms" that liberals have traditionally been identified with. In part, this would be a question of self-preservation, since an atmosphere of liberal tolerance is likely to be more conducive to the growth of such "radical" groups than one of repressive conservatism. In part, it is a way to develop the conditions for future communalism, since many of the "disadvantaged" will have to pass through a stage of greater individual affluence before appreciating this to be the empty victory it is. And in part, it is simply a way to respond to what one's neighbors feel to be their needs of the moment.

If the basic expression of social change is held to be the communal work place, however, the group is likely to devote most of its outside energies to strengthening the position of other such groups, and to creating bonds between them. In their early stages, many communal work places will be undercapitalized and overoptimistic, and they will need all the help they can get to survive. Beyond this, there are a number of experiments which only such groups can carry out in finding the lineaments of a new social order—patterns for exchanging goods, for making decisions affecting groups of communes, and so on. Many of these areas have already been addressed by the alternative-seekers of recent years. In practice, their attempts have generally foundered on the instability and limited aspirations of contemporary communes. But they may illustrate broad approaches that communal work places could refine for their own use.

Exchanging Information. The most fully realized aspect of intercommunal cooperation in recent years has been the exchange of information. Among the many magazines that have provided news of the movement are *Communities, The Green Revolution, Lifestyle!, The Black Bart Brigade, Vocations for Social Change,* and *The Mother Earth News.* In addition, newsletters have been proposed, if not always long sustained, to serve communes in particular regions: "KALIFLOWER" for groups in the San Francisco Bay area (Berke, 1970:13), the Rainbow Family's "Smoke Signal" in New York City (NASCO, 1972:1), a round-robin newsletter initiated by Downhill Farm for nearby groups in Maryland and Pennsylvania (Jerome, 1972b:12–13). Gatherings of greatly divergent degrees of formality have been held all over the country: the weekly meetings of Beansprout (a federation of Boston-area communes), Twin Oaks's annual summer conference for those interested in forming communes of their own, workshops on a variety of subjects sponsored by such groups as the Heathcote Center and Community Service, and a staggering assortment of more impromptu gatherings allowing people simply to keep in touch with one another. Presumably, communal work places will wish to pursue all these methods for sharing experiences and information.

Exchanging People. Several years ago, Michael Bennett proposed a system of "exchange programs" between rural and urban communes: "People in the city would then be educated in the fundamentals of farming and country life, and the country people could come to the city to get themselves together in ways which require the resources the city has to offer" (1970: 33). In fact, the communal life style proved an endless succession of such "exchanges," as people roamed restlessly from group to group. The education in a variety of life patterns which this process involves is something that communal work places might wish to explore among themselves, if less restlessly. And there is a variation of the process which could be equally valuable: more established work places could "loan" experienced members to newer groups in need of assistance. The kibbutzim have long done this on a major scale. And in more modest form, the Cooperative League of the USA offers similar services to its members through its "cousin co-op" plan (Voorhis, n.d.:14).

The routine possibility for exchanging members among communal work places might serve another useful function as well. There is no guarantee that any particular assortment of people will "work" as a commune, however important it is to the group to achieve this. Communal work places will differ greatly in tone from one to another, and individuals may not find their appropriate place on the first attempt. If it is considered normal to experience other groups around some pattern of exchange, people will be freer over time to find their niches without feeling they are only floating through the process. Obviously, this sort of activity could only take place around the edges of a basically stable "family" group, or we would simply be back in the transient world of the counterculture. But within limits, a mechanism of this sort could play an important role in helping people find the "we" with which they are most comfortable.

Financial Support. In addition to exchanging counsel, there are more material forms of support which alternative groups have tried to supply each other. The Madison (Wisconsin) Sustaining Fund began in 1971 to collect a 1 percent tax on sales of participating commercial groups, the proceeds to be distributed among various community service organizations (Wind, 1972:23).* The Homer Morris Fund was established in the mid-1950s to provide short-term loans to intentional communities (Morgan, 1972:18); comparable efforts have been made more recently elsewhere (*Communitas,* 1972). And there have been several attempts to create systems of mutual insurance against financial disaster, so that community money need not be drained off in payments to conventional insurance companies (Sloane, 1972:5; CNVA, 1973). In the absence of a strong financial base—or a psychological feeling of "community" strong enough to bring forth significant amounts of cash—most of these attempts have come to little. But they illustrate possibilities that groups of communal work places might wish to pursue further.

There are other forms of financial support which these work places might supply each other. A communal business, and particularly one whose members are learning new productive skills and trying to tap unfamiliar markets, may require some time to get on its financial feet. During such a period, there are at least two ways in which other groups might help. First, if the fledgling commune's products were of use to them, they might guarantee a certain volume of purchases until other markets were established. In a roughly parallel context, Charles Hampden-Turner (1970) has called such a strategy "political marketing," and it might be enough in itself to ease the new group through its most difficult months.

---

* Attempts to create similar funds have since been made in other areas, including Washington, D.C. (Morris, 1973:4).

Were more than this required, a variant might see established groups agreeing initially to pay somewhat more than the "market" price for the goods involved. This is roughly analagous to the way in which developing countries have erected protective tariff barriers around their "infant industries," with domestic purchasers paying higher than world prices until the industries reached competitive maturity. In the case of an association of communal work groups, the "tariff" would be informal, consisting of the felt psychic cost of buying from a cheaper "foreign" (conventional) supplier rather than from a fellow commune in need. In developing countries, many infant industries never did become competitive, and this technique has lost some of its early appeal. But as discussed below, communal groups might wish to employ it anyway.

Joint Projects. In July of 1972, people involved in three alternative magazines—*Alternatives, Communitarian,* and *Communitas*—hatched a plan for one of the more ambitious intercommunitarian ventures of recent years. By that December, they had merged their respective publications into a single magazine, *Communities,* in cooperation with three other community groups around the country. For their first issue, business affairs were handled in Virginia, distribution and part of the editing in Ohio, additional editorial work in California, design and typesetting in Rhode Island, and preparation of a brochure to announce the publication in Michigan. Undaunted by such complexity, this group of groups not only continued to get copies of the magazine to subscribers but began to publish books as well, notably a guide to legal questions affecting intentional communities. None of this represents "communal work" as we have defined it in this book, but it suggests that projects beyond the scope of a single communal work place might be carried out in association with other such groups.

Most communal work places, however, will prefer to keep the total productive process more fully within view, rather than fragmenting it in the manner familiar from corporate experience. Perhaps more logical in terms of joint effort is cooperation in acquiring goods and services that no one group could as easily, or as cheaply, provide for itself. A Santa Fe community school, for example, has proposed formation of a national legal service to coordinate and support legal actions growing out of experiments in alternative education (Nagel, 1973:8); communal work places might well wish to create an equivalent service of their own. Group health care might be provided through an association of communes. Neighboring groups might join in forming a school for their children. And cooperative purchases of food, tools, and other goods would be likely both to reduce the price of these and to form closer ties between the groups involved.*

Exchange of Goods and Services. A work collective in Florida has proposed that "we all initiate our own Alternate, non-profit, humanistic economy, one in which we distribute, produce, buy and sell to ourselves as many of our daily needs as possible—keeping our money within our movements, organizations, and media. It is . . . an economy within an economy" (Lang, n.d.:3). To provide the information base for this alternate economy, groups like Community Market (1973) and the New World Coalition (1972) have prepared catalogs of goods produced by various alternative groups. Jack McLanahan has suggested creation of a National Coordination Office to help move such goods from one group to another (n.d.:16). As a Community Market survey discovered, however, the possibility for such exchange is for the moment sharply limited, since a large proportion of goods now produced are luxury items (1973:25). But as a greater range of communal work places enters the picture, an "alternate economy" will become increasingly feasible.

In addition to "keeping our money within our movements," the alternate economy would provide the basis for experimenting with patterns for exchanging goods and services other than the impersonal ones that the "market" provides. Barter is the most obvious of these "new" forms, and it offers several advantages. As Charles Morrow Wilson has pointed out, "Barter . . . survives by that wonderful personalized magic called good will. It draws neighbors and communities closer, it improves understanding, tolerance, and respect among bartering participants" (1960:9). And since no money changes hands, it is extremely difficult for the authorities to collect sales or income taxes on such transactions.** Barter is difficult to extend to large numbers of isolated trading partners, however. At least in the early stages, such groups will presumably rely on the market to provide guidelines to appropriate terms of trade. But even here, market prices will readily be

---

* In part to facilitate such cooperative purchases, several East Coast communes have proposed establishment of an "Intercommunity Transportation Authority" which could truck goods to and from distant markets (Judy, 1973:10).

**Many alternative groups have already found themselves bartering at least some of their products for needed items, and an Akron group created a "service exchange" through which people can apply their own skills in return for services from others (Miller, 1973: 24).

modified by such factors as the desire to support new work places, and experimentation with more humane patterns of trade will continue.

Communal work places will have an advantage in searching for such
patterns, since the drive for "efficient" economic solutions will lack the
compulsiveness attached to this in the outside world. As noted in Chapter
11, a communal work place requires little more than a level of material
comfort adequate to sustain the search for more personal forms of growth.
It will therefore be relatively easier for such groups, say, to support the
"infant industries" of others. It is conceivable that even a somewhat "inef-
ficient" network of work places, with industries never reaching far beyond
"infancy," could live largely off trade among its own members. Given a
sufficient degree of common identification and shared purpose, it would
seem relatively unimportant that each group as a result consumed less than
if most commercial relationships were maintained with, and on the terms
of, the business world outside. And whatever their degree of external com-
petitiveness, communal work places need feel no overriding requirements
for imposing a fine calculus of profitability on their trading relationships
with each other.

A Confederation of Communal Work Places. All the above measures implemented, we would have in essence a confederation of communal work
places. Existing within, but to a significant degree independent of, the larger
capitalistic framework, such a confederation would comprise an "alternate
society" with potential for being generalized to the society as a whole.
Limited efforts have been made in the past to bring alternative groups together in this way. A "Fellowship of Intentional Communities" existed more
than twenty years ago, for example, and an abortive attempt was made in
1970 to bring the fellowship back to life (*Green Revolution,* 1970:6). A
California group has written more recently of a federation which would
link large numbers of other communitarian villages to the one they plan
for themselves (Communitarian Village, n.d.:1–2). The constituent units
of these efforts, however, have been the sorts of loose communities which
represent only a minimal departure from existing social patterns, and this
has been reflected in the lack of either real content or staying power in
their federations. A confederation of communal work places, on the other
hand, would build on stronger units with greater aspiration for social change
—and would itself be stronger as a result.

We should note this: as the organism of social change reaches outward
from communal work place to federation of communes, intensely difficult

issues arise. Beyond an extremely limited point, for example, the exchange of goods between any number of producing groups must involve some sort of coordinating mechanism less personal than the barter approach. According to Howard Sherman, *"Either* competition in the market must make most of these decisions *or* a very large bureaucracy must make them" (1972: 311). Sherman poses a gloomy choice, but preferable alternatives have yet to be devised. Similar problems are inherent in the political arena, where regional groups of work places will have to find some way of dealing with issues of common concern without simply reproducing the meaningless "representative" structures we have today. In the absence as yet of any significant number of serious communal groups, it is premature to speculate on what solutions to these problems might be. We can only record our intuition that solutions can be found—and our assurance that the finding will be a long, demanding process.

And yet, it is perhaps the most worthwhile endeavor upon which we could embark. Martin Buber has said this:

> The prime conditions for a genuine society can be summed up as follows: it is not an aggregate of essentially unrelated individuals, for such an aggregate could only be held together by a 'political,' i.e. a coercive principle of government; it must be built up of little societies on the basis of communal life and of the associations of these societies. . . . In other words: only a structurally rich society can claim the inheritance of the State. (1958:80)

Buber is thinking precisely of those "little societies" which integrate work, play, living, education—in other words, of the sort of communal work place this book is about. To establish such work places is thus to serve a double function. We lay the foundations for growing as a society beyond the structural impoverishment in which we now live. And whatever the immediate outcome of this larger struggle, we carry it out in a communal way that allows us in the process to grow far beyond what we were before. We will have to reach deep within ourselves to find the resources to do these things, but they can be done.

Bibliography

Abraham, W. E. 1962. *The Mind of Africa.* Chicago: University of Chicago Press.

Adelman, Stan. n.d. Letter to the editor. *Journal of the New Harbinger,* no. 6.

Adizes, Ichak. 1971. *Industrial Democracy: Yugoslav Style (The Effect of Decentralization on Organizational Behavior).* New York: Free Press.

Alcott, James. 1971. *A National Proving Ground: Minnesota Experimental City.* Minneapolis: Minnesota Experimental City. Reprint from *AIA Journal,* November.

Alley, Rewi. 1974. "The Cultural Revolution in Education." *Far East Reporter,* February.

Allison, R. Bruce, ed. 1972. *Humanizing Our Future: Some Imaginative Alternatives.* Hinsdale, Ill.: The School of Living Press.

Alperovitz, Gar. 1972. "Socialism as a Pluralist Commonwealth." In Edwards, Reich, and Weisskopf, 1972.

Alternatives! Foundation. 1971. *Making Communities.* San Francisco.

American Friends Service Committee. 1972. "Land Trusts." *Synergism,* July.

Anarchist Commune. 1973. "The Anarchist Commune." *Communes: Journal of the Commune Movement* (U.K.), April.

Anderson, Bill, n.d. "The Law Commune." In New Vocations Project, n.d.

Arguelles, Jose, and Arguelles, Miriam. 1972. *Mandala.* Berkeley: Shambala Publications.

Armah, Ayi Kwei. 1972. *Why Are We So Blest?* Garden City, N.Y.: Doubleday.

Arnold, Eberhard. 1967. *Why We Live in Community.* Rifton, N.Y.: The Plough Publishing House.

Arnold, Emmy. 1964. *Torches Together.* Rifton, N.Y.: The Plough Publishing House.

Atcheson, Richard. 1971. *The Bearded Lady*. New York: John Day.

Bach, Richard. 1970. *Jonathan Livingston Seagull*. New York: Macmillan.

Baer, Steve. 1973. "Solar House." *Alternative Sources of Energy,* March.

Baird, Bruce. 1971. "ONE: Building Community in a Warehouse." In New Vocations Project, 1971.

Barkai, Haim. 1971. *The Kibbutz: An Experiment in Microsocialism.* Jerusalem: Hebrew University Department of Economics, November.

Benello, C. George, and Roussopoulos, Dimitrios, eds. 1971. *The Case for Participatory Democracy: Some Prospects for a Radical Society.* New York: Viking.

Bennett, Michael. 1970. "The Alternative." *The Mother Earth News,* September.

Berke, Joseph. 1970. "Bay Area Notes." *Alternate Society,* September.

Bettelheim, Bruno. 1969. *The Children of the Dream: Communal Child-Rearing and American Education.* London: Collier-Macmillan.

Bevier, Thomas. 1971. "The Group." *The Mother Earth News,* July.

Bishop, Claire Huchet. 1950. *All Things Common.* New York: Harper.

Blumberg, Paul. 1968. *Industrial Democracy: The Sociology of Participation.* New York: Schocken.

Bookchin, Murray. 1971. *Post Scarcity Anarchism.* Berkeley: Ramparts Press.
———. 1972. "The Crisis of Our Environment." In Edwards, Reich, and Weisskopf, 1972.

Borkenau, Franz. 1971. "The Spanish Cockpit." In Shatz, 1971.

Boudreau, Eugene. 1973. *Buying Country Land.* New York: Collier.

Bourdet, Yvon. 1970. *La délivrance de Prométhée.* Paris: Editions Anthropos.

Bouton, Brian. 1973. "Community and Land Trust." *Communities,* February.

Brace Research Institute. 1972. *Annual Report.* Ste. Anne de Bellevue, Quebec. June.
———. 1973. *Publications List* (Miscellaneous Report no. M.17). Ste. Anne de Bellevue, Quebec. May.

Bradford, David, and Bradford, Eva. 1972. *A Model for a Middle Class Commune.* Stanford, Calif. Spring. Mimeographed.

Briscoe, Robert. 1972. "The Invisible Co-ops." *Journal of the New Harbinger,* July.

Buber, Martin. 1958. *Paths in Utopia.* Boston: Beacon.

Burns, John. 1972. "China Restoring Exams in Her Schools." *New York Times,* September 25.

Cambridge Institute. 1970. *Prospectus for Cambridge Institute New City Project.* Cambridge, Mass. September 8. Mimeographed.

Cascade Collective. 1972. *Cascade: A Magazine of Alternatives Northwest.* Portland, Oreg. Spring.

Case, John. 1972. "Vision of a New Social Order." *The Nation,* February 14.
———, and Hunnius, Gerry. 1971. *Workers and the Community: Self-Management in the CDC.* Cambridge, Mass.: Center for Community Economic Development. July.
Casey, William J. 1971. *Lawyer's Desk Book.* Rev. 2d ed. New York: Institute for Business Planning.
———, et al. 1971. *The Real Estate Desk Book.* 4th ed. New York: Institute for Business Planning.
Castaneda, Carlos. 1968. *The Teachings of Don Juan: A Yaqui Way of Knowledge.* New York: Ballantine.
———. 1971. *A Separate Reality: Further Conversations with Don Juan.* New York: Simon & Schuster.
Catholic Rural Life and Intermediate Technology Development Group. 1968. *Populorum Progressio to the Third World: A Symposium on Intermediate Technology in Development.* Rome: Caritas Internationalis.
CCAS. *See* Committee of Concerned Asian Scholars.
CeCoCo. n.d. *Guidebook for Rural Cottage and Small Industries.* Osaka, Japan.
Center for Community Economic Development. 1971a. *Growth Industries and Project Selection: An Introduction for Community Development Corporations.* Cambridge, Mass. September.
———. 1971b. *Profiles in Community Based Economic Development.* Cambridge, Mass. January.
Cépède, M. 1971. "Part-time Farming and Industrialization of Rural Areas." In Klatzmann, Ilan, and Levi, 1971.
Charlie. n.d. "Beansprout." *Commune-ication,* no. 2.
Chase, Stuart. 1969. *The Story of Toad Lane.* Chicago: Cooperative League of the U.S.A.
Chermayeff, Serge, and Alexander, Christopher. 1963. *Community and Privacy: Toward a New Architecture of Humanism.* Garden City, N.Y.: Doubleday Anchor.
Clarke, Robin. 1973. "Technology for an Alternative Society." *Lifestyle!,* February.
———, and Clarke, Janine. 1972. "Soft Technology: Blueprint for a Research Community." *Undercurrents,* May.
CNVA. *See* Community for Nonviolent Action.
Cody, Harriett Mary, and Sadis, Harvey Joseph. 1973. "Marriage Contract of Harriett Mary Cody and Harvey Joseph Sadis." *Ms.,* June.
Committee of Concerned Asian Scholars. 1972. *China: Inside the People's Republic.* New York: Bantam.
Communauté de travail Marcel Barbu. 1946. *Des hommes libres.* Valence.
Communitarian Village. n.d. *Communitarian Village.* Oroville, Calif. Brochure.
Communitas. 1972. "Why *Communitas?*" July.

Communities. 1972. "Editorial." December.

Community Fellowship. 1970. *An Intentional Community Handbook.* Yellow Springs, Ohio: Community Service, Inc.

Community for Nonviolent Action. 1973. "Fire Pledge." *Direct Action for a Nonviolent World,* April 9.

Community Market. 1973a. *The Community Market Cooperative Catalog.* New York: Knopf.

―――. 1973b. "Economics Clearinghouse: A Community Market Survey." *Communities,* October–November.

―――. n.d. "Welcome to Community Market." *Communities,* no. 3.

Connolly, Edward. 1971. *Deer Run.* New York: Scribners.

Conroy, Sarah Booth. 1972. "Security Is a Warm Yurt." *Washington Post,* August 20.

Cooperative League of the U.S.A., The. n.d. *In a Big Co-op Can Members Really Control Policies?* Chicago, Ill., and Washington, D.C.

Dahl, Robert A. 1970. *After the Revolution: Authority in a Good Society.* New Haven: Yale University Press.

Dalton, George, ed. 1968. *Primitive, Archaic, and Modern Economies: Essays of Karl Polanyi.* Garden City, N.Y.: Doubleday Anchor.

Daniels, Lee. 1972. "Reviewing Jonathan Kozol's *Free Schools.*" *New Schools Exchange Letter,* April 15.

Daubier, Jean. 1970. "The Chinese Cultural Revolution." *Monthly Review,* October.

Davidson, Sara. 1970. "Open Land." *Harper's,* June.

De Baggio, Thomas. 1972. "Legal Insurance." *Saturday Review of the Society,* October.

Delespesse, Max. 1972. "La contestation de la propriété privée et l'enseignement de Jésus." *Courrier communautaire international,* March–April.

―――, and Tange, André, eds. 1970. *Le jaillissement des expériences communautaires.* Paris: Fleurus.

―――. 1971. *Des communautaires témoignent.* Paris: Fleurus.

Della Femina, Jerry. 1970. *From Those Wonderful Folks Who Gave You Pearl Harbor: Front-Line Dispatches from the Advertising War.* New York: Pocket Books.

Dennison, George. 1969. *The Lives of Children.* New York: Random House.

Desanti, Dominique. 1970. *Les socialistes de l'utopie.* Paris: Petite Bibliothèque Payot.

Desroche, Emmanuel. 1972. *Le mochav shitoufi.* Unpublished manuscript.

Desroche, Henri. 1971. *The American Shakers: From Neo-Christianity to Presocialism.* Amherst: University of Massachusetts Press.

Diamond, Stephen, 1971. *What the Trees Said.* New York: Dell.

Donna. 1974. Letter. *Leaves of Twin Oaks,* January.

Douart, Georges. 1961. *Du kolkhoze au kibboutz: sur les chantiers de l'amitié.* Paris: Plon.

Drake Publishers, Inc. 1973. *How to Start Your Own Small Business.* New York.

Dubos, René. 1968. *So Human an Animal.* New York: Scribners.

Duckworth, E. H. 1951. "A Visit to the Apostles and the Town of Aiyetoro." *Nigeria,* no. 36.

East Street Gallery. 1973. "East Street Gallery." *Communities,* no. 3.

Edel, Matthew. 1970. *Community Development Corporations.* Cambridge, Mass.: Center for Community Economic Development, September.

Edwards, Richard C.; Reich, Michael; and Weisskopf, Thomas E. 1972. *The Capitalist System: A Radical Analysis of American Society.* Englewood Cliffs, N.J.: Prentice-Hall.

Eisenmenger, Robert W. 1967. *The Dynamics of Growth in New England's Economy, 1870–1964.* Middletown, Conn.: Wesleyan University Press.

Erisman, Alva Lewis. 1972. "China: Agricultural Development, 1949–1971." In United States Congress, 1972.

Fairfield, Richard. 1971. *Communes, U.S.A.* San Francisco: Alternatives Foundation.

———. 1972a. *Communes, Europe.* San Francisco: Alternatives Foundation.

———. 1972b. *Communes, Japan.* San Francisco: Alternatives Foundation.

Fein, A. 1971. "The Kibbutz and Problems of Agro-Industrial Integration." In Klatzmann, Ilan, and Levi, 1971.

Fessenden (Reginald A.) Educational Fund. 1973. Combined edition of *Radio Times and Alternative Radio Exchange,* Spring.

Financial Publishing Company. n.d. *Compound Interest and Annuity Tables.* 3d ed. Boston.

Finkle, Jason L., and Gable, Richard W. 1966. *Political Development and Social Change.* New York: Wiley.

Fraser, Douglas. 1968. *Village Planning in the Primitive World.* New York: Braziller.

French, David. 1971. "After the Fall: What This Country Needs Is a Good *Counter* Counterculture Culture." *New York Times Magazine,* October 3.

———. 1972. "Community as a Failure of Communes." In Allison, 1972.

———, and French, Elena. 1972. "Research on Intentional Communities in the United States." *Communautés: Archives internationales de sociologie de la coopération et du développement,* July–December.

———. 1973. "Co-ops vs. Cooperation." *Journal of the New Harbinger,* March.

Fromm, Erich. 1968. *The Revolution of Hope: Toward a Humanized Technology.* New York: Harper Colophon Books.

Fuller, R. Buckminster. 1969. *Operating Manual for Spaceship Earth.* New York: Simon & Schuster.

Gal, D. 1971. "The Process of Industrialization at the Village Level: The Spread of Industrialization and Its Promoting Factors." In Klatzmann, Ilan, and Levi, 1971.

Galbraith, John Kenneth. 1967. *The New Industrial State.* New York: New American Library.

———. 1972. "Galbraith Has Seen China's Future—And It Works." *New York Times Magazine,* November 26.

Garcia, Jerry. 1972. Interview. *Rolling Stone,* February 3.

Gardner, Joyce. 1970. "Cold Mountain." *Alternate Society,* October.

Garrett, J. C. 1968. *Utopias in Literature Since the Romantic Period.* Christchurch, New Zealand: University of Canterbury.

Gatrell, V. A. C., ed. 1969. *Robert Owen:* A New View of Society *and* Report to the County of Lanark. Baltimore: Penguin.

Genesee Co-op. 1972. "Some Words About Us." *Synergism,* March.

Gergen, Kenneth J. 1972. "Multiple Identity: The Healthy, Happy Human Being Wears Many Masks." *Psychology Today,* May.

German Foundation for Developing Countries. 1972. *Development and Dissemination of Appropriate Technologies in Rural Areas.* Berlin.

Gintis, Herbert. 1970. *On Commodity Fetishism and Irrational Production.* Cambridge, Mass.: Harvard Institute of Economic Research, Discussion paper no. 121, May. Mimeographed.

———. 1972. "Toward a Political Economy of Education." *This Magazine Is About Schools,* Spring.

Givens, Cornbread. 1972. "Breaking the Cycle of Poverty." *Journal of the New Harbinger,* September.

Godding, Jean-Pierre. 1972. "Les Ujamaa, villages communautaires de Tanzanie." *Courrier communautaire international.* November–December.

Goldman, Irving. 1961. "The Zuni Indians of New Mexico." In Mead, 1961.

Goldstein, Lee. 1974. *Communes, Law, and Commonsense: A Legal Manual for Communities.* Boston, Mass.: New Community Projects.

Goldwasser, Janet, and Dowty, Stuart. 1973. "Chinese Factories Are Exciting Places!" *Far East Reporter,* February.

Goodman, Paul. 1972. "Politics Within Limits." *New York Review of Books,* August 10.

Goodman, Percival, and Goodman, Paul. 1960. *Communitas.* New York: Random House.

Gorman, Clem. 1971. *Making Communes.* Bottisham, Cambs. (U.K.): Whole Earth Tools.

Gottschalk, Shimon. 1971. *Rural New Towns: Toward a National Policy.* Cambridge, Mass.: Center for Community Economic Development, July.

Gougaud, Henri. 1971. *Nous voulons vivre en communauté.* Paris: Bélibaste.

Gould, Peter. 1972. *Burnt Toast.* New York: Ballantine.

Graubard, Allen. 1972. *Free the Children: Radical Reform and the Free School Movement.* New York: Pantheon.

Greenburg, Dan. 1972. "My First Orgy." *Playboy,* December.

Greene, Wade, and Golden, Soma. 1971. "The Luddites Were Not All Wrong." *New York Times Magazine,* November 21.

Greenfield, Robert. 1972. "Beyond Taos: The Lama Foundation." *Rolling Stone,* September 28.

Green Revolution. 1970. "Fellowship of Intentional Communities." March–April.

Greenway, Robert, and Rasberry, Salli. n.d. Letter. *New Schools Exchange Newsletter,* no. 60.

Grierson, Denham. 1971. *Young People in Communal Living.* Philadelphia: Westminster.

Grindrod, Bary. 1971. "The Marvelous Chicken-Powered Motorcar!" *The Mother Earth News,* July.

Grossman, Gregory. 1967. *Economic Systems.* Englewood Cliffs, N.J.: Prentice-Hall.

Guérin, Daniel. 1970. *Anarchism.* New York: Monthly Review Press.

Guillain, Robert. 1971. "La Chine après la révolution culturelle." *Le Monde,* September 22.

Gurley, John W. 1970. "Maoist Economic Development: The New Man in the New China." *The Center Magazine,* May.

Hampden-Turner, Charles. 1970. "A Proposal for Political Marketing." *Yale Review of Law and Social Action,* Winter.

———. n.d. *The Factory as an Oppressive Environment.* Cambridge, Mass.: Center for Community Economic Development.

Hanson, Royce. 1971. *New Towns: Laboratories for Democracy.* New York: The Twentieth Century Fund.

Haq, Mahbub ul-. 1971. "Employment in the 1970s: A New Perspective." *International Development Review,* no 4.

Harrington, Michael. 1972a. *Socialism.* New York: Bantam.

———. 1972b. "We Few, We Happy Few, We Bohemians." *Esquire,* August.

Hawthorne, Edward P. 1971. *The Transfer of Technology.* Paris: Organization for Economic Co-operation and Development.

Hayden, Dolores. 1973. "The 'Social Architects' and Their Architecture of Social Change." *Journal of Applied Behavioral Science,* nos. 2–3.

Heathcote Community. n.d. *A Descriptive List of Intentional Communities.* Freeland, Md.

Hedgepeth, William, and Stock, Dennis. 1970. *The Alternative.* New York: Macmillan.

Herlihy, James Leo. 1971. *The Season of the Witch.* New York: Avon.

Hinds, William Alfred. 1961. *American Communities.* New York: Corinth Books.

Hine, Robert V. 1966. *California's Utopian Colonies.* New Haven and London: Yale University Press.

Hirschman, Albert O. 1967. *Development Projects Observed.* Washington, D.C.: Brookings Institution.

——. 1970. *Exit, Voice, and Loyalty: Responses to Decline in Firms, Organizations, and States.* Cambridge, Mass.: Harvard University Press.

Hoffman, Abbie. 1968. *Revolution for the Hell of It.* New York: Dial.

——. 1969. *Woodstock Nation.* New York: Vintage.

Horowitz, Irving Louis, ed. 1964. *The Anarchists.* New York: Dell.

Horvat, Branko. 1971. "Yugoslav Economic Policy in the Post-War Period: Problems, Ideas, Institutional Developments." *The American Economic Review,* June.

Hoselitz, B. F. 1971. "Types and Locations of Industries in Developing Countries." In Klatzmann, Ilan, and Levi, 1971.

Houriet, Robert. 1971. *Getting Back Together.* New York: Coward, McCann & Geoghegan.

Hovemann, Glenn. 1972. "Alpha." *Communitas,* July.

Huberman, Leo, and Sweezy, Paul M. 1968. *Introduction to Socialism.* New York: Monthly Review Press.

Hunnius, Gerry. 1971. "The Yugoslav System of Decentralization and Self-Management." In Benello and Roussopoulos, 1971.

——. 1973. "Workers' Self-Management in Yugoslavia." In Hunnius, Garson, and Case, 1973.

——; Garson, G. David; and Case, John, eds. 1973. *Workers' Control: A Reader on Labor and Social Change.* New York: Vintage.

Ineson, George. 1971. "Taena." In Delespesse and Tange, 1971.

Infield, Henrik. 1955. *Coopératives communautaires et sociologie expérimentale: esquisses pour une sociologie de la coopération* (adaptation française par Henri Desroche). Paris: Editions de Minuit.

Intermediate Technology Development Group. 1968. *Conference on the Further Development in the United Kingdom of Appropriate Technologies for, and Their Communication to, Developing Countries.* Conference report. London.

International Independence Institute. 1972. *The Community Land Trust: A Guide to a New Model for Land Tenure in America.* Cambridge, Mass.: Center for Community Economic Development.

Jackson, J. Hampden. 1962. *Marx, Proudhon and European Socialism.* New York: Collier Books.

Jackson, Sarah. 1972. *Economically Appropriate Technologies for Developing Countries: A Survey.* Washington, D.C.: Overseas Development Council.

Japan Kibbutz Association. 1969. *Collectives in Japan.* Tokyo. October.

Jeffries, Vernon. 1972. "Thoughts About the Dark Sides of Cooperatives." *Synergism,* May.

Jerome, Judson. 1972a. Interview. *Communitas,* July.

————. 1972b. "Would You Believe a Newsletter?" *Communitas,* July.

Joll, James. 1964. *The Anarchists.* New York: Grosset & Dunlap.

Judy. 1973. "ICTA." *Leaves of Twin Oaks,* November.

Kagawa, Toyohiko. n.d. *Brotherhood Economics.* Ann Arbor, Mich.: North American Student Cooperative Organization. (Originally published 1936.)

Kane, Cheikh Hamidou. 1969. *Ambiguous Adventure.* New York: Collier Books.

Kanovsky, Eliyahu. 1966. *The Economy of the Israeli Kibbutz.* Cambridge, Mass.: Harvard University Press.

Kanter, Rosabeth Moss. 1971. "Some Social Issues in the Community Development Corporation Proposal." In Benello and Roussopoulos, 1971.

————. 1972. *Commitment and Community.* Cambridge, Mass.: Harvard University Press.

Katz, Elia. 1971. *Armed Love.* New York: Holt, Rinehart and Winston.

Kaysen, Carl, and Turner, Donald F. 1959. *Antitrust Policy: An Economic and Legal Analysis.* Cambridge, Mass.: Harvard University Press.

Kaysing, William. 1972. *How to Live in the New America.* Englewood Cliffs, N.J.: Prentice-Hall.

Kieninger, Richard. 1972. "Observations." *Stelle Letter,* January.

Kinkade, Kathleen. 1973. *A Walden Two Experiment: The First Five Years of Twin Oaks Community.* New York: Morrow.

Kirkland, Will. 1973. "Trusting People." *Journal of the Institute for the Study of Nonviolence,* April–May.

Klatzmann, Joseph; Ilan, Benjamin Y.; and Levi, Yair, eds. 1971. *The Role of Group Action in the Industrialization of Rural Areas.* New York: Praeger.

Koinonia Partners. n.d. *Koinonia Partners.* Americus, Ga.

Krimerman, Leonard I., and Perry, Lewis, eds. 1966. *Patterns of Anarchy: A Collection of Writings on the Anarchist Tradition.* Garden City, N.Y.: Doubleday Anchor.

Kriyananda. 1968. *Cooperative Communities: How to Start Them and Why.* Nevada City, Calif.: Ananda Publications.

Kroeber, Theodora. 1970. *Ishi in Two Worlds: A Biography of the Last Wild Indian in North America.* Berkeley: University of California Press.

Kropotkin, Pëtr. n.d. *Mutual Aid: A Factor of Evolution.* Boston: Extending Horizons Books.

Lama Foundation, The. 1971. *Be Here Now*. San Cristobal, N.M.

Lang, Jerome D. n.d. *Towards an Alternate Economy*. Coral Gables, Fla.: Alternate Economy. Mimeographed.

Langer, Elinor. 1972. "Alienation: Inside the New York Telephone Company." In Edwards, Reich, and Weisskopf, 1972.

Lawrence, Paul R., and Lorsch, Jay W. 1967. *Organization and Environment: Managing Differentiation and Integration*. Boston: Division of Research, Graduate School of Business Administration, Harvard University.

Laye, Camara. 1954. *The Dark Child*. New York: Farrar, Straus & Giroux.

Lebret, L.-J., and Desroches, H.-Ch. 1946. *La Communauté Boimondau*. L'Arbresle (Rhone): Editions économie et humanisme.

Lee, Dallas. 1971. *The Cotton Patch Evidence: The Story of Clarence Jordan and the Koinonia Farm Experiment*. New York: Harper & Row.

Lee, Dorothy. 1959. *Freedom and Culture*. Englewood Cliffs, N.J.: Prentice-Hall.

Leon, Dan. 1969. *The Kibbutz: A New Way of Life*. Elmsford, N.Y.: Pergamon Press.

Leontief, Wassily. 1973. "Socialism in China." *Atlantic Monthly*, March.

Leviatan, Uri. n.d. *The Industrial Process in the Israeli Kibbutzim: Problems and Their Solution*. Ruppin, Israel: Ruppin Institute. Mimeographed.

Lilly, John C. 1972. *The Center of the Cyclone: An Autobiography of Inner Space*. New York: The Julian Press.

Luckywalla, El. 1971. "Coming to Our Senses." *Black Bart Brigade*, November.

MacKillop, Andrew. 1972. "Wind Power." *Undercurrents*, Autumn–Winter.

Mair, Lucy. 1964. *Primitive Government*. Baltimore: Penguin.

Mallet, Serge. 1970. "Bureaucracy and Technology in the Socialist Countries." *Socialist Revolution*, May–June.

Manuel, Frank E. 1962. *The Prophets of Paris*. New York: Harper & Row.

Margolies, Rick. 1972. "Building Communes." *Alternatives: Communal Living*, Summer.

Margolis, Richard J. 1972. "Coming Together: The Cooperative Way, Its Origins, Developments and Prospects." *The New Leader*, April 17.

Marin, Peter. 1970. "The Free People." *This Magazine Is About Schools*, Spring.

Marks, Paul J. 1969. *A New Community: Format for Health, Contentment, Security*. The Questers Project.

Martin, John D. 1969a. *A Goldmine of Information (Home Income Guide* supplement). La Mesa, Calif.: Vocational Education Enterprises.

———. 1969b. *The Home Income Guide: Over Six Hundred Ways to Make Money at Home*. La Mesa, Calif.: Vocational Education Enterprises.

Mary. 1973. "Turnover." *Leaves of Twin Oaks*, June–July.

Massachusetts Institute of Technology. n.d. *Adaptation of Industrial and Public Works Technology to the Conditions of Developing Countries: Report of Activities*. Cambridge, Mass. Mimeographed.

Mazrui, Ali A. 1971. *The Trial of Christopher Okigbo.* New York: The Third Press.

Mbiti, John S. 1969. *African Religions and Philosophy.* London: Heinemann Educational Books.

McLanahan, Charles J. 1972. *A Look at Life: 60/73 of the Way Through.* January. Mimeographed.

————. n.d. "Reflections on the Co-op Challenge." *Journal of the New Harbinger,* no. 5.

McLean, Rebecca F. 1970. *Secrets of Saving Money.* La Mesa, Calif.: Vocational Education Enterprises.

McRobie, G. 1971. "Technologies for Rural Industrialization in Developing Countries." In Klatzmann, Ilan, and Levi, 1971.

McWhirter, Norris, and McWhirter, Ross. 1973. *Guinness Book of World Records.* New York: Bantam.

McWilliams, Wilson Carey. 1973. *The Idea of Fraternity in America.* Berkeley, Los Angeles, London: University of California Press.

Mead, Margaret, ed. 1961. *Cooperation and Competition Among Primitive Peoples.* Boston: Beacon.

Mehnert, Klaus. 1972. *China Returns.* New York: Dutton.

Meister, Albert. 1958. *Les communautés de travail: bilan d'une expérience de propriété et de gestion collectives.* Paris: Entente Communautaire.

Melman, Seymour. 1970. "Industrial Efficiency Under Managerial vs. Cooperative Decision-Making." *Review of Radical Political Economics,* Spring.

Melville, Keith. 1972. *Communes in the Counter Culture: Origins, Theories, Styles of Life.* New York: Morrow.

Meulemeester, Michel de. 1971. "Les villages communautaires." In Delespesse and Tange, 1971.

Miller, Dale. 1973. "FIGHTing in Akron." *Black Bart Brigade,* September.

Miller, Kate, and Swift, Casey. 1972. "De-Sexing the English Language." *Ms.,* Spring. (Preview issue.)

Miller, Tom. 1970. "Paolo Soleri and His Arcological Cities." *Rolling Stone,* April 30.

Millikan, Max F., ed. 1967. *National Economic Planning.* New York: Columbia University Press.

Mishan, E. J. 1969. *Technology and Growth: The Price We Pay.* New York: Praeger.

Modern Utopian. 1971. *Modern Man in Search of Utopia.* San Francisco: Alternatives Foundation.

Moffat, Gary. 1971. "Community Heritage in Western Civilization." *Alternate Society,* August–September.

Moral, Herbert R. 1972. *Buying Country Property.* Charlotte, Vt.: Garden Way Publishing Co.

Morgan, Arthur E. 1953. *Industries for Small Communities—With Cases from Yellow Springs.* Yellow Springs, Ohio: Community Service, Inc.

Morgan, Griscom. 1972. "Pioneering a People's Fund." *Journal of the New Harbinger,* June.

Morris, David. 1973. "Fund Sought to Help Regenerate Community." *The Daily Rag* (Washington, D.C.), October 26.

Mosher, Craig R. 1973 "ONE: An Urban Community." *Journal of Applied Behavioral Science,* March–June.

Mother Earth News, The. n.d. *The Mother Earth News Research Center* (Mother's reprint no. 87). Madison, Ohio.

Mumford, Lewis. 1962. *The Story of Utopias.* New York: Viking.

Mungo, Raymond. 1970. *Total Loss Farm: A Year in the Life.* New York: Dutton.

Myrdal, Jan, and Kessle, Gun. 1972. *China: The Revolution Continued.* New York: Vintage.

Nagel, Ed. 1973. "Legal Assistance for Alternative Schools." *New Schools Exchange Newsletter,* May 15.

Nakane, Chie. 1970. *Japanese Society.* Berkeley: University of California Press.

NASCO. *See* North American Student Cooperative Organization.

Nearing, Helen, and Nearing, Scott. 1970. *Living the Good Life: How to Live Sanely and Simply in a Troubled World.* New York: Schocken.

Neihardt, John G. 1961. *Black Elk Speaks: Being the Life Story of a Holy Man of the Oglala Sioux.* Lincoln: University of Nebraska Press.

Neubauer, Peter B., ed. 1965. *Children in Collectives: Child-Rearing Aims and Practices in the Kibbutz.* Springfield, Ill.: Charles C Thomas.

New Alchemy Institute—East. n.d. *The New Alchemists.* Brochure. Woods Hole, Mass.

New American Movement. 1971. "The New American Movement!" *Black Bart Brigade,* November.

New Community Projects. 1972. "The Politics of Housework." *Commune-ication,* no. 2.

————. n.d. "All in the Family." *Commune-ication.*

Newsweek. 1972. "The Four-Day Weekend." October 9.

New Vocations Project. 1971. *Working Loose.* San Francisco: American Friends Service Committee.

————. n.d. *Seed People.* San Francisco: American Friends Service Committee.

New World Coalition. 1972. *Shop the Other America.* Boston.

Nir, Henry. 1968. *Living in a Kibbutz.* New York: Kibbutz Aliya Desk.

Nordhoff, Charles. 1966. *The Communistic Societies of the United States.* New York: Dover. First published 1875.

North American Student Cooperative Organization. 1972a. "Lifestyles: The Rainbow Family Inter-Tribal Communications Center." *Monthly News of Co-op Communities,* September.

———. 1972b. "Representative Structures for Student Co-ops." *Monthly News of Co-op Communities,* November.

———. 1973. *Board of Directors Candidates: Statements of Qualifications.* Ann Arbor, Mich.: NASCO.

Noyes, John H. 1966. *History of American Socialisms.* New York: Dover. First published 1870.

Nyerere, Julius K. 1967. "The Arusha Declaration and TANU's Policy on Socialism and Self-Reliance." *The Nationalist* (Tanzania), February 14.

Oakland Co-op. 1972. "Consumer/People Oriented." *Journal of the New Harbinger,* July.

Oglesby, Carl, ed. 1969. *The New Left Reader.* New York: Grove Press.

Oppenheimer, Martin. 1971. "The Limitations of Socialism: Some Sociological Observations on Participatory Democracy." In Benello and Roussopoulos, 1971.

Orleans, Leo A. 1972. "China's Science and Technology: Continuity and Innovation." In United States Congress, 1972.

Owen, Robert. 1970. *Report to the County of Lanark: A New View of Society.* Baltimore: Penguin.

Pahana Town Forum. 1972. *Town Prospectus.* Santa Barbara, Calif. Winter.

Paulus, Jacques. 1969. "Society of Brothers." In Delespesse and Tange, 1969.

Peace and Conflict Research Programme (University of Lancaster). 1973. "The Chile Community: A Proposed Socio-Ecological Experiment." *Undercurrents,* Spring.

Pelletier, Wilfred. 1971. "Childhood in an Indian Village." *Alternate Society,* January.

People's Yellow Pages Collective. 1972. *The People's Yellow Pages.* 2d ed. San Francisco. (1st ed., 1971.)

Petersen, James. 1973. "Lessons from the Indian Soul: A Conversation with Frank Waters." *Psychology Today,* May.

Philadelphia Citywide Co-op Organization (Education Caucus). 1972. "Operating Principles." *Journal of the New Harbinger,* February.

Pinch of Love. 1972. "A Pinch of Love." *Synergism,* May.

Pinto, Udar. 1973. Interview. *East West Journal,* November.

Platt, John. 1972. "What's Ahead for 1990." *The Center Magazine,* July–August.

Pyronnet, Jo. 1970. "L'Arche." In Delespesse and Tange, 1970.

Rabin, A. I. 1965. *Growing Up in the Kibbutz.* New York: Springer.

Radin, Paul. 1957. *Primitive Man as Philosopher.* New York: Dover.

Rangan, Kasturi. 1971. "A Utopian Town in India Built on a Dream." *New York Times,* October 16.

Rasberry, Salli, and Greenway, Robert. 1970. *Rasberry Exercises: How to Start Your Own School . . . And Make a Book.* Sebastopol, Calif.: Freestone Publishing Co.

Raskin, Marcus G. 1971. *Being and Doing.* New York: Random House.

Rassemblement Communautaire Français. 1946. *Vie communautaire . . . liberté vraie.* Valence: Cité Donguy-Hermann.

Reed, Roy. 1973. "Conformity Backfires for a Commune." *New York Times,* September 22.

Reich, Charles A. 1970. *The Greening of America.* New York: Random House.

Reim, Tari. 1970. "Or a Chance to Get It Together?" *Rolling Stone,* March 19.

Reinhold, Robert. 1971. "MIT to Study Ways to Use Technology to Aid Poor Nations." *New York Times,* November 26.

Revel, Jean-François. 1970. *Without Marx or Jesus: The New American Revolution Has Begun.* New York: Dell.

Richman, Barry M. 1969. *Industrial Society in Communist China.* New York: Random House.

Riesman, David. 1954. *Selected Essays from Individualism Reconsidered.* Garden City, N.Y.: Doubleday Anchor.

Roberts, Ron E. 1971. *The New Communes: Coming Together in America.* Englewood Cliffs, N.J.: Prentice-Hall.

Robertson, Constance Noyes. 1970. *Oneida Community: An Autobiography, 1851–1876.* Syracuse: Syracuse University Press.

———. 1972. *Oneida Community: The Breakup, 1876–1881.* Syracuse: Syracuse University Press.

Rosenman, H. 1971. "The Process of Industrialization at the Village Level: Structural and Organizational Patterns of Industrial Enterprises." In Klatzmann, Ilan, and Levi, 1971.

Rosenthal, Jack. 1971. "A Tale of One City." *New York Times Magazine,* December 26.

Rosner, Menahem. n.d. *Worker Participation in Decision-Making in Kibbutz Industry.* Ruppin, Israel: Ruppin Institute.

Roszak, Theodore. 1969. *The Making of a Counter Culture.* Garden City, N.Y.: Doubleday.

———. 1972. *Where the Wasteland Ends: Politics and Transcendence in Post-industrial Society.* Garden City, N.Y.: Doubleday.

Roussopoulos, Dimitrios. 1971. "The Organizational Question and the Urban Commune." In Benello and Roussopoulos, 1971.

Salpukas, Agis. 1973. "Jobs Rotated to Fight Boredom." *New York Times,*
    February 5.

Sautois, Michel. 1971. "Nomadelfia." In Delespesse and Tange, 1971.

Schaberg, Jim, and Silha, Stephen. 1972. "New World City . . . Syntropy and
    Learning." *The Foundation Journal,* no. 2.

School of Living. 1973. "Alternate Power Seminar." *The Green Revolution,* June.

Schumacher, E. F. 1971. "Buddhist Economics." *Alternate Society,* January.

Schuster, Eunice Minette. 1931–1932. "Native American Anarchism: A Study
    of Left-Wing American Individualism." *Smith College Studies in History,*
    October–July.

Seashore, Stanley E., and Barnowe, J. Thad. 1972. "Collar Color Doesn't Count."
    Psychology Today, August.

Shabecoff, Philip. 1973. "Percy Says U.S. Is on 'Brink of a Major Breakthrough'
    in Attempt to Change Ideas on Work." *New York Times,* March 27.

Shaffner, Susan. 1972. Quoted by R. Fairfield. *Alternatives Journal,* October 1–15.

Shatz, Marshall S., ed. 1971. *The Essential Works of Anarchism.* New York:
    Bantam.

Shaw, Arthur. 1970. "The Plowboy Interview." *The Mother Earth News,* July.

Sherman, Howard. 1972. *Radical Political Economy: Capitalism and Socialism
    from a Marxist-Humanist Perspective.* New York: Basic Books.

Shortney, Joan Ranson. 1971. *How to Live on Nothing.* Richmond Hill, Ontario:
    Pocket Books.

Skinner, B. F. 1948. *Walden Two.* New York: Macmillan.

Slater, Philip. 1970. *The Pursuit of Loneliness: American Culture at the Breaking
    Point.* Boston: Beacon.

Sloane, Cliff. 1972. "Insurance System for Co-ops." *Synergism,* October.

Small Business Administration. *See* United States Small Business Administration.

Smith, Dennis. 1972. *Report from Engine Co. 82.* New York: Pocket Books.

Society of Brothers. 1963. *Children in Community.* Rifton, N.Y.: The Plough
    Publishing House.

Speck, Ross V. 1972. *The New Families: Youth, Communes, and the Politics
    of Drugs.* New York: Basic Books.

Spiro, Melford E. 1970. *Kibbutz: Venture in Utopia.* New York: Schocken.

Spradley, James P., and McCurdy, David W., eds. 1971. *Conformity and Conflict:
    Readings in Cultural Anthropology.* Boston: Little, Brown.

Stein, Barry. 1971. *The Community Context of Economic Conversion.* Cambridge,
    Mass.: Center for Community Economic Development.

Stelle Group. 1970. *Stelle: A City for Tomorrow.* Chicago. May.

Stern, Sol. 1973. "The Kibbutz: Not by Ideology Alone." *New York Times
    Magazine,* May 6.

Steven. 1973a. "The Labor Credit System." *Leaves of Twin Oaks,* June–July.

————. 1973b. "So You Think Twin Oaks Is a Behaviorist Community." *Leaves of Twin Oaks,* June–July.

————. 1974. "On Change at Twin Oaks." *Leaves of Twin Oaks,* January.

Sturm, Douglas. 1971. "The Kibbutzim and the Spirit of Israel: An Interpretative Essay." In Teselle, 1971.

Sugihara, Yoshie, and Plath, David W. 1969. *Sensei and His People: The Building of a Japanese Commune.* Berkeley: University of California Press.

Sundancer, Elaine. 1972. "Life on a Country Commune." *Communitas,* September.

Swan, Jon. 1972. "The 400-Year-Old Commune." *Atlantic Monthly,* November.

Swann, Bob. 1973. Interview. *Lifestyle!,* June.

Teil, Roger du. 1946. *Vie communautaire . . . liberté vraie: la communauté vue par un intellectuel.* Valence: Rassemblement Communautaire Français.

Terrill, Ross. 1972. *800,000,000: The Real China.* New York: Dell.

Teselle, Sallie, ed. 1971. *The Family, Communes and Utopian Societies.* New York: Harper Torchbooks.

Theobald, Robert. 1970. *An Alternative Future for America II.* Chicago: The Swallow Press.

This Magazine Is About Schools. 1971a. "Editorial Statement." Summer.

————. 1971b. "Editorial Statement." Fall-Winter.

Thomas, Irv. 1971. "Black Bart Philosophy." *Black Bart Brigade,* November.

————. 1972. "Black Bart Philosophy." *Black Bart Brigade,* April.

Tilmann, Richard. 1972. Letter. *Journal of the New Harbinger,* November.

Time. 1970. "Economic Growth: New Doubts About an Old Ideal." March 2.

————. 1972. "Profits on the Kibbutz." July 3.

————. 1973. "The Graying of America." September 17.

Toffler, Alvin. 1970. *Future Shock.* New York: Random House.

Trotscha, Peter. 1971. "Cultural Change and the Co-op." *Journal of the New Harbinger,* October.

Twin Oaks Community. 1972. *Experimenting with Walden Two: The Collected Leaves of Twin Oaks, Issues 1–15.* Louisa, Va.

————. n.d. *Twin Oaks.* Louisa, Va.

Udy, Stanley H., Jr. 1959. *Organization of Work: A Comparative Analysis of Production Among Nonindustrial Peoples.* New Haven: HRAF Press.

————. 1970. *Work in Traditional and Modern Society.* Englewood Cliffs, N.J.: Prentice-Hall.

United Nations, Department of Economic and Social Affairs. 1972a. *Appropriate Technology and Research for Industrial Development: Report of the Advisory Committee on the Application of Science and Technology to Development on Two Aspects of Industrial Growth.* New York.

————. 1972b. *Transfer of Operative Technology at the Enterprise Level: Report of an Interregional Expert Group on Its Meeting Held in New York from 21 to 26 June 1971.* New York.

United States Bureau of the Census. 1972. *Statistical Abstract of the United States: 1972.* Washington, D.C.: U.S. Government Printing Office.

United States Congress, Joint Economic Committee. 1972. *People's Republic of China: An Economic Assessment.* Washington, D.C.: U.S. Government Printing Office.

United States Department of Health, Education, and Welfare. 1973. *Work in America.* Cambridge, Mass.: MIT Press.

United States Internal Revenue Service. 1971a. *Preliminary Report, Statistics of Income—1969, Individual Income Tax Returns.* Washington, D.C.: U.S. Government Printing Office.

————. 1971b. *Statistics of Income, 1967—Corporation Tax Returns.* Washington, D.C.: U.S. Government Printing Office.

United States Office of Education. 1972. *Vocational Instructional Materials for Trade and Industrial Occupations Available from Federal Agencies.* Washington, D.C.: U.S. Government Printing Office.

United States Small Business Administration. 1972a. *Choosing the Legal Structure for Your Firm* (Management Aids for Small Manufacturers #80). Washington, D.C. Reprint.

————. 1972b. *Steps in Incorporating a Business* (Management Aids for Small Manufacturers #111). Washington, D.C. Reprint.

————. n.d. *Starting a Small Business in Vermont: A Brief Guide About Some of the Legal Obligations.* Montpelier, Vt.

Valenti, Chiara. 1972. "Le grandi famiglie." *Panorama* (Italy), August 31.

Vanek, Jaroslav. 1971. *The Participatory Economy: An Evolutionary Hypothesis and a Strategy for Development.* Ithaca, N. Y.: Cornell University Press.

Van Gelder, Lindsay. 1972. "The Most Unforgettable Employer We've Ever Met." *Ms.,* October.

Vermont News Service. 1973. *Vermont People's Yellow Pages 1973–1974.* Plainfield, Vt.

Volunteers for International Technical Assistance. 1970. *Village Technology Handbook.* Schenectady, N.Y.

Voorhis, Jerry. n.d. "On Building an Open, Just, and Creative Society." *Journal of the New Harbinger,* no. 5.

Watson, Bill. 1971. *Counter-Planning on the Shop Floor.* Cambridge, Mass.: Radical America.

Webber, Everett. 1959. *Escape to Utopia: The Communal Movement in America.* New York: Hastings House.

Weisskopf, Thomas E. 1972. "The Problems of Surplus Absorption in a Capitalist Society." In Edwards, Reich, and Weisskopf, 1972.

Weisskopf, Walter A. 1971. *Alienation and Economics.* New York: Dutton.

Wheeler, Harvey. 1972. "Technology: Foundation of Cultural Change." *The Center Magazine,* July–August.

Wheeler, Howard. 1972. "New Vrindaban: The Making of a Village." *The Mother Earth News (Lifestyle!* supplement), July.

Wheelright, E. L., and McFarlane, Bruce. 1970. *The Chinese Road to Socialism: Economics of the Cultural Revolution.* New York: Monthly Review Press.

Wilhelm, Richard (trans.). 1967. *The I Ching or Book of Changes.* London: Routledge & Kegan Paul.

Wilson, Charles Morrow. 1960. *Let's Try Barter: The Answer to Inflation and the Tax Collector.* New York: Devin-Adair.

Wind, J. J. 1972. "Community Chipping." *Journal of the New Harbinger,* June.

Winfield, Bill. 1970. "The People's Grocery." *The Mother Earth News,* July.

Wood, John; Eastman, Anthony; and Carden, Murray. 1972. "Eco-Unit." *Undercurrents,* Autumn–Winter.

Woodcock, George. 1962. *Anarchism: A History of Libertarian Ideas and Movements.* Cleveland: World.

———. 1971. "The Manipulated." *Alternate Society,* February–March.

Yablonsky, Lewis. 1968. *The Hippie Trip.* New York: Pegasus.

Yankee Dairy News. 1972. "A Statement of Policy." July.

Yaswen, Gordon. 1971. "Sunrise Hill." *Alternate Society,* April.

Yogananda, Paramahansa. 1969. *Autobiography of a Yogi.* Los Angeles: Self-Realization Fellowship.

Zablocki, Benjamin. 1971. *The Joyful Community.* Baltimore: Penguin.

Zilles, Marsha. 1973. "Home on the New Alchemy Farm." *Alternative Sources of Energy,* January.

Index